W9-BSH-390

The Student
and His Professor

The Student and His Professor

JOHN HANNAH, RALPH AIGLER
AND THE ORIGIN
OF THE MICHIGAN STATE-
MICHIGAN RIVALRY

———

David J. Young

Copyright © 2015 by David J. Young
DJY Publishing, LLC
All rights reserved under International
And Pan-American Copyright Conventions

ISBN-13: 9780692362419
ISBN-10: 069236241X

Cover design: Anna Young
ayoungdesign.com

For I know well the plans I have in mind for you,
says the Lord,
plans for your welfare, not for woe!
plans to give you a future full of hope.
When you call me, when you go pray to me,
I will listen to you.
When you look for me,
you will find me.
Yes, when you seek me with all your heart,
you will find me with you, says the Lord,
and I will change your lot.

Jeremiah 29: 11-14
New American Bible

Table of Contents

Acknowledgments

———

FOLLOWING COMPLETION OF MY FIRST work, *Arrogance and Scheming in the Big Ten: Michigan State's Quest for Membership and Michigan's Powerful Opposition*, I acknowledged the profound role archivists Brian Williams (Bentley Historical Library, University of Michigan) and Portia Vescio (Michigan State University Archives and Historical Collections) played in aiding that endeavor. They were extremely helpful during this project as well. Thank you.

My Medicare Brigade—a core group of patients who happen to be gifted writers and critics—assisted me once again during this latest undertaking. When called to the task, they eagerly proofed my work. Thank you to Reverend John (University of Illinois, Western Theological Seminary) and Eileen (Hope College) Nordstrom, Professor Emeritus Don Williams of Hope College (Muskingum College, The Ohio State University), and Professor Emeritus James Johnson of Loyola (Xavier University, Loyola University of Chicago). Julia Sanders was the only Spartan among the retirees. She enrolled at Michigan State College of Agriculture and Applied Science and graduated from Michigan State University of Agriculture and Applied Science!

Don Hahn (University of Michigan times two), a semi-retired attorney, also read through the manuscript. Although eligible for Medicare, he wasn't included in the group—Don receives his health care from another physician in town!

Jeff Kinzel (Northwestern, University of Michigan Law School, Wharton School of Business) has been a friend since childhood back in East Lansing. He co-manages a private equity fund based out of Chicago and New York. I am fortunate that his mother, who held a master's degree in English Literature, insisted he memorize those grammar rules most of us have long since forgotten. Fortunately, Jeff still enjoys writing and editing. I could always count on him for help with challenging syntax questions.

Tom Murdoch and his support staff (Murdoch Marketing) kindly assisted me in updating my website (www.msu-umbig10.com). Thanks for your help.

Anna Young, my niece, assisted me in the cover graphics (ayoungdesign.com). It took quite a few iterations, but we finally got it right! You are a very talented young lady.

Michael Young was extremely helpful in providing counsel on challenging technical aspects of the Word program. Patience is a virtue and Mike is blessed with a lot of it. You are a truly gifted young man.

Andy and Christopher, unlike brother Mike, had no direct role in my project other than an occasional inquiry about its status. As trivial as that might seem, they had a knack for asking during moments of creative despair, when I felt like hovering my cursor over the document, right-clicking the mouse, and sending the entire project to the trash bin. Their pep talks were invaluable.

And finally, Margaret deserves special mention. Not once did she waver in her encouragement and support during my six-year ordeal—researching and writing two books while maintaining a full-time medical practice. Thank you for putting up with a silly dreamer.

David J. Young
May 16, 2015

Prologue: The Myth

———

MICHIGAN STATE College of Agriculture and Applied Science was admitted into the Intercollegiate Conference of Faculty Representatives[1] in May of 1949. Urban legend had it that the University of Michigan worked feverishly, behind the scenes, to prevent President John Hannah's college from gaining membership. And strangely enough, the University of Notre Dame, my alma mater, was intermixed in the myth—the Irish were given kudos for aiding the Spartans' cause. In the fall of 2008, in large part due to historical curiosity, I began to research the topic. The end result was my first book, *Arrogance and Scheming in the Big Ten: Michigan State's Quest for Membership and Michigan's Powerful Opposition.*

Much to my surprise, after visiting various archives about the conference, I discovered that that myth, originally shared with me by Michigan State Executive Vice President Jack Breslin, our family neighbor back in the mid-1970s, was not quite accurate. There was no doubt that Notre Dame aided the Spartan cause, in large part by its willingness to resurrect a gridiron relationship with the college. The long-term agreement—the Spaghetti and Meatballs Contract[2]—was unprecedented. At the time, most schools signed two-year home and home agreements with a suitor. President John Hannah, however, wanted more: a guaranteed extended relationship with Notre Dame to complement the long-running series Michigan State maintained with the University of Michigan. Having two prominent competitors would ensure that his

Spartans gained headlines in the sports section of national newspapers at least twice a year. The press coverage was an invaluable marketing tool. Michigan State needed to attract affordable post-doctorates from prominent graduate programs in order to sustain its novel curricular and research initiatives on campus. And in Hannah's opinion, there was no better help-wanted ad than favorable press!

The unusual contract with Notre Dame also forced the State Board of Agriculture to expand Macklin Field to 52,000 seats. The Irish had ended their relationship with the Aggies following the 1921 football season—it was all about the money. Simply stated, Old College Field accommodated at most 4,000 fans. The widely popular Notre Dame was capable of filling much larger stadia. The added dollars from competing in front of crowds exceeding 60,000 were critical for the small Catholic university's bottom line. But if Michigan Agricultural College ever expanded its seating capacity beyond 30,000 customers, the Holy Cross priests were more than eager to renew a gridiron relationship.[3]

The popular urban myth also maintained that the University of Michigan opposed the land-grant college's membership into the Big Nine. But as archival documents bore out, that aspect of the story couldn't be further from the truth. In point of fact, behind closed doors in mid-May of 1949, when it really mattered, the Wolverine's powerful faculty representative to the conference, Professor Ralph Aigler, twisted some arms to assure Michigan State was the unanimous selection to replace the University of Chicago. Prior to that tally, however, there was no doubt that the Wolverine athletic leader had orchestrated some intriguing schemes to prevent the Spartans from assuming the seat vacated by the Maroons a few years earlier. And in retrospect, he had some pretty valid reasons.

I BEGAN my research into this topic in the early fall of 2008. At the time, Bentley Historical Library associate archivist Brian Williams encouraged me to skim over some papers retained by Professor Aigler of the Michigan Law School. His deceased wife's family had just released thousands of letters and documents that dated back 100 years. Brian was confident I would find my answer somewhere in those 17 boxes.

Of course, I had no idea who Ralph Aigler was let alone the significant role he had played in the story of Michigan athletics. But after spending a few hours flipping through some files and reading a couple of letters, I realized that this man was a giant in intercollegiate sport history. Brian was right: the answer to my question was undoubtedly located in the backroom stacks at the Bentley. What I didn't appreciate, however, until many months later, was another storyline interposed among those letters—the fascinating 34-year relationship between Professor Aigler and President John Hannah. Their gentlemanly feud, borne out of differing convictions on the role of financial aid in amateur athletics, would play a major role in transitioning a lopsided, politically mandated intrastate football series into a bona fide rivalry.

FOR THOSE who have read *Arrogance and Scheming in the Big Ten,* the first few chapters of this work will seem familiar. I had to find a way to summarize for the uninitiated John Hannah's quixotic quest for membership in the Intercollegiate Conference of Faculty Representatives—commonly referred to as the Big Nine or Western Conference[4] at the time. The third chapter is dedicated to Professor Ralph Aigler—he deserved a richer, more thorough biographical sketch than what was revealed in my first book. The remainder of *The Student and His Professor* explores the adversarial relationship between Hannah and Aigler in the context of four historical events: Michigan State's pursuit of the conference seat vacated by the University of Chicago, the Probation of '53, the Paul Bunyan Trophy controversy, and the intrastate "name change" civil war.

Arrogance and Scheming in the Big Ten intentionally included footnotes. I wanted to avoid being charged with favoritism in this long-standing intrastate squabble—after all, I spent my formative years in East Lansing before departing for Notre Dame. The current layout, however, will use endnotes to allow the story to flow more like an historical novel rather than a history textbook. But for the curious few, do take an occasional peek at some of the references—there are interesting tidbits (italicized) interspersed among many of those citations.

Cast of Characters

Aigler, Ralph William: alumnus, *University of Michigan (UM);* professor; faculty representative, *UM*

Blommers, Paul: professor; faculty representative, *State University of Iowa (SUI)*

Brandon, Arthur: director of university relations, *UM*

Brattin, Claud Lamar: alumnus, *UM*; professor, *Michigan State College (MSC)*

Breslin, Jacwier: alumnus, *MSC*; assistant alumni field director, *MSC*

Brody, Clark: alumnus, *The State Agricultural College (TSAC)*; chairman, State Board of Agriculture (SBA), *MSC*

Bunyan, Paul: mythical lumberjack, *MSC, MSU, UM*

Byers, Walter: assistant commissioner; executive director of NCAA

Crisler, Herbert Orin: athletic director, *UM*

Dirks, Henry: professor and dean, *MSC*

Dunn, R. Glen: alumnus, *UM*; staff attorney, attorney general's office

Emmons, Lloyd: professor and dean; faculty representative, *MSC*

Erickson, Claud Robert: alumnus, *TSAC*; consultant engineer, *MSC*

Guerre, George: alumnus, *MSC*; assistant alumni field director, *MSC*

Hannah, John Alfred: alumnus, *Michigan Agricultural College (MAC)*; president, *MSC*

Harden, Edgar: professor and dean; faculty representative, *MSC*

Hatcher, Harlan Henthorne: president, *UM*

Hovde, Frederick: president, *Purdue University*

Kavanaugh, Thomas: Michigan attorney general, 1954-57

Larkins, Richard: athletic director, *The Ohio State University*

Martin, Ed: retired FBI agent; Intercollegiate Conference

Michigan Mole: *UM* alumnus living underground about East Lansing

Millard, Frank: alumnus, *UM;* Michigan attorney general, 1951-54

Morrill, James Lewis: president, *UMn*

Morrill, Justin: congressional representative, Vermont, 1855-67; sponsor of Morrill Land-Grant College Act of 1862

Mueller, Frederick: alumnus, *TSAC*; member, SBA, *MSC*

Munn, Clarence: head football coach, *MSC*; athletic director, *MSC*

Niehuss, Marvin: professor; vice president, *UM*

Reed, William: associate commissioner

Ruthven, Alexander Grant: president, *UM*

Searl, Russell: alumnus, *UM*; staff attorney, attorney general's office

Shaw, Robert Sidey: president, *MSC*

Smith, Howard Remus: alumnus, *TSAC*

Stason, E. Blythe: professor and dean; *UM*

VanderVoort, Edward: alumnus, *UM*; Lansing business owner

Williams, G. Mennen: alumnus, *UM;* governor, State of Michigan

Wilson, Kenneth: second commissioner, Intercollegiate Conference

Yost, Fielding: head football coach, *UM*; athletic director, *UM*

Young, Ralph: athletic director, *MAC, MSC*

Chronology of Events

———

1817: Catholepistemiad Michigania founded

1821: Catholepistemiad Michigania renamed University of Michigan

1837: University of Michigan relocates to Ann Arbor

1855: The Agricultural College of the State of Michigan (ACSM) founded

1862: Morrill Land-Grant Act passed/ACSM renamed The State Agricultural College (TSAC)

1885: Ralph William Aigler born

1902: John Alfred Hannah born

1905: Intercollegiate Athletic Association of the United States founded; renamed NCAA, 1912

1906: Amateur Code of Ethics defined (revised 1916)

1908: Michigan withdraws from Big Nine/Decade of Defiance begins

1909: TSAC renamed Michigan Agricultural College (MAC)

1917: Michigan rejoins Big Ten

1921: Hannah attends UM as an undergraduate law student/ Taylorville-Carlinville Scandal

1922: Hannah transfers to MAC

1925: MAC renamed Michigan State College of Agriculture and Applied Science (MSC)

1929: MSC hires James Crowley as coach/Iowa Probation/Stock Market Collapse

1932: Yost-Young confidential "scrimmage game" understanding

1935: Hannah becomes secretary of the college and secretary of the State Board of Agriculture/Southeastern Conference codifies the "athletic" scholarship

1937: *first* MSC conference membership rejection

1938: Michigan hires Herbert Orin Crisler as coach and assistant athletic director/Dirks-Erickson Handshake Contract

1940: Crisler assumes athletic directorship

1941: Hannah becomes president of MSC/Jenison Awards approved

1943: *second* MSC conference membership rejection

1945: Kenneth Wilson becomes commissioner of conference/Jenison Awards program expanded/WWII ends

1946: University of Chicago withdraws from Big Ten/*third* MSC conference membership rejection/Spaghetti and Meatballs Contract/MSC hires Clarence Munn as coach

1947: Jenison Awards program expanded/*fourth* MSC conference membership rejection

1948: Sanity Code approved/MSC ends Jenison Awards program/*fifth* MSC conference membership rejection/bungled Purdue investigation/ Macklin Stadium expansion dedication/MSC tentatively approved for conference membership

1949: Committee of Three recommendation/MSC officially approved for conference membership/MSC participates in Big Ten competition in all sports but football/George Guerre hired as assistant alumni field director/Guerre Hand-Slap/bungled Ohio State investigation

1951: Crisler becomes aware of Spartan Foundation-Century Club/ Breslin Letter

1952: Telegram Probation threat/Wilson procrastination/Hannah Christmas Eve letter

1953: Telegram Probation enforced/Probation of '53/MSC inaugural season in Big Ten football/Paul Bunyan Trophy controversy/MSC cochampion of Big Ten football/MSC selected to represent conference in Rose Bowl/Wilson visit to East Lansing

1954: MSC wins Rose Bowl/Munn resigns as coach/Munn selected athletic director/name change controversy—round #1

1955: name change controversy—round #2/Centennial Year celebration/MSCAAS renamed Michigan State University of Agriculture and Applied Science/Ralph Aigler retires from UM

1964: death of Ralph Aigler/Michigan State University of Agriculture and Applied Science renamed Michigan State University

1969: John Hannah retires from MSU

1991: death of John Hannah

2014: (O'Bannon federal court decision)

2015: (NCAA effectively sanctions employment contracts for student athletes)

The Student and his Professor

JOHN HANNAH, RALPH AIGLER
AND THE ORIGIN
OF THE MICHIGAN STATE-
MICHIGAN RIVALRY

CHAPTER 1

Still in Control

———

No (member) university shall compete with any
non-conference institution...unless both compete
under Conference rules of eligibility.

<small>HANDBOOK OF THE INTERCOLLEGIATE CONFERENCE[1]</small>

THEY MET FOR THE FIRST time in September of 1921. It was one week
into the academic year. The student, a transfer from Grand Rapids
Community College—a feeder school for the University of Michigan—
was randomly chosen by the professor. Despite completing all required
readings, he was ill-prepared for what followed. Over the next ten minutes, while utilizing didactic dialogue, the professor would challenge
him on some arcane question pertaining to procedural law, totally unrelated to the class assignment. Fortunately for the student, the session
ended abruptly. The bell outside the amphitheater announced the end
of the 75-minute lecture.

Professor Ralph Aigler signaled for the young man to come forward.
They shook hands. He was impressed with the student's presence—the
relentless questioning was intended not only to gain knowledge on the
subject but also to promote disciplined, rational responses under fire—
invaluable forensic skills for promising lawyers. And based on what he

noted that morning, the professor predicted a very bright future for his student. Nine months later, John Hannah would drop out of law school.

MICHIGAN STATE College first applied for membership into the Western Conference (Big Ten) in May of 1937. Dusting off its Nebraska Response of 1908, the Faculty Representatives Committee decided that "it was the sense of the conference that it [was] inexpedient to en-large...at [the] time."[2] Professor Ralph William Aigler of the University of Michigan probably played a role in that rejection. Regardless of his personal reasons for opposing the Spartan initiative, it was the right decision for the conference's ruling body. There was no need to expand to 11 members.

Undaunted by that initial rejection, Michigan State and President John Hannah would try four additional times over the next 11 years before finally hitting pay dirt with round six. In each instance, the Wolverine faculty representative would influence the outcome.

If the long ordeal proved anything, it was how a dynamic young college president persevered against incredible odds, including standing up to perhaps the most powerful faculty leader in the history of the Intercollegiate Conference, to finally achieve a critical strategic plan for his alma mater.

JOHN ALFRED Hannah was promoted to the presidency of Michigan State College in July of 1941. Within four months, he would request permission from his trustees, the State Board of Agriculture, to offer student-athletes financial aid—his controversial Jenison Awards.[3] The proposal was based on his concept of justice and fairness—at least it seemed that way.[4]

President Hannah had been troubled by the hypocrisy that pervaded higher education, especially as it applied to subsidies for college athletes. He gained that conviction while previously serving in President Robert Sidey Shaw's administration as college secretary, effectively the chief operating officer. Economic hardship was pervasive in the aftermath of the '29 stock market collapse. Most students, athletes included, struggled to finance a college degree. Part-time jobs, both on and off campus, were hard to come by.

Faced with dwindling enrollment, the State Board of Agriculture approved a financial aid program.[5] The school would offer grants, scholarships, and loans to needy students. And the only qualification, beyond financial duress, was that the applicant didn't participate in intercollegiate sports! There were historical reasons for this unusual requirement.

The nascent National Collegiate Athletic Association,[6] in response to play-for-pay schemes destroying the game of football at the time, proposed a code of ethics in 1906. It was later revised in 1916. Students were obligated to pledge allegiance to the concept of pure amateur play—a signed vow to not accept money for competitive play during their three years of eligibility.[7] The NCAA's intent was straightforward: ensure a level playing field on both sides of the line of scrimmage. And as a corollary, recruiting was also forbidden. The practice, especially in the hands of overzealous coaches, alumni, and boosters, invariably included dollar enticements. Over time, grants, loans, academic scholarships—even training table meals—were considered financial aid contrary to the amateur code of ethics.

Many schools professed loyalty to the unenforceable NCAA honor code—reality proved otherwise. Unscrupulous coaches, mindful that job security correlated with gridiron success, devised novel schemes to circumvent it. Administrators, aware of the illegal practices, often looked the other way. After all, winning football was good for the bottom line. But in the end, the student beneficiary's concept of "moral behavior, right living, and common decency" was skewed.[8] And for institutions of higher learning, charged with educating future leaders, this was unacceptable.[9]

President Hannah's solution to this pervasive practice was a dose of integrity and realism. His institution would offer grants to incoming Spartan football players. The Jenison Awards would cover room, board and tuition. And consistent with his character, the program would be totally transparent. He would trumpet his plan to the public. Awardees would be cited in the college's financial aid brochure along with recipients of traditional scholarship grants.[10]

Hannah acknowledged that most football players were not the brightest lights in a classroom. But they were good, hard-working young men eager to get an education and earn a diploma. To deny them monetary assistance while Michigan State benefitted financially from their gridiron skills was an injustice.[11] How could these young men compete in the classroom if limited free time, away from the practice field, was devoted to part-time jobs rather than to studies?

At the time the president gained approval for his novel proposal, the only person outside of East Lansing even remotely aware of Michigan State's financial aid program was Professor Ralph Aigler of the University of Michigan. In the faculty representative's opinion, the dollars were an illegal subsidy. The practice was contrary to the spirit of the amateur code; it also violated the Intercollegiate Conference's handbook on rules and regulations for the college athlete.

Aigler would argue that Hannah's motive was self-serving. There were no honorable intentions in awarding Jenison grants. The college president was merely scheming to boost his school's football fortunes by steering talent towards East Lansing and away from Ann Arbor.[12] [13] And in hindsight, the law professor's conjecture was absolutely correct—at least in December of 1941!

At first glance, John Hannah's proposal appeared altruistic. But the man also loved college football—a game he became acquainted with while briefly attending the University of Michigan law school back in 1921. The weeklong buildup in anticipation of the Ohio State game that year utterly fascinated him. The enthusiasm and excitement demonstrated by students, faculty, and town folk was captivating.[14] Two decades later, he planned to import that culture to his campus. And the surest way to accomplish that feat was by occasionally defeating the gridiron juggernaut located 60 miles away—an historically rare occurrence since the series began back in 1898.[15]

Hannah's financial aid program was never fully implemented. The outbreak of World War II effectively put the plan on hold. The War Department forbade schools training army and ROTC candidates, such as Michigan State, from participating in intercollegiate athletics. As a consequence, the football program was mothballed for almost two years. But following a successful build-up in military personnel just prior to D-Day, the army brass declared an end to its ban. The Spartans were back in action later that fall.

And to jump-start the football program, in May of 1945 President Hannah would expand his Jenison Awards. He cited "some of the problems of maintaining intercollegiate athletic teams to compete credibly with other (renowned) institutions…." as his reason.[16] He was referencing the University of Michigan!

Back in Ann Arbor, after hearing about this latest ploy on Hannah's part, Professor Ralph Aigler was beside himself. Adding to his frustration, there was little he could do to thwart the seemingly dishonorable actions of a highly respected college leader.[17]

THE PRACTICE of subsidizing Michigan State athletes actually predated the Jenison Awards by well over a decade. In early August of 1929, the college hired James "Sleepy Jim" Crowley to lead the Spartans. The State Board needed a young, dynamic leader to arouse the school's hibernating football program. And in the interest of aiding its new coach, the administration made available student loans that he could offer to qualified high school seniors. In Crowley's hands, it proved to be a very effective recruiting tool.

Ralph Aigler first became aware of the Spartan subsidy scheme a few years later. High school seniors were bypassing Ann Arbor and spending four years in East Lansing instead. As a direct consequence, the traditionally successful Wolverine football program fell on hard times. But what really troubled the lawyer were the implications of Michigan State winking at Crowley's antics. The school was violating a Big Ten "contract" it was expected to honor in order to compete against his

Wolverines.[18] [19] Unfortunately, as Aigler knew only too well, the contract was unenforceable. Lacking any means to even file a complaint with the impotent NCAA, the law professor had no recourse but to take matters into his own hands. He would pursue vigilante justice, a time-tested conference practice to quietly discipline a rogue competitor.

Over the next few years, Aigler would successfully impose a conference-scheduling boycott against the Spartans. And in the spring of 1937, behind closed doors, he ensured that his nine colleagues sitting on the Faculty Representatives Committee denied Michigan State membership in the conference.[20]

Uncertain of Professor Aigler's role, if any, in stymying those past Spartan initiatives,[21] the Michigan State administration pressed forward with its strategic plan. With Hannah now in control, the school decided to pursue membership once again—but this time with the support of its sister-state institution. In a letter ghostwritten by President Hannah, Spartan Athletic Director Ralph Young asked Herbert "Fritz" Crisler for his help in promoting an application.[22] [23] It was an odd request coming from a manager charged with overseeing an athletic department. With Ralph Aigler away on sabbatical and unavailable for advice, Crisler sought the counsel of his president. Alexander Ruthven agreed—this was a political issue involving relations between two large publically funded institutions, a question more appropriate for the University Regents rather than the Board in Control of Intercollegiate Athletics.[24] Hannah's preliminary request for Michigan's support of a Spartan application ended on that note.

THE WOLVERINES' attitude towards a Spartan application for membership in the conference would suddenly change in March of 1946. The University of Chicago had just announced plans to withdraw from the Big Ten. John Hannah, mindful of the potential scheduling headaches for nine athletic directors, immediately penned a note to President Alexander Ruthven.[25] He had violated institutional protocol in writing directly to the university leader for one reason: Professor Ralph Aigler.

The lawyer wielded too much influence in the athletic department over in Ann Arbor. Perhaps communicating directly with Ruthven might gain him that Wolverine sponsorship he desperately needed for a successful Spartan membership initiative.

Alexander Grant Ruthven assumed the presidency of the University of Michigan shortly after the market crash of 1929. His first decade in office proved challenging as he struggled to maintain institutional solvency. No department, including athletics,[26] was immune from budgetary cuts. Financial stability also took precedence during his second decade in office as he tried to balance the books during the war years. Decreased enrollment, in large part due to the deployment of so many young men overseas, taxed the school's main revenue stream—tuition. Federal dollars from various military training programs offered short-term support.[27] But following the end of hostilities, empty classrooms were no longer an issue. The president now needed additional revenue to finance infrastructure expansion to accommodate thousands of veterans planning to resume studies for degrees held in abeyance.

And therein lay the problem for President Ruthven. John Hannah, as he knew only too well, controlled state government in Lansing. The man was extremely popular with legislators on both sides of the aisle. He had gained that rapport while serving as college secretary a decade earlier. It was Hannah's job to lobby politicians for state tax dollars. Needless to say, he was very effective.[28] [29] Adding to Ruthven's challenge, current Governor Harry Kelly was impressed with the Spartan president; he also considered him a close friend.[30] Mindful of the college administrator's influence among powerbrokers inside the State Capitol, Ruthven appeared to have no option but to honor Hannah's request for Wolverine support in his strategic initiative.

He shared Hannah's letter with Ralph Aigler and Fritz Crisler. Professor Aigler, mindful of Ruthven's predicament, agreed to go along with his boss's plan. He and his director would support a Spartan application—but with strings attached.[31] Hannah's administration must demonstrate to their satisfaction complete compliance with the

Intercollegiate Handbook. In other words, all current forms of subsidies for athletes must be revoked.[32] The "Ruthven Decree" was announced to the press shortly thereafter.

BOLSTERED BY the University of Michigan's promise, Michigan State tendered an application for Western Conference membership in May of 1946. And once again, much to John Hannah's surprise, it experienced rejection—its third time in nine years.

As it turned out, in the immediate postwar era, there were too many pressing issues confronting the conference. And in Professor Aigler's opinion, replacement of the University of Chicago was not a priority. Mindful that the college was about to tender an application for membership shortly after the Ruthven Decree, he adeptly orchestrated a plan that would not embarrass Michigan and its president. The lawyer let it be known to a few confidants that the Wolverines would offer support for a Spartan initiative—but in spirit only.[33] [34] Unaware of the confidential agenda for that spring conference meeting, a frustrated John Hannah could only conclude that Michigan's athletic leadership, Ralph Aigler in particular, was not trustworthy.[35]

Later that year, President Hannah felt it was time for new direction in the football program. Despite ample acquired talent, the Spartans were simply not performing at the level he and his board had projected. In early December, Clarence "Biggie" Munn was hired to replace Charlie Bachman. And in January of 1947, to assist his new coach's endeavors, the president expanded the number of Jenison Awards Munn could dispense each year.[36]

Four months later, Hannah met with the Big Nine Faculty Representatives Committee during its spring meeting in Highland Park, Illinois. Previous attempts at directly interacting with the men that made decisions on conference membership size had failed for various reasons. But now, due to his dogged determination, he finally had an opportunity to argue his case before Ralph Aigler's colleagues. Perhaps his persuasive presence might gain the votes needed to assume the seat vacated by Chicago—and in a setting Aigler would have little control over.

Hannah's presentation was impressive. The faculty leadership, however, would defer to their athletic directors on the question of conference size. The men charged with drafting schedules remained confident that there was still no need to replace the Chicago Maroons. The Faculty Representatives Committee respected that decision.[37] [38]

The University of Michigan athletic leadership played no direct role in the Highland Park rejection. John Hannah, of course, would argue differently. The pattern was all too familiar. Fritz Crisler, in Hannah's opinion, no doubt had a major say in that debate behind closed doors.[39]

IN ALL fairness to Ralph Aigler and Herbert Crisler, the Intercollegiate Conference had valid reasons for tabling the latest Spartan application in the spring of 1947. At the time, the faculty leadership was focused on a very controversial issue—scholarships for non-scholar athletes.

Financial aid for students with physical rather than intellectual fitness was a concept spreading like a cancer across the country just prior to the Second World War. The practice originated in the Deep South. By the late 1930s, the Purity Movement was conceived in an attempt at treating the disease. And as expected, Professor Ralph Aigler was one of its principals. The chemotherapy—cautiously empowering the NCAA to discipline schools violating the spirit of its amateur code of ethics—failed for one glaring reason: home rule.[40] Back in 1906, in order to encourage membership in the fledgling organization, the NCAA founders assured schools the right to monitor their own compliance with the national association's rules and regulations. Years later, many colleges and universities, especially those south of the Mason-Dixon line, had no plans to abdicate that God-given right, especially in the interest of upholding an outdated and unrealistic amateur code.[41] Pearl Harbor, however, put a damper on the debate that followed the quick demise of the Purity Code.

Following the end of hostilities overseas, as anticipated, the subsidy issue cropped up again.[42] [43] By now high school seniors, with the approval of their parents, were effectively selling their athletic services to the highest bidder. Aigler and other amateur zealots, in an attempt at bringing "sanity" to the financial aid madness pervading the country, resurrected the old Purity Movement. And by the spring of 1947, the Intercollegiate Conference leadership was ready to discuss the provisional document, the Sanity Code, soon to be advanced by the NCAA. The Michigan professor was confident that the draft, effectively permitting academic scholarship for qualified student athletes, would become the law of the land within six months when NCAA members would gather in plenary session and cast their votes on the measure.[44] [45]

Professor Aigler wanted the Big Nine Faculty Representatives to not only approve the Sanity Code draft; he also wanted his conference to exceed the proposed NCAA benchmark for scholarship aid by rewriting the Intercollegiate Handbook to reflect that intent.[46] [47] [48] The May meeting in Highland Park was intended primarily for that reason.[49] Michigan State's application—let alone a debate on conference expansion back to ten members—was not a priority at the time.

MICHIGAN STATE College sought membership in the Western Conference once again in May of 1948. Unlike the previous four applications, the Spartan administration played no direct role in this one.

Back in March of 1946, John Hannah had written to members of the Council of Ten—the presidents representing all conference schools. The University of Chicago had just announced plans to withdraw from the organization; Hannah wanted to alert the university leaders of his desire to one day join their group.

The Michigan State president's letter prompted a notable response from Ann Arbor—the Ruthven Decree. What he didn't expect, however, was a letter from President James Lewis Morrill of the University of Minnesota. The two men had been close friends for a number of years. Morrill was unaware of Hannah's interest in joining the conference. He promised his support should the need arise.[50] One year later, after experiencing his fourth rebuff, John Hannah took his friend up on the offer.[51] [52]

By now, President Hannah was more than ever convinced that Ralph Aigler and Fritz Crisler were working behind the scenes to stymie his grand plans for Michigan State. Their recent public pronouncements of support were meaningless.[53] The president was dumbfounded. He had absolutely no way to counter Aigler and Crisler's control of debate (and votes) within the Big Nine.

Hannah shared his latest frustration with the Minnesotan. A Buckeye by both birth and degree, Lew Morrill learned early on to never trust a Wolverine.[54] He was more than willing to help out.

A few days later, Morrill wrote to his athletic leadership, Faculty Representative Henry Rottschaefer and Athletic Director Frank McCormick, and expressed a personal interest in aiding Hannah's cause. He asked for their assistance.[55]

The following spring, Michigan State tendered its fifth application for membership in the Intercollegiate Conference. The University of Minnesota orchestrated the initiative—neither Lew Morrill nor John Hannah was aware of it.[56]

As it turned out, both McCormick and Rottschaefer planned to submit separate motions in support of Hannah's quest at the upcoming May of '48 conference meetings.[57] [58] [59] Unfortunately neither Gopher had communicated with the other, let alone President Morrill, about their respective plans. In fact, the only one who knew exactly what was going on didn't even work for the University of Minnesota. Ralph Aigler had been informed of the agenda for both meetings a few weeks in advance by conference Commissioner Kenneth Wilson. Mindful of McCormick and Rottschaefer's separate intentions, he met with his athletic director. After mulling over the poorly conceived Minnesota plan, the Michigan Men devised a clever scheme to counter it.

Fritz Crisler would argue among his colleagues that he could not support McCormick's motion to expand membership, and thereby support Michigan State, until the college demonstrated full compliance with the Intercollegiate Handbook, consistent with Ralph Aigler's amended Ruthven Decree.[60] His fellow directors would no doubt line up behind him. Aigler, on the other hand, would deputize Illinois Faculty Representative Frank Richart to do his dirty work. The Wolverine leader feared exposure—embarrassing leaks to the press of a collaborative Michigan effort to foil the latest Spartan initiative. And so, a well-coached Richart would raise concerns among his faculty colleagues virtually identical to Crisler's.[61]

Needless to say, the Wolverine ploy prevailed without a glitch. The McCormick (and Rottschaefer) Miscue ended on that note.[62]

But, as had been the case in all-previous Spartan rejections, there was a valid reason for Aigler's plan to block any meaningful discussion on conference expansion. And once again, it all had to do with the Sanity Code, legislation that had recently been approved by the NCAA.

One year earlier, during the spring meetings in Highland Park, the conference leadership revised the Big Nine handbook. An academic scholarship for qualified student athletes was approved—at least in principle. Incoming freshman would now be eligible for financial aid. Professor Aigler, mindful of the political significance of this radical policy change for the Intercollegiate Conference, moved that the commissioner monitor member compliance with the provisional rule and report back to the Faculty Representative Committee the following spring. Wilson's eventual findings, however, were unexpected. Most schools had failed the final exam—including the University of Michigan.[63]

Recognizing the significance of the report cards he would soon be handing out, the commissioner sought counsel from the author of the controversial conference legislation. Ralph Aigler felt that the spring meeting should be devoted to this embarrassing discovery.[64] As a consequence, there would be little time for other agenda items—including debate on a Spartan petition for membership.

JOHN HANNAH first heard about the Spartan's failed fifth application a few days after the fact. In violation of conference rules on confidentiality, a Minnesota mole, perhaps Lew Morrill, had shared with
Hannah concerns that two conference leaders had expressed regarding
the Spartans' lack of compliance with their Intercollegiate Handbook.
What he didn't reveal was the other, more troublesome reason for cut-
ting off debate. The Wilson Report was too controversial to leak out to
anyone, including Morrill's good friend. Lacking that additional background information, all Hannah could conclude was what he had previously shared with Morrill—as long as the Wolverines were in control
of all debate, there would be little chance for Michigan State to gain
membership in the Big Nine.[65] [66]

James Lewis Morrill was not quite as pessimistic. Although he too
was convinced that Michigan was conniving behind closed doors to hinder the latest Michigan State application, the Minnesota president was
confident—given time and some good old-fashioned scheming on his
part—that the Wolverine influence could be thwarted.[67] After all, the
McCormick (and Rotschaefer) Miscue, in his opinion, had failed for
lack of coordinated planning between Minnesota and Michigan State
College.[68]

The Morrill Plan was brilliant.[69] He would personally politic members of the Council of Nine regarding John Hannah's initiative; if committed to the cause, Morrill asked that they share that intent with their
faculty representatives. In effect, he planned to circumvent bylaws on
questions of conference membership and size—a responsibility traditionally reserved for the faculty, not the presidents.[70] [71] As a consequence, Ralph Aigler's influence, so effective behind closed doors in
past debate, would be neutralized.

After hearing about his friend's shrewd plan, Hannah proposed an
amendment. He requested that Minnesota, rather than Michigan, make
the motion to admit Michigan State into the Intercollegiate Conference.
Hannah would also have President Fred Hovde, another close friend,
encourage his Purdue Boilermaker faculty representative to second the

motion, thereby ensuring a vote take place. Professor Aigler would be totally caught off guard.[72] Adding to the Spartan leader's intriguing proposal, the ploy would also force the powerful Wolverine to show his cards in this complicated poker game. Hannah reminded Morrill that ever since the Ruthven Decree of '46, Professor Aigler had openly supported Michigan State's cause. A nay vote on his part could prove very embarrassing for the University of Michigan if word was ever leaked to the press.

On December 12, 1948, Minnesota Faculty Representative Henry Rottschaefer proposed that Michigan State College be admitted into the Big Nine. Later that evening, by telephone, Lew Morrill and John Hannah would celebrate a rare victory for both schools over the Wolverines.[73] And somewhat surprisingly, for an institution that had experienced five rejections in 11 years, the sixth vote was unanimous—at least that was the tally shared with the press.[74]

As it turned out, Ralph Aigler was not to be outsmarted after all. Michigan State was only provisionally selected to replace the University of Chicago. Based on his confidential "Aigler Amendment" to Rottschaefer's motion, an ad hoc Committee of Three would make an unannounced visit to East Lansing to verify Spartan compliance with the Intercollegiate Handbook. Four stipulations were spelled out; the faculty expected a perfect score.[75] A final vote on membership would follow the committee's report and recommendation.[76]

Professor Ralph William Aigler, it appeared, was still in control.

CHAPTER 2

Only a Matter of Time

———

"One thing I regret is that, before calling for a vote [on the
Aigler Amendment to the Rottschaefer motion], I did not point
out the embarrassing position we might be in if the [Committee
of Three] investigation shows an unsatisfactory condition
continuing at [Michigan State]. Frankly, I doubt that it will,
but that is a possibility, if the action we took means anything."

PROFESSOR FRANK RICHART, UNIVERSITY OF
ILLINOIS; 17 DECEMBER 1948[1]

MICHIGAN STATE COLLEGE WAS NOT a popular choice to replace the
University of Chicago. Most Big Nine coaches and athletic directors
were upset over the Faculty Representative Committee's decision. And it
all had to do with financial aid and past administrative antics.

One year earlier, in January of 1948, President Hannah terminated
the controversial Jenison program. He had no choice. The Sanity Code
had just been approved by the NCAA membership. Only athletes demonstrating benchmark scholarship could now receive financial aid. The
rule, however, was proactive. Colleges could continue to honor contracts
with currently enrolled students.[2] Regardless of that decision, at issue
for conference coaches was competitive fairness. [3] [4] [5] [6] Spartan Head
Coach Biggie Munn's football program was loaded with a very talented

group of upperclassmen still legally on the dole. Why should they be obligated to compete against hired talent?

The athletic directors, on the other hand, questioned how a school with Michigan State's reputation ever gained admission. Non-conference schools were required to sign a contract that obligated adherence to the Intercollegiate Handbook rules on recruiting and eligibility. It was now well known that Michigan State had clearly ignored the obligation while continuing to compete on the gridiron against the University of Michigan over the past few decades. Why should the Spartans now embrace conference doctrine? Regardless of the December vote, heavily influenced by nine presidents, the college was clearly not welcomed.[7]

Shortly after the controversial December Decision, the athletic directors met to hammer out football schedules for the next three years. Mindful of how divisive the faculty representatives' vote to admit Michigan State was among coaches and athletic directors, Michigan's Fritz Crisler proposed his "Asterisk Motion." Assuming the Spartans were ultimately admitted into the conference, it would deny them claim to conference football crowns until all current Jenison awardees had exhausted their eligibility. The Spartans could participate in Big Ten play—it just wouldn't count. His colleagues supported the proposal.[8]

Four months later, the Committee of Three visited East Lansing. The college was found compliant with only two of four criteria necessary for sanctioned membership.[9] Fifty percent on any test, especially a final examination, was a failing grade in the opinion of four professors sitting on the Faculty Representatives Committee. In their opinion, the Spartans should get no credit for this college course on handbook policies. Based on the Aigler Amendment approved back in December, Michigan State's membership should be formally renounced.

The conference leaders now found themselves in a real quandary. To reject the college after unanimously (albeit provisionally) approving it only a few months earlier would prove embarrassing to a proud association of nine pre-eminent academic research institutions—a public relations nightmare unlike any other experienced by the Intercollegiate Conference during its first 50 years.[10]

Fortunately, the solution was simple, due in large part to the somewhat surprising but levelheaded actions of Professor Ralph William Aigler of the University of Michigan.

THE FATE of Spartan athletics was one of the last items on the agenda for the Friday afternoon meeting in Evanston.[11] Following completion of that session, Commissioner Kenneth Wilson met with reporters. He announced that Michigan State College of Agriculture and Applied Science was now a bona fide member of the Western Conference. The tally was unanimous, just like the provisional vote back in December. The entire conference family—faculty representatives, athletic directors, and coaches—eagerly welcomed the pioneer land-grant college into the Big Ten.[12]

Wilson's comments, in hindsight, were a ruse, a classic spin. What actually took place inside the Orrington Hotel on May 20, 1949, was quite another story.

Law Professor Ralph Aigler was keenly aware of conference procedure for a vote of this nature. Bylaws merely required a simple majority to change membership.[13] In other words, Michigan State needed just five consenting nods to assume the seat vacated by the University of Chicago. But after the Committee of Three report, confirmation was no longer a certainty. The four faculty skeptics were not going to budge. Fritz Crisler's Asterisk Motion, which had satisfied the pessimistic coaches and directors earlier that day, failed to appease the intransigent minority.

As he glanced around the conference table, Professor Aigler realized that an equal number of colleagues either favored or opposed the formal admission of Michigan State into the Big Nine.[14] [15] [16] In an ironic twist, the fate of Spartan athletics, at least for the foreseeable future, now rested in the hands of John Hannah's nemesis.

In years past, Ralph Aigler might have relished this unique opportunity. But times had changed. His boss, President Alexander Ruthven, had asked him to support the Spartans initiative three years earlier. Aigler's only requirement, oft repeated to a cynical press corps, was that Michigan State demonstrated complete compliance with the Intercollegiate Handbook.[17] And for the most part, it had. The two deficiencies noted by the Committee of Three were minor; they could be easily addressed before the upcoming academic year. He was content with its recommendations.

What Aigler now feared, however, was the backlash he might encounter if the decision proved unfavorable for John Hannah. As President Ruthven had reminded him a few years ago, the Aggie was extremely popular. Political leadership, press, and citizenry held him in high regard.[18] [19] In fact, Hannah was so greatly respected that prominent Republicans would ask him to run for governor a few years later.[20] [21] [22]

Professor Aigler, on the other hand, was not treated quite as kindly by the press. It probably had to do with his professional background as an attorney.

Steeped in the practice of confidentiality, Aigler maintained tight lips (for the most part) on controversial decisions involving the conference or his university. Reporters crucified him for his silence following a controversial 1929 investigation of illegal subsidy practices at the State University of Iowa; the humiliating probation and scheduling boycott were devastating for the school and its athletic program.[23] [24] Likewise, his refusal to answer questions regarding the termination of Michigan head coach Harry Kipke following the '37 football season rubbed sportswriters and naysayers the wrong way.[25]

John Hannah's recent and well-publicized quest for membership in the Big Nine didn't help Aigler's public image either. The law professor's lukewarm, if not ambiguous statements regarding support for the Spartans, dating back to the 1946 Ruthven Decree, put him at odds with reporters forced to interpret his legalese. Frustrated by his seemingly equivocal if not evasive responses, the media chose to challenge his integrity and character instead.[26] [27] It was undeserved.

But putting aside Professor Aigler's personal issues with members of the regional press, what really troubled the legal scholar, as he peered around the room, was how this story and his role in it might play out in major newspapers about the country. The prominent conference leader had reason to be concerned.

At about same time the faculty representatives were gathering to debate the Committee of Three findings, an issue of far greater significance for Ralph Aigler was brewing on the national scene. The Sanity Code, his legacy to intercollegiate sport, was under siege. Simply stated, a small number of schools were planning to challenge the Purity Movement legislation aimed at curbing subsidies for non-scholar athletes.[28] [29] [30] Their outwardly altruistic reasons for defying the code, if cleverly conveyed by prominent, sympathetic reporters and editors, could profoundly influence national debate on the controversial issue. And it wouldn't be hard to do. Aigler and his cohorts, at least within some circles, were perceived as insensitive to the poor student athlete trying to make ends meet while competing in the classroom and on the practice field.[31]

Aigler needed that media on his side with this impending debate over a revised definition of the amateur athlete. This inopportune Spartan vote, if misconstrued by the press, could be used to challenge his relevance as an amateur leader, even among his conference brethren that he had so adeptly influenced in years past.[32] [33] [34] [35] After all, there was no irony lost in this story involving Michigan State. John Hannah, until expediency required otherwise, was a well-known proponent of athletic grants. His reasons were eloquently outlined in his plenary address before the NCAA brethren three years earlier.[36] It was all about institutional hypocrisy—profess a conviction but practice otherwise. And in the process, hard-working young men were being taken advantage of by money-grubbing colleges and universities.

It appeared Professor Aigler had no options in this Spartan vote. He had to ensure that Michigan State was officially and finally approved for membership into the Western Conference. His four colleagues on the Faculty Representatives Committee must not be allowed to control a final vote on a well-publicized, five-month-old promise over a few minor, easily remedied deficiencies.

And so, Ralph William Aigler did what he did best behind closed doors—some good old-fashioned arm-twisting. Begrudgingly, the four defiant academicians conceded. Shortly after the decision, Commissioner Wilson announced the decision to the press outside.[37] [38]

FOUR WEEKS in advance of the Committee of Three visit to East Lansing, Professor Ralph Aigler and Athletic Director Fritz Crisler were already resigned to the fact that John Hannah would achieve his strategic objective, regardless of the committee's findings.[39] The two would now focus their attention on parenting a "problem child."[40] [41]

The college, in Aigler's opinion, lacked administrative leadership committed to the Intercollegiate Handbook. Its president was considered the greatest offender.[42] He was viewed as a crafty manipulator, willing to use any tactic, including dollars, to gain an athletic tradition at Michigan State.[43] [44] [45] [46] The loss of the Jenison Program was a considered a minor setback for Hannah and his sidekicks; the two Wolverine leaders were confident that an alternative subsidy scheme, certain to aid recruiting efforts, would soon evolve underground near campus.

And so, trusting no outside oversight organization, Aigler and Crisler would take it upon themselves to monitor activities around East Lansing.[47] [48] A few loyal alumni living in the community would aid the cause. All rumors would be shared with the commissioner's office.[49] [50]

Professor Ralph Aigler was facing mandatory retirement within six years. Nothing would please the old Wolverine more than to finally catch his adversary in the act before his tenure in Ann Arbor ended. And in Aigler's opinion, it was only a matter of time.[51] [52]

CHAPTER 3

King of the Hill

—

"A person who takes the position that all change means
progress irkes [sic] me as much as one who takes the position
that progress is made without change.... I don't know whether
to call myself a liberal conservative or a conservative liberal.
I do believe that one should hold to his present course until
he is reasonably sure that things will be better if one were
to travel another road...this is my basic philosophy."

PROFESSOR RALPH W. AIGLER; CIRCA NOVEMBER 1953[1]

RALPH WILLIAM AIGLER HAD LITTLE time for play during his youth.
Born February 15, 1885 in Sandusky County, Ohio, the youngest of
William and Mary Isabelle Aigler's four children, Ralph was raised on
a farm. He spent most of his childhood helping the family milk cows,
gather eggs, and clear the farmyard.[2] School was a break from the daily
routine.

Ralph's first experience with organized sports occurred during high
school in nearby Bellevue. He ran track for one season.[3] The youngest
Aigler, however, was a better student than athlete. He graduated second
in a class of twelve in the spring of 1901 while receiving honors notice.[4]
Three years later, he quit his job as an assistant cashier at a local bank.[5]
After heeding advice from his older brother Allan, Ralph moved to Ann

Arbor.[6] He planned to follow in his sibling's footsteps and study the law at the University of Michigan.

Following graduation in 1905, Allan returned to Bellevue and hung out his shingle. And like his father, a successful farmer and businessman, he soon became quite involved in business affairs about the community. He helped found and later presided over a local bank and a regional telephone company—both critical to the economic development of the region. He was also active in Republican politics. Allan was elected Huron County prosecutor. He later represented northwest Ohio in the state legislature from the 30th senatorial district. Bill Aigler's son would eventually serve in Columbus as president pro-tem and majority floor leader.[7] And for one day in 1930, due to vagaries of the state constitution, he was actually governor of Ohio![8]

Unlike his brother, Ralph had no interest in returning to his hometown let alone involving himself in local and state politics after graduation in the spring of 1907.[9] [10] [11] Intrigued with the big city, he accepted a job in Chicago with Rosenthal and Hamill. He planned to practice contract law.[12]

A few months after moving to Illinois, Michigan law Professor Edson Sunderland contacted his former student. The University of Michigan regents had recently approved a new part-time position as instructor in the Practice Court. The salary was $1200 per year. Promotion to professorship and full tenure was virtually a guarantee within three years if he remained interested in teaching.[13] The offer was hard to turn down. Over the next three years, Aigler would commute between Chicago and Ann Arbor.

As promised by Sunderland, Aigler was eventually promoted to full professor in 1910. By now, fully ensconced in academic law, he resigned his position with Rosenthal and Hamill and moved back to Michigan. And like brother Allan, he would soon find himself actively involved in politics and leadership—but at a university rather than in county and state government.

RALPH AIGLER first became acquainted with Fielding Yost and Michigan Football a year following his graduation.[14] Prior to that time, he had little interest in extracurricular sporting events taking place about campus. The Bellevue native was more focused on his legal studies. But by chance, on a Saturday afternoon in the fall of 1908, he happened to attend a football game at Ferry Field. The law department instructor was spellbound. Over the next 46 years, Aigler would rarely miss a gridiron contest in Ann Arbor.

Acknowledging his affection for the game, the young professor's introduction to Wolverine football was significant for another reason. In January of that same year, the University of Michigan withdrew from the Intercollegiate Conference of Faculty Representatives. The decision by the Board in Control of Athletics was controversial, to say the least. Just about everyone in town had an opinion. The lingering dispute peaked his interest in attending that first football game. The experience prompted him to thoroughly research the controversy. And by November of 1912, a well-informed Aigler, now passionate about the honorable intentions of the conference founders, would find himself caught up in a highly charged debate that just would not go away.

AS A member of the Intercollegiate Conference it helped found in 1895, the University of Michigan was obligated to maintain an oversight board, dominated by faculty, charged with ensuring that athletic integrity remained intact at all levels of the institution. The intent of the founders was to have academicians, protected by tenure, guard the best interests of students involved in extracurricular sporting activities.

Following the tragic 1905 college football season, one marked by a number of deaths and serious injuries on campus gridirons about the country, the conference leadership—influenced by President Theodore Roosevelt's call to action—modified its handbook. Rules of engagement were revised to make the game safer to play. Many of those changes, at least in the opinion of Wolverine students, would profoundly impact Fielding Yost's juggernaut currently dominating Big Nine play. The student body cried foul and demanded action to counter the decisions of the ruling Faculty Representatives Committee. A few delegates met with the university regents and president in January of 1907.

Shortly after that meeting, the regents petitioned the Board in Control of Athletics. Siding with the students, they demanded that Michigan withdraw from the Western Conference. Board members protested. The action by the regents—influencing responsibilities reserved for tenured faculty—was a major violation of conference bylaws. In defiance, the Board in Control took no action. Ten months later, the university regents, now swayed by student petitions overwhelmingly in favor of withdrawal, moved to reconstitute the recalcitrant athletic board. No longer would academicians maintain a majority number of seats. In mid-January of 1908, lacking faculty control of athletics, the University of Michigan formally withdrew from the Big Nine.

In retaliation for the unprecedented action, the Intercollegiate Conference of Faculty Representatives declared a scheduling boycott against its former member. No school was allowed to compete against the wayward Wolverines until they returned to the fold. Popular rivalries with Minnesota, Illinois, and Chicago were held in abeyance.

The boycott proved to be highly successful. Michigan Football suffered during the interim Decade of Defiance (1908-1917). As a consequence, certain factions of students, athletes included, circulated petitions requesting a return to conference affiliation. Informal debates cropped up about campus. But it was a planned gathering held at the Michigan Union in November of 1912 that caught the attention of the university community and town folk alike.

The debate centered on repatriation with the Intercollegiate Conference. During that dinner engagement attended by students and faculty, senior law student Frank Murphy, representing a large segment of the student body, demanded concessions from the conference before the Wolverines should entertain any invitation to return to the Big Nine.

A young Professor Ralph Aigler was asked to speak on behalf of the faculty. He noted that Murphy's points were off the mark. Rather than discuss concessions or retribution for past actions impacting Yost and his football team, Aigler argued that the debate should focus on the faculty regaining control of athletics at the university. After all, the university's six-year experiment in regent/alumni/student control of the athletic board was a proven failure.[15] [16]

Professor Aigler's comments created a stir, especially among the regents. Quite suddenly, a little known law professor was being quoted in the *Michigan Daily* and regional newspapers. By the spring of 1913, faculty peers, acknowledging his leadership skills in the aftermath of that debate, chose him to serve as one of their token representatives on the Board in Control of Athletics.[17] Over the next few years, he would sway student opinion in his favor. Petitions demanding change followed. The students desperately wanted the Wolverines back where they thrived—the Intercollegiate Conference. And the only way to assure that invitation was by regaining faculty control of all athletic policy at the University of Michigan. The regents capitulated to the latest student demands.

In June of 1917, at the request of the Board in Control, Professor Ralph Aigler met with the Western Conference faculty representatives in Chicago to announce the regents' decision. Shortly after reading his statement, the University of Michigan was unanimously welcomed back into the conference. And in acknowledgment of his leadership role in that action, the board selected him as its faculty representative to the Big Ten. Aigler would maintain that seat for the next 38 years.[18] In recognition of his contribution to Wolverine athletics, the legal scholar, with absolutely no skills in any sport, would be awarded an honorary "M" monogram. Many years later, he would be posthumously inducted into the University of Michigan's Athletic Hall of Honor for his role in regaining a tradition.[19]

AS INSTRUCTOR in the Practice Court, Ralph Aigler's job description included a number of mundane tasks that his supervisor, Professor Edson Sunderland, no longer had the time for. Essentially Aigler was asked to do secretarial work—it was his job to ensure that students understood courtroom procedure while studying case law.

Sunderland, perhaps sensitive to the basic tasks being asked of Aigler, embellished certain duties of the new position. He clearly wanted his former student to sign up. "The most difficult part of the work is the arrangement of jury cases, and it is absolutely indispensable that [you] develop facility in that line. Some dramatic sense, imagination and knowledge of the law are all necessary. It would be expected that in two or three years [you] would be able to arrange from a third to half of the cases." He polished off the job description by noting that the opportunity would "bring you into intimate touch with almost every branch of the substantive law."[20]

The recently appointed instructor proved to be one of the "most effective" teachers in the department despite holding down a job no one else wanted.[21] [22] [23] There were reasons for his popularity. He actually included a little wit and humor into a generally dull subject.[24] Aigler also enhanced the learning experience. Recognizing the inadequacies of the current program, he published a casebook series to assist students. Topics covered included bankruptcy, titles, negotiable papers, and banking.[25] Decades later, his texts were still widely circulated in law school programs about the country. But perhaps the most significant reason for Aigler being so well liked by his students was his willingness to befriend them and offer career counseling.[26] Many maintained contact with their mentor for years following graduation.

Being affiliated with the pre-eminent University of Michigan Law School, tenured professors were expected to publish scholarly works. Aigler was no exception. But compiling a casebook was by no means considered sufficient for a program of Michigan's repute. In time, he would transition away from the Practice Court. Real property and commercial law became his area of expertise. He ultimately gained a national reputation—Aigler penned over one hundred scholarly law review articles on these subjects during his long stay in Ann Arbor. And in recognition of his role in drafting a title-clearance law for Michigan, his name was attached to the McShane-Aigler act.[27] Many other states adopted its legal principles.[28]

Much like his father and older brother, the professor was a natural leader. His assumption of the faculty representative position was one clear-cut example. But he found time for serving in other leadership roles as well. Early in his career, he was selected as secretary-treasurer of the prestigious Association of American Law Schools. Aigler would eventually serve as its president.[29] He was also quite active in the American Bar Association.[30] In short order, recognizing his skills as an administrator, a number of prominent programs would offer him their deanship. Suitors included Colorado, Iowa, Ohio State, Arizona, Cincinnati, and Pittsburgh.[31] [32] [33] Perhaps anticipating the retirement of Dean Henry M. Bates, his mentor, Aigler remained in Ann Arbor.[34] A few years later, the University of Michigan regents would bypass him for that promotion in favor of another colleague on the faculty.

In addition to job offers from prominent law schools, Ralph Aigler was also recruited for the presidency of the University of Arizona. After much soul searching, he turned it down.[35] [36]

In acknowledgement of his scholarly repute and his skills in the lecture hall, several law schools—Stanford, Columbia, Harvard, the University of Southern California, and Cornell—offered him visiting professorships. And following retirement, Aigler would accept appointments as a part-time lector at Hastings College of Law and the University of Arizona.[37]

Early on in his tenure as Michigan's faculty representative, Professor Aigler recognized the potential his position on the Board in Control might play in steering athletic policy within the Big Ten. A law degree and persuasive tongue certainly didn't hurt his cause![38] In acknowledging the influential role he gained for the university, the board would nominate him on 12 consecutive occasions to serve three-year terms as its representative to the conference.[39] Mandatory retirement in the spring of 1955 would end the streak.[40]

Utilizing forensic skills, the lawyer would skillfully manipulate, if not dominate debate during conference gatherings in Chicago. His colleagues, usually professors of science, engineering or some branch of the liberal arts, lacking his gift of persuasive argument, often deferred to him.[41] [42] [43] [44] [45] And the first two commissioners of the conference, John Griffith and later Kenneth Wilson, mindful of that influence, realized that it was always critical to have Ralph Aigler in their court. They often sought his confidential counsel on challenging questions involving conference management.

As his influence and power grew, in part due to the athletic renown of the university he represented, the professor would assume a bully pulpit at the national level as well. Aigler became the voice for pristine amateur practices as spelled out in the NCAA constitution.[46] His passion for fairness in competition would ultimately earn him kudos, at least in some circles, for drafting the controversial Sanity Code legislation. Unfortunately for the prominent Purity Movement leader, his legacy to college athletics experienced a quick demise. The NCAA membership wasn't quite ready for the recently empowered organization to monitor regional recruiting and subsidizing practices. Despite that disappointing setback, he would continue to challenge college and university leaders to remain focused on their mission—they were educators and researchers, not purveyors of entertainment for the mass public.[47] [48] The well being of the student must always take precedence.

Professor Aigler served his university in other ways as well, while maintaining his seat on the Board in Control of Athletics.[49] Fielding Yost was physically and mentally declining during his final years in office. Acknowledging those deficiencies, a few regents approached the lawyer and requested that he assume responsibility for critical decisions traditionally reserved for the director. He would effectively run the athletic department from his law office in Hutchins Hall for almost two years.[50]

Under the professor's savvy leadership, the university eventually hired Herbert Orin Crisler as assistant director of athletics and head football coach in January of 1938.[51] [52] Crisler played a major role in resurrecting the proud Wolverine tradition in the aftermath of the tainted Harry Kipke years.[53] The coach would ultimately assume leadership of the department following Yost's retirement a few years later.

Ralph Aigler, like his father and brother, was a conservative Republican. He was outspoken in his opposition to most of President Franklin Roosevelt's initiatives. The New Deal was no exception.[54] [55] The moral fabric of society was being undone by liberalism.[56] Communist insurgency on college campuses—Ann Arbor in particular—greatly troubled him.[57] [58] Despite those concerns, he eschewed public office. The professor opted instead to share his wisdom with confidants; but he was always willing and eager to speak out if requested.[59] [60]

In his limited free time, the Bellevue, Ohio native enjoyed attending professional sporting events in nearby Detroit. The Tigers and Red Wings were a passion.[61] [62] The Detroit Lions were another matter. Obsessed over the professional creep into college football, he wanted nothing to do with the National Football League franchise![63] [64] Adding to his disdain for the Sunday afternoon version of football, he considered it "insufferably dull."[65]

Ralph and his wife Helen were the parents to one daughter. Helen passed away from breast cancer in January of 1943. Three years later, he married Eileen Maloney.[66] They remained together until his death in 1964.

DESPITE AN amazing career as an academician, perhaps Professor Ralph Aigler's most notable accomplishment, at least for alumni and fans, was his role in advancing the Michigan-Ohio State series into a classic rivalry ending the college football season.

In October of 1897, Ohio State University waged a battle on the gridiron against the University of Michigan for the first time. Sixteen years later, the Buckeyes could claim two "practical" victories—better known as ties.[67] In the opinion of many Wolverines fans, it was time to terminate the biennial contract with their neighbor south of the border.

As it turned out, Michigan's Decade of Defiance did temporarily end the series following the 1912 game. Ohio State had just signed on to become a member of the Intercollegiate Conference earlier that year. But due to handbook rules, the Buckeyes were unable to maintain a gridiron relationship with the former member of the Big Nine.

Five years later, the conference boycott was lifted. Thanks to Ralph Aigler, the aimless Wolverines found their way back home. By November, Michigan was once again a member of the Western Conference. The series between the schools resumed the following season. And as expected, Fielding Yost's Wolverines soundly defeated the Buckeyes in Columbus.

Ohio State would finally earn its first victory over Michigan in October of 1919. Two years later, Coach John Wilce could proudly claim a three-game winning streak.

Impressed with the Buckeye's recent success in the interstate series with his Wolverines, Faculty Representative Aigler wrote to Ohio State Athletic Director Lynn St. John. Acknowledging that the early-season contest was "no longer a practice game" for Michigan before the start of conference play (now that Ohio State was also a member), the law professor proposed that the schools compete during the final weekend of the season—a Saturday traditionally reserved for one's true rival. St. John, perhaps miffed by Aigler's choice of words, turned him down. That date belonged to the University of Illinois.[68] [69]

Undaunted by the rejection, the turncoat Ohioan again approached St. John a decade later. By now, the Buckeyes could claim six victories over Michigan since the football relationship was resumed in 1918. This time, St. John capitulated.[70] Scheduling contracts were signed the following spring. The Fighting Illini would be relegated to the weekend before the finale. And so, in large part due to the foresight and persistence of Ralph Aigler, the strange series with Ohio State became a bona fide rivalry as of November 23, 1935. Eight decades later, it remains one of the greatest annual brawls in all of college football.

UNLIKE OHIO State's Lynn St. John, Michigan State's Ralph Young would have eagerly accepted an offer from Professor Aigler to close out the season with the Wolverines, regardless of venue. The Scrimmage Game weekend, the season opener, failed to give the intrastate contest the recognition his boss, President John Hannah, sought for the land-grant college and its athletic program. Any date other than that last Saturday in September would have sufficed. Michigan, negotiating from a position of dominance at the time, would not relent on that frequent Spartan request. Ralph Aigler wanted nothing to do with elevating the politically mandated series to rivalry status.[71] And unbeknownst to Michigan State administrators, he had some pretty good reasons.

The State Agricultural College first challenged the University of Michigan on the gridiron in 1898 at Regents Field in Ann Arbor. Fifteen years later, under the tutelage of John Macklin, the Aggies would use a proven recipe for success—suspect eligibility standards and perhaps a little bit of rough play—to finally defeat the Wolverines.[72] Macklin quit coaching two years later following his fifth straight winning season, a campaign that included another victory over Fielding Yost. Alumni and loyal fans, only too familiar with Michigan's dominance in the series, were devastated by his decision.

Over the next decade the Aggies struggled on the football field. Shortly following the 1921 season, desperate for a field marshal to turn its fortunes around, the college offered an employment contract to Knute Rockne. After considerable reflection, the Notre Dame coach declined. Despite the rejection, Rockne remained in close contact with a few administrators at Michigan Agricultural College (MAC)—Dean Robert Shaw in particular.[73] That cordial, ongoing relationship with the legendary Irish coach would ultimately benefit the college; it would also profoundly impact Michigan State's relationship with the University of Michigan—at least in the eyes of a law professor in Ann Arbor.

In March of 1926, influential Aggies affiliated with the Detroit Alumni Club met with President Kenyon Butterfield. The college's strict recruiting and eligibility rules, instituted following the departure of Coach John Macklin, had devastated a once successful program. Frustrated with the poor performance of the football team, they proposed a "reorganization of the Athletic Board in Control."[74] Faculty control of the council was hindering the Spartans' ability to compete, especially against Michigan.[75]

In response to the alumni petition, the State Board of Agriculture formed an ad hoc committee "to study the whole question of athletics."[76] And by November, President Butterfield was ready to act. The Athletic Council was reconstituted—faculty presence was effectively diminished to minority status; alumni and students now ruled. A physical education curriculum to complement a growing intercollegiate athletic program at the college was approved. [77] Coaches could now offer marginal students an opportunity to attend Michigan State and earn a degree in its school of education.[78] The academic program—a proven means to build a football team—was a crafty scheme pioneered by certain Big Ten schools to circumvent onerous conference handbook rules on eligibility.[79] The Spartans would model their physical education program after one used by the State University of Iowa.[80]

The following season, after another disappointing gridiron campaign, Coach Ralph Young was asked to resign and focus his attention on managing the athletic department. The action was consistent with recommendations suggested by the Detroit Alumni Club one year earlier.

Lansing native Harry Kipke was hired to coach the Spartans. After one successful season, he resigned his post to accept the job at Michigan, his alma mater. Athletic director Fielding Yost's brazen ploy angered the Spartan administration and its new president, Robert Sidey Shaw. Yost not only negotiated with Kipke without gaining Shaw's permission—a common courtesy sanctioned by Big Ten leaders just a few years earlier—he did so during the late spring, only three months before the start of the 1929 season.[81] As a consequence of Yost's poaching, Michigan State was now placed in the unenviable position of trying to hire a coach at the last minute.[82]

The Spartans had acquired Harry Kipke's services for one reason: develop a winning tradition like Michigan's. Frustrated with the recent treatment provided the school by Yost, Robert Shaw turned towards South Bend and a trusted friend named Rockne. The college president would now embrace the Fighting Irish model for success.[83]

As it turned out, Knute Rockne and Fielding Yost had maintained a running feud for years.[84] Angered by his nemesis' breach of conference protocol at Michigan State's expense, the Notre Dame athletic director and head football coach took it upon himself to aid his friends in East Lansing.[85] [86] He offered to Director Ralph Young the names of several men with Fighting Irish blood. The coaching legend was confident that anyone on the list would serve the college well. [87] By mid-July, Michigan State had its man. James Harold Crowley, one of Rockne's famed Four Horsemen, signed a three-year contract a few weeks later.[88] [89] Saturday afternoon victories would soon follow.

The All-American quickly realized, however, that his sideline skills gained through past association with Rockne and Notre Dame were not sufficient to sustain a winner following that first season. He needed more talent. And therein lay the problem for law Professor Ralph Aigler of the University of Michigan.

For three decades, the Wolverines dominated intercollegiate football. Its tradition for gridiron excellence was second to none. And with the completion of Michigan Stadium in 1927, Michigan coaches could offer gifted athletes an additional reason for moving to Ann Arbor—competing in front of 85,000 spectators. Michigan State, by comparison, lacked a football tradition. And College Field, recently expanded, sat at most 20,000 fans with bleachers added.[90] The Spartans had a tough sell.

The amateur code of ethics (1906 and later 1916) re-defined the college game.[91] Proselyting (recruiting) and subsidizing student athletes were strictly forbidden. Eligibility standards were upgraded.[92] Most conferences professed allegiance—at least in principle—to NCAA rules.[93] The Southern Conference, however, failed to subscribe. Recruiting, financial aid packages, and booster support were means towards an end—winning football and institutional pride.[94] [95] And with the NCAA lacking disciplinary powers at that time, little could be done to counter the practice.[96] Prior to his arrival in East Lansing, Sleepy Jim Crowley was an assistant coach at the University of Georgia.[97] He departed Athens well versed in recruiting and subsidizing.

Not long after the Horseman trotted into town, Michigan State—eager to assist its Rockne protégé—created a loan fund intended for all students, athletes included.[98] A booster club, promoted by the new coach, soon followed. Sleepy Jim, in short order, was recruiting top-notch talent to East Lansing.[99] By the end of his second season on the sidelines, the young coach was a proven winner. Shaw's investment was paying off.

In the meantime, back in Ann Arbor, stories began circulating among the athletic leadership about amateur code and Big Ten contract violations taking place under Crowley's watch.[100] However, there was very little Ralph Aigler could do about the rumors. Consistent with NCAA rules, the college—unaffiliated with a conference—monitored its own compliance.[101]

Undeterred by that historic loophole, the lawyer had a few remaining options he could use to quietly discipline the outlaws.[102] In theory, he could enforce a Big Ten contract effectively signed by the Spartans. It obligated non-conference programs to honor the Intercollegiate Handbook—strict rules consistent with the amateur code.[103] Noncompliance could justify his severing the current scheduling agreement and all future football competition with Michigan State.[104] But he was also aware that state taxpayers demanded the game. As a consequence, he was left with no legal recourse to stand behind.[105] [106]

Vigilante justice—disciplining the college outside the constraints of due process—was another option for the lawyer.[107] [108] The penalty was harsh: without explanation, avoid contracting future football games with the Spartans. The financial repercussions of not competing in Michigan Stadium would send a message to the administration in East Lansing.

But once again, there was no way the professor could end the popular intrastate series.[109] The press would hound him for an explanation. Regardless of his cautiously worded response, sportswriters would speculate on why the Wolverines failed to contract with the college. Inevitably, Michigan would be ridiculed in the papers for appearing pompous and sanctimonious towards the Spartans—especially if the real reason was ever discovered. The law professor appeared to be in a real bind.

Sleepy Jim Crowley was extremely successful during his four-year tenure in East Lansing. Winning records were now an expectation among the students and alumni. And although he failed to defeat the Wolverines, the coach did tie Michigan on two occasions—moral victories in a series marked by far too many losses.

In January of 1933, Crowley would tender his resignation to accept a job at Fordham University in the Bronx. Although Spartan fans were initially angered over the announcement, it was probably fortuitous that the coach had moved out East.[110] [111] [112]

A few weeks following the press release, the North Central Association (NCA), an accrediting agency for institutions in the upper Midwest, investigated Michigan State College. In addition to monitoring compliance with regional academic standards, the NCA also evaluated the role athletics, as a part of a physical education department curriculum, played in student development.[113]

Two months later, President Robert Shaw would receive the highly confidential report. Michigan State College was in violation of a number of NCA standards. There was an "overemphasis on intercollegiate athletics" at the school. Skilled athletes were being recruited and illegally subsidized through loans and jobs. Grades were "uniformally [sic] high" in comparison to those of non-athletes. Coach Crowley, in particular, was cited for his lack of leadership and prolonged absence from the campus. As an associate professor in physical education, he provided little to "the educational [experience] or character building program" for college students.[114] (In hindsight, integrity may not have been one of Crowley's stronger suits—at least at that time. Unbeknownst to the investigator, the coach claimed a diploma from the University of Notre Dame on his resume, a requirement for any tenured faculty appointment. In point of fact, he never graduated from ND.) [115] [116] [117] [118] Michigan State was at-risk for public censure due to its various NCA violations,[119] a devastating blow for an institution struggling with enrollment numbers and financial solvency during the early Depression.

Acknowledging that the coach was no longer an employee, the accrediting agency appeared to grant Shaw some leniency. The college would be tentatively credentialed pending a review of its corrective actions for the remaining infractions.[120]

Aware that the North Central Agency had investigated Michigan State, Professor Ralph Aigler was certain that the college would finally be disciplined for violation of NCA standards—standards consistent with the Big Ten handbook. With censorship or probation a foregone conclusion, he could, at least temporarily, sever a relationship with the non-conference program and avoid repercussions from the press and certain state politicians. The Big Ten schools, after all, had recently agreed to cancel contracts with programs disciplined by the NCA for noncompliance with its strict standards.[121] Aigler was feeling smug—and rightly so.

But when the accrediting agency announced that Michigan State passed its review with flying colors, the law professor was absolutely beside himself. He concluded that the NCA was not only inept but also incapable of monitoring athletic practices at institutions—Michigan State included.[122]

And so, in response to that seemingly sham NCA investigation, Ralph Aigler would take it upon himself to covertly discipline the land-grant college whenever the opportunity arose. Over the next two decades, while questionable recruiting and subsidizing practices continued unchecked in East Lansing, he would organize a conference-scheduling boycott, share rumors with colleagues about lax administrative oversight at the college, and use his persuasive tongue, behind closed doors, to hinder the Spartans' ultimate quest—membership in his conference.

IN SEPTEMBER of 1918, an extremely bright young man from Manistee moved to East Lansing. Four years later Claud Robert Erickson would graduate from Michigan Agricultural College with a degree in mechanical engineering.[123] Although having little interest in athletics,[124] he would one day orchestrate a booster scheme that would not only gain for him an unexpected notoriety but also profoundly embarrass the leadership of his alma mater. It would also afford Professor Ralph Aigler an opportunity he had been patiently waiting for dating back 20 years—a chance to finally and definitively discipline the outlaw institution located 60 miles away.

CHAPTER 4

A Call to Duty

—

An amateur athlete is one who participates in competitive
physical sports only for the pleasure and the physical, mental,
moral and social benefits directly derived therefrom.

ARTICLE 6: NCAA CONSTITUTION OF 1916[1]

TWO DAYS FOLLOWING THE DECEMBER '48 announcement that Michigan
State was chosen to replace the University of Chicago, Professor Frank
Richart wrote a letter to John Hannah. It was his "pleasant duty," as
chairman of the Faculty Representatives Committee, to welcome the
Spartans into the Western Conference. The research engineer, an expert in structural concrete, tempered his comments by noting that that
decision was not yet cemented into place. The conference leadership
expected full compliance with its Intercollegiate Handbook. There remained four conditions that had to be addressed to their satisfaction
before the Spartans could claim affiliation.[2] And the issue of greatest
concern was Hannah's subsidy program for non-scholar athletes, financial aid still in effect for upperclassmen.

The Big Nine leadership wanted to make it very clear to President
Hannah that membership in their exclusive club was not without cost.
And it all had to do with the recently approved NCAA Sanity Code and
a revised Intercollegiate Conference Handbook consistent with that
law.

The historic NCAA legislation, drafted in large part by Michigan law Professor Ralph Aigler, required that all members abide by benchmark regulations on financial aid for athletes.[3] [4] Failure to comply with the law of the land placed an institution at-risk of dismissal from the national association. Adding bite to its bark, schools "in good standing" were required to "schedule intercollegiate contests only with institutions which (sic) conduct their athletic programs in conformity with [the revised NCAA constitution]."[5] In other words, contracting with an outcast program, perhaps in the interest of preserving an old rivalry, placed that school at-risk of being denied prized privileges of membership—participation in NCAA-sponsored events. [6] [7]

President Hannah was faced with a real conundrum. On the one hand, maintaining his controversial Jenison program could lead to Michigan State being banished from the national organization. Lacking that affiliation would no doubt force prominent regional programs, most notably Notre Dame and Michigan, to sever contractual relationships with the Spartans. [8] Rescinding the financial aid program, on the other hand, could profoundly impact talent flow to East Lansing—critical for his football program's ascent to the next level of national competition.

The Spartan leader, challenged by the ramifications of non-compliance with the Sanity Code, chose to terminate the subsidy program in January of 1948.[9] Future freshmen athletes that failed to measure up to the NCAA benchmark for scholarship would be denied grants. Current upperclassmen, however, were allowed to continue receiving Jenison dollars until their eligibility was used up. It was consistent with an NCAA ruling that allowed schools to honor contracts signed with students prior to January.[10]

But that would all change by late December. Michigan State was now a provisional member of the Intercollegiate Conference. In order to attain official membership, the college had to abide by Big Ten financial aid standards—far more restrictive than the national Sanity Code criteria. Only students graduating in the upper quarter of their high school class could apply for academic scholarships.[11] [12] Most current Spartan varsity athletes failed to measure up to that benchmark.

Hannah was once again left in a quandary. He had to comply with Big Nine rules if he were to pass muster with the Committee of Three investigators coming to town sometime in the next few months. Yet he also felt an obligation to those 100 young men that had been promised financial aid. Unfortunately for the president, his college had few if any options left to assist the kids. Work-study opportunities were non-existent at that time of the year. And off campus jobs were a rarity so soon after Christmas.

Ralph Aigler had anticipated this dilemma. Yet he felt no empathy. This was John Hannah's problem. He created it. He can fix it. And in private conversation, he shared as much.

> Frankly, I [am convinced]... that Hannah and his associates at Michigan State [had failed to] realize just what it means for them to live up to Conference rules. Their attention was centered upon the prestige that they thought would come from being a member of our Conference.[13]

The pressure for his administration to now find some alternative means to fulfill those contractual promises was undoubtedly immense. The law professor was confident that some "sub rosa scheme, the existence of which will be difficult to detect," would eventually take shape in East Lansing.[14] Unbeknownst to Aigler, the plans were already in the works.

CLAUD ROBERT Erickson grew up in Manistee, Michigan shortly after the turn of the century. He was an extremely bright boy and excelled in the classroom. He also displayed some character and grit. His parents struggled financially while trying to raise a family in a lumber town noted for its economic booms and busts. Claud worked part-time jobs throughout high school to help them out. Immediately following graduation, he assumed a full-time position in town rather than move on to college. Erickson continued to share part of his pay with the family. Not long after hiring on as a laborer, however, a few co-workers realized that he had a brighter future away from the sawmills. They encouraged him to reconsider his decision to remain in Manistee.[15] Four years later, in the spring of 1922, he completed his studies in mechanical engineering at Michigan Agricultural College.[16][17]

Time spent in East Lansing proved challenging for the student. Erickson struggled to find the means to support himself. At one point he contemplated dropping-out of school. Perseverance, a trait gained from his earlier years in Manistee, ultimately helped him land a part-time job at a power plant in Lansing. The dollars covered living expenses near campus.[18] In addition, certain faculty members, mindful of his financial plight, "chipped in to keep him in school."[19] That unexpected kindness left an indelible mark on him. It also endeared Erickson to his alma mater.

Following graduation, Claud took on a full-time position at the Lansing Board of Water and Light. Over the next decade he would earn additional graduate professional degrees in mechanical, electrical, and civil engineering from Michigan State College while attending classes in off hours.[20][21][22] Taking advantage of his advanced training, Erickson assumed greater responsibilities at the municipality. He ultimately became general manager and a member of the governing board. The Aggie was also very active in national and regional engineering associations during a professional career that spanned 53 years. In recognition of his distinguished service to its organization and to the community, the Board of Water and Light affixed his name to its new Delta Township power plant in 1971.

Leadership appeared to be a passion for Claud Erickson. Away from work, he was quite active in guiding many volunteer organizations. He also sat on various community boards, serving as either member or chairman.[23]

In June of 1982, the alumni board of the Michigan State University College of Engineering announced plans to recognize a distinguished graduate. Claud Robert Erickson was its first recipient. To this day, his name remains associated with the annual award.

When John Hannah was promoted to president of Michigan State College, his vision was to transition the school into a major land-grant institution. He wanted the faculty, students, and alumni to serve their communities, their country, and ultimately the world through outreach, consistent with the educational philosophy of Justin Morrill. And in pursuing that commitment, he was confident that all participants would gain a greater appreciation and respect for their university.

President Hannah once asked a prominent Michigan Agricultural College graduate, one who had lived a life of service to his community and country, why Aggie and Spartan alumni continued to support their alma mater? Claud Erickson's response, based on his personal experience, was predictable. Recalling the kindness, encouragement, and generosity offered to him by a number of professors during financially challenging undergraduate years, he commented, "Because they love the university that offered them the hand of friendship and the open door of opportunity."

(As will be seen, Erickson's hand of friendship—clasped with a wad of dollars—would one day humiliate his alma mater and its proud administration.)

IN OCTOBER of 1938, Secretary of the College John Hannah was asked by President Robert Shaw to hire an engineering consultant capable of overseeing "the development and operation of heating, power and other utility facilities on the campus."[24] He sought the counsel of engineering Dean Henry Dirks. Claud Erickson was highly recommended "as the outstanding person in the country for this type of service."[25] That was quite a compliment coming from a professor with Ivy League credentials.

Secretary Hannah asked that Dirks work out a contract with his former graduate student. After ironing out a few wrinkles concerning fees, the two engineers consummated the agreement with a handshake; nothing was documented in writing. Erickson agreed to serve the college administration as a formal consultant focused on monitoring infrastructure repair and new construction projects. He would be provided a flat stipend "paid at a rate of $1,500 per year effective December 1st, 1938."[26] Erickson would also receive a small percentage of final project costs—not an insignificant amount when dealing with multimillion-dollar bids.

Assuming a contract consistent with college business practices had been drafted and signed between the two engineers, Secretary Hannah gave his cursory approval. He had never discussed with Dirks the finer details of the understanding. The State Board, based on its secretary's recommendation, effectively rubber-stamped a handshake agreement. Hannah's failure to request a copy of the contract proved to be a rare, yet costly, miscue for the young administrator.

The first project assigned to Claud Erickson involved expansion plans for the power plant adjacent to Macklin Field. It was a major strategic undertaking. Future infrastructure growth south of the Red Cedar River was predicated on the success of this endeavor. And as anticipated by Dean Dirks, Erickson handled it with aplomb. He entertained construction proposals and weighed various bids. Secretary Hannah approved his recommendations. He then monitored the huge project. Eighteen months later, following completion of work at the site, Erickson presented his invoice to the college secretary. John Hannah was taken aback, if not miffed, by what he read. The bottom line was totally unexpected.[27]

In addition to Erickson's annual base fee of $1,500 for project oversight, the consultant also tacked on his invoice a 1.5 percent surcharge ($1,700) for the current power plant revision. The added fee was not consistent with a retained contract the college had with a large architectural firm also involved in the project.[28][29]

Frustrated with failing to locate the signed document spelling out the agreement, the college secretary met with the dean of engineering. Much to Hannah's surprise, Dirks lacked a copy as well. The contract, he pointed out, was based on a promise and a handshake. And to the best of his recollection, that tack-on fee was consistent with their understanding. Hannah had no recourse but to honor the legally binding contract.

The secretary called a meeting with the consultant. The college would respect the Dirks-Erickson agreement and honor the consultant's current and future invoices, regardless of project costs. Hannah merely insisted that the understanding now be appropriately documented. And in appreciation for Hannah respecting the original handshake contract, Erickson agreed to offer a rebate—at least it sure appeared that way. The engineer would write out a check, approximately 18% of any invoice, to Michigan State each time he received payment from the college. It was understood that the benefaction was always "to be used as the College Administration desires." His only request was that there "be no publicity concerning [the] gift."[30]

(That boilerplate note, occasionally showing up in State Board minutes announcing a payment to and coinciding gift from Erickson, would one day pique the curiosity of a recently appointed board member from Grand Rapids. Frederick Mueller's reading of the contract during the spring of 1950 would bear some historical significance for Michigan State and its consultant.)

The experience of negotiating with the college secretary was an enlightening one for the public works engineer. The savvy young administrator impressed the consultant. If Erickson planned to maintain his lucrative contract with the college, it was quite obvious that he must remain in John Hannah's good graces.

One year following written affirmation of the original Dirks-Erickson Handshake Contract, Secretary Hannah would replace the retiring Robert Shaw as president of Michigan State College. Six months later, in early December of 1941, the United States would find itself at war. All construction projects on campus were suddenly put on hold. And for Claud Erickson, that meant his services would not be needed, at least for the duration of conflict overseas.

THE END of the Second World War was only a matter of time. Munich was under allied control by early May of 1945. Within a few months, Tokyo would surrender as well. Back home, Americans were beginning to celebrate. One year earlier, however, the mood was not quite as optimistic. Hitler's Wehrmacht was holding its own in Europe and the Japanese, despite some recent setbacks, remained equally defiant. D-Day was still a closely guarded secret.

Despite the somber news from overseas, a few leaders in Washington were confident that the Allies would eventually prevail. Anticipating that outcome, the United States Congress passed the Servicemen Readjustment Act, better known as the GI Bill in early June of 1944. President Franklin Roosevelt signed it into law two weeks later. The intent of legislative leaders was to avoid the unfortunate treatment Great War veterans experienced after returning from Europe a few decades earlier.

The GI Bill was "seen as a genuine attempt to thwart a looming social and economic crisis" about the country.[31] The president, signing the historic law, was also sending a clear message to colleges, universities, and trade schools. The government needed help in educating and training millions of servicemen soon to be returning to an economy in transition back to peaceful times.

Michigan Republican Governor Harry Kelly, unlike politicians in Washington, was way ahead in planning for that day. In mid-January of 1943, shortly after his inauguration, the Great War veteran audaciously proposed the use of surplus income tax revenue to finance a Veterans Trust Fund. The invasion of Normandy was still a year and a half away. It didn't matter. Kelly wanted dollars readily available to aid returning soldiers. Memories of 1919 were still fresh in his mind.

While serving as secretary of the college during the late 1930s, it was John Hannah's job to lobby the legislature on behalf of Michigan State. The future college president considered all politicians working in Lansing as friends. But his relationship with Kelly was special. The two became very close after their first encounter. Mutual respect for each other's leadership skills topped the list. It didn't hurt matters that they shared similar political convictions. Ancestry may have also entered into the mix. Although Hannah's father was of Scottish Presbyterian descent, his mother, Mary Malone, was pure Irish Catholic. [32] And for a man named Kelly, that all but sealed the deal!

As their relationship evolved, the shrewd leaders realized how they might use each other to accomplish grander political goals. The governor would lean on his friend's statewide popularity to gain passage of critical legislation. Hannah could assure him key votes from rural politicians, regardless of party affiliation—his years as an agriculture extension service agent positioned him well to deliver on a promise. [33] [34] [35] And the college president would take advantage of his association with the head of state to gain insider knowledge about pending legislative action, the most significant being appropriations. [36] The "Victory Building Program" was perhaps the best example.

By the end of the war, Kelly's 1943 Veterans Trust Fund was well endowed with over $50 million. Mindful of his commitment to returning soldiers, the governor proposed the Victory Building Program. Half of the sequestered fund was to aid indigent veterans and their families; the remainder was to be set aside to "underwrite a substantial State building program to meet the accumulated and anticipated needs for educational buildings and for State-operated facilities such as hospitals." [37]

John Hannah began planning for the future of his institution within months of the Allied assault on Normandy, largely due to his awareness of Kelly's plan. Projections were that Michigan State would double its enrollment to 12,000 within a few years; many of those students would be returning veterans. [38] His close relationship with the governor allowed him to predict with some certainty the availability of state funding for various construction projects necessary to accommodate that influx. [39]

Mindful that the Victory Building Program would be enacted and dollars made available shortly after January 1, 1946, Hannah had his staff complete applications for funds well in advance of the roll call on the proposed bill. His board had already approved architectural and engineering plans for future projects based on promises for funding from Governor Kelly. Construction contracts followed. Hard-hat crews would begin digging around campus by late February![40] [41] Needless to say, Michigan State, well prepared for the dollar dole-out,[42] received a very healthy share from the state legislature.[43] [44]

And so, by May of 1945, it came as no surprise to the State Board of Agriculture that President Hannah requested that the college resurrect its relationship with Claud Erickson. His services were desperately needed to ensure that all these projects, including yet another expansion of the power plant near the stadium, remained on schedule and under budget.[45] [46] [47] The Lansing Board of Water and Light engineer was up to the task. He eagerly resumed his moonlighting arrangement with the college.

Less than a year later, State Board minutes would note receipt of a "statement from Claud Erickson in the amount of $6,000 for work that he had done on the married veterans' trailer court."[48] It was his first oversight job in four years. And in gratitude for the work, as well as the timely payment, the consultant confidentially gifted his alma mater $1000, consistent with an old rebate understanding. College Secretary Karl McDonel, Hannah's right hand business administrator, sent a note of appreciation a few days later on behalf of the president and the board. [49] [50]

Over the next three years, Claud Erickson would bill Michigan State $52,200 for his services. Based on the relative value of money, he received over $500,000 for moonlighting.[51] And in appreciation for the opportunity to work with his alma mater, the engineer would rebate $11,675—equivalent to $112,000 in 2014. That 1938 handshake with Dean Dirks ultimately proved to be a very lucrative for the Aggie!

Although Erickson's business practice, while contracting with a public domain, appeared suspect by today's standards, it was not out of the norm at that time. Gifting was an effective means of marketing services and solidifying relationships. And there was no doubt that the consultant provided a first-class product; other than Secretary Hannah's initial concerns with the fee arrangement, no other complaint was ever filed by the administration.

Erickson's largesse would abruptly end in January of 1949.[52] There was no clear-cut explanation—he was still receiving jobs.[53] In hindsight, the timing may have had something to do with the recent, provisional admission of Michigan State into the Intercollegiate Conference and the termination of its residual Jenison program—a mandatory requirement for membership.

ON JANUARY 28, 1949, only two days before Secretary McDonel would receive the final confidential gift to the State Board from engineering consultant Claud Robert Erickson, the University of Michigan faculty representative to the Big Nine wrote a long letter to Commissioner Ken Wilson and Professors Paul Blommers of Iowa and Kenneth Little of Wisconsin. Ralph Aigler wanted to educate the ad hoc Committee of Three about Michigan State's past transgressions. The law professor didn't want the upcoming investigation of the college to be in vain. The school's official membership in the Western Conference, as he reminded the three investigators, was predicated on their committee performing a thorough inspection of Spartan compliance with the Intercollegiate Handbook. Acknowledging that past misconduct was not at issue, awareness of old behavior might still offer clues about remaining improprieties as they poked about campus in the near future.

Aigler's greatest concern, dating back to the decision by the Faculty Representatives Committee to conditionally select the Spartans, was how the college administration might deal with severing subsidies to almost 70 upperclassmen currently enrolled in the Jenison program.[54] The recently revised conference handbook permitted institutional dollars for valid scholars only—young men graduating in the top 25 percent of their high school class. Most of the Jenison awardees, based on his understanding, were clearly ineligible.

Presumably, with the beginning of the term following our actions of December, and that would be just after January [of

1949], those [athletic] scholarships were terminated. I need not emphasize to you three men what a drastic step that would be considered to be, particularly by the young men who have been enjoying that easy income and then find it taken away from them. I have some evidence that a considerable dispute has arisen on the campus over at East Lansing in this respect.

It must be perfectly obvious that the pressure to find some alternative way of taking care of these athletes will be tremendous. You men on the committee can easily learn whether they have been taken off the Jennison [sic] list. It will not be so easy for you to learn whether the aids have been continued in some more subtle form....

Knowing the situation as I know it, there are going to be strong pressures [in] East Lansing to cut corners, particularly in such things as these Jennison [sic] scholarships. [55]

In May of 1949, following its three-day investigation, the Committee of Three would offer its recommendations to the faculty representatives. Behind closed doors at the Orrington Hotel in Evanston, Illinois, the leadership would heatedly debate Michigan State's failure to fulfill all four remaining requirements for membership. But in the end, in large part due to Professor Ralph Aigler's powers of persuasion, the college would be officially and finally welcomed into the Big Nine.

In response to the favorable decision, President John Hannah promised prompt action on the two remaining deficiencies.[56] Unfortunately, the conference and Commissioner Kenneth Wilson took him at his word. The most significant shortcoming, failure to ensure faculty control of the Spartan Athletic Council, was not adequately addressed by his administration.[57] [58] Four years later, in the aftermath of a very embarrassing chapter in the college's history, Hannah would finally correct that deficiency.[59] [60]

A FEW months in advance of Michigan State's official acceptance into the Big Nine, an Aggie—perhaps out of duty to his alma mater—took it upon himself to form a foundation. At one time, the college graduate had been challenged by education costs. If not for the financial generosity of a few professors, he would have dropped out of Michigan Agricultural College. It now appeared the right time to give back to his alma mater. That misguided decision by Claud Erickson, to offer under-the-table assistance to student athletes, would prove Ralph Aigler prescient—at least it surely seemed that way.

CHAPTER 5

Prelude to Probation

———

COMMISSIONER JOHN GRIFFITH WORKED FEVERISHLY over the preceding week to ensure that all arrangements were in place for the faculty, directors, and head coaches soon to arrive in Chicago. He thanked his small staff for their perseverance in assisting him. They would gather Thursday morning to tie up loose ends before conference dignitaries began checking in later that afternoon.

Griffith arrived at the office about 6:30AM. He planned to gather thoughts on his opening comments for the Friday evening plenary session. The phones would start ringing in a few hours—interruptions were a certainty throughout the day. There was no better time to organize thoughts. Two hours later, one of the secretaries, shortly after her arrival, found the commissioner slumped over on his desk. He was without a pulse.

Word of John Griffith's sudden death spread quickly among the Western Conference leadership. Despite the tragic news, the faculty representatives, athletic directors, and coaches all agreed to convene the following day for the first session of planned meetings. Griffith would have wanted it that way.

PRIOR TO the Second Great War, back in the mid-1930s, a number of universities and colleges were recruiting talented athletes to enroll in school by offering subsidies. The University of Pittsburgh adopted the practice. Pay-for-play, as Panther coaches soon discovered, was a sure way to win football titles.[1] To stem the tide, the NCAA responded with its Purity Code. Unfortunately for the authors of that historic legislation, there was no means to enforce it; the NCAA remained impotent to act on outcasts.[2] [3]

Shortly after the Purity Code demise, the Japanese attacked Pearl Harbor. And within a few months, the military would contract with colleges and universities to assist in training young men for deployment overseas. Debate on novel payment schemes intended to circumvent an amateur ideal under siege, was placed on hold as everyone focused on winning a war rather than a Saturday afternoon football game.

Recognizing the invaluable role competitive sport might play in encouraging conditioning and promoting esprit de corps among inductees, the military effectively assumed control of all athletic activities on campuses, intercollegiate team sports included.[4] As a consequence, conference rules on scheduling and eligibility were suspended. Students were transferred to various colleges or bases for basic training, ROTC instruction, or pre-flight school preparation. And if the inductee was an athlete of varsity caliber, he was encouraged to participate with the service team sponsored by that college or military base. It was considered a part of his patriotic duty.

The unprecedented training program was highly successful. Millions of young men were expeditiously deployed due to collaboration among college administrators, athletic directors, and coaches, all eager to aid the military cause. By spring of 1944, the War Department was confident in its projections; the manpower currently in uniform was more than adequate to defeat both Germany and Japan. There was no longer a need for housing and training new soldiers and seamen on college campuses. Implicit in that announcement was that de facto military control of intercollegiate athletics would soon end.

With that backdrop in mind, only five months after the successful Allied landing along the northern coast of France, Professor Ralph

Aigler decided that it was the right time to begin discussing the implications of all these recent military developments on conference practices.

John Griffith's untimely death in early December of '44, however, put that debate on hold. The more pressing concern for the men about to gather at the Sherman Hotel that weekend was finding a replacement for their highly regarded commissioner.[5]

HERBERT ORIN Crisler graduated from the University of Chicago in the spring of 1922. His original intent was to earn a science degree and later attend medical school; at least that was his plan until he met Amos Alonzo Stagg.[6] His football coach, an imposing figure despite diminutive stature, proved to be quite a mentor. Crisler would change career plans and pursue physical education and coaching.[7] [8]

Following graduation from the Midway, Fritz Crisler accepted a job as an assistant to Coach Stagg. The University of Minnesota, desperate for a man of integrity to run its program, later hired the 31-year-old prodigy to serve as combined head football coach and athletic director. After two years, he resigned to assume similar responsibilities at Princeton. In late December of 1937, Professor Ralph Aigler, de facto athletic director of the University of Michigan at the time, negotiated Crisler's controversial move to Ann Arbor.[9] [10] He would assume leadership of the football program the following spring. Three years later, he inherited the athletic director's office.

Crisler was a gifted leader. Extremely bright, articulate, and impassioned—he captivated an audience. The Wolverine was also quite an accomplished businessman.[11] Balancing budgets and managing employees proved no challenge for him. He quickly gained the respect of his colleagues within the university and about the conference.[12]

Acknowledging his various attributes, it came as no surprise to the Big Ten faculty representatives that Fritz Crisler was the athletic directors' first choice to replace the recently deceased John Griffith.[13] It also came as no surprise to those conference leaders that he declined their offer. His current position in Ann Arbor, leading a premier athletic program, provided him with greater opportunity to impact the course of intercollegiate policy.[14] [15]

Following Crisler's decision, the Athletic Directors Committee, charged with hiring a replacement for the commissioner, compiled a short list of alternative candidates. Northwestern athletic director Kenneth "Tug" Wilson was its first choice, in large part due to influential Buckeye director Lynn St. John. Aware of his friend's interest in the position, the elder statesman essentially guaranteed him the appointment.[16] [17]

As it turned out, Wilson was bored with his current job in Evanston. After 20 years at Northwestern, he was ready for a change. And based on what the Wildcat director knew about John Griffith's seemingly straightforward responsibilities, Wilson was confident that he was the right man for the position.

As a former Olympian in track and field, he had another reason for wanting Griffith's office. Wilson maintained a dream to one-day serve on the United States Olympic Committee.[18] The title of Big Ten commissioner carried with it a certain prestige, deservedly or not, that might gain him a presence among that elite group of businessmen, politicians, and benefactors.[19]

The athletic directors, influenced by Lynn St. John's backroom politicking, offered the position to their colleague.[20] The faculty representatives were surprised by the decision. Wilson wasn't even on their wish list of prospective candidates.[21] And based on experience, they had some valid reasons.

One representative felt that Wilson was too "easily influenced by dominating personalities" to effectively carry out the job.[22] As a professor of psychiatry at the University of Wisconsin Medical School, Dr. William Lorenz was without doubt qualified in making that clinical assessment! Others leaders, including Ralph Aigler, questioned his overall leadership skills. Despite a long tenure as Northwestern's athletic director, he had never displayed a knack for taking charge among his colleagues, let alone spearheading a project.[23] [24] [25]

Regardless of the faculty representatives' private concerns, conference bylaws mandated that the athletic directors interview and hire their employee. The Faculty Representatives Committee was charged with merely approving the selection. And so, in mid-March of 1945, Kenneth Leon Wilson was anointed commissioner of the Intercollegiate Conference of Faculty Representatives.

THE STRATEGIC issues that Professor Ralph Aigler wanted to discuss back in December, placed on hold due to John Griffith's unexpected death, were finally addressed during a special March gathering in Chicago.[26] Top on his list of concerns was financial aid to student athletes—the athletic scholarship. With the end of the war seemingly in sight, Aigler forecasted the resumption of a contentious national debate on subsidies for young men gifted with greater physical rather than scholarly attributes.

Revenue-generating college sports had become a very big business by the early 1920s. The pressure to succeed, not only for athletic directors and coaches, but administrators as well, was immense. The University of Pittsburgh's success during the previous decade, well documented in a muckraking expose in the *Saturday Evening Post,* proved that inducements do work. The two articles humiliated the highly regarded institution.[27] [28] But the message was loud and clear: schools like Pittsburgh were willing to sell their souls in order to be winners. They just didn't want to burn in hell for it. So in the immediate post-war era, Aigler anticipated a collaborative effort by a core group of Eastern and Southern schools to again try to legitimize the practice. And the surest way to accomplish that end was by controlling the influential press.[29] With that in mind, he felt it was critical that amateur purists be well prepared for that impending debate.

Within a few years, a massive influx of student-soldiers would be returning to college campuses following honorable discharge from the armed forces. Mindful of the proven football talent in that pool, athletic leaders forecasted an unprecedented recruiting opportunity for unscrupulous coaches.[30] It was a sure-fire way to either salvage or advance a career. All a coach needed was access to dollars; the GI Bill provided an unexpected source. The federal dollars guaranteed any returning student veteran, athletes included, tuition and living allowance. The "temptation to 'sweeten the pot'" for that unprincipled coach was obvious.[31] And for some honorably discharged soldiers returning to a wife—and an unexpected three-year old—those additional dollars might prove difficult to turn down.

The implications of all this federal money being promised to veterans with residual athletic eligibility were profound. At the very least, the government grants, recently approved by Congress, now cast a favorable light on the concept of financial aid for college athletes.[32] The Purity Movement, Aigler reasoned, might have to reconsider its "quixotic" stance opposing all forms of assistance. Times were a-changin.' Public opinion, he feared, was tilting in favor of the amateur code revisionists. If the government can give students, including some with athletic skills, dollars to attend school, why can't a college or a booster club? Compromise might be necessary if pay-for-play—the feared professional creep into the popular college game—was to be held in check.[33] [34]

In addition to concerns regarding the government's role in effectively legitimizing financial aid for non-scholar athletes, growing spectator interest in professional football also troubled Professor Aigler.

The National Football League was founded in the early 1920s. Over the next two decades, it struggled to gain a weekend following. In large part due to a few highly recognized college athletes eager to compete on Sunday afternoon for paychecks, the game gradually grew in popularity.[35] [36] At the time Western Conference leaders were meeting in March of 1945, there was rumor that a group of wealthy investors was about to form another league—the All-American College Conference. A bidding war with the NFL for limited collegiate talent was predicted.[37] The faculty representatives were concerned that some well-known veterans, with residual varsity eligibility, might consider earning a salary from a professional club rather than completing a degree from a university.[38]

And to make the discussion even more challenging for those Big Ten leaders gathered in Chicago, many fans considered college conferences as nothing more than semi-professional leagues, in operation merely to prepare athletes for Sunday competition.[39]

The Michigan law professor's solution to all these threats on the amateur game, at least in the spring of '45, was to propose a revision of the conference handbook. An ad hoc committee that included Aigler was assigned the task of making a more relevant statement on recruiting and subsidizing in the immediate post war years.[40] The powerful Wolverine would also contact members of the old Purity Movement. There needed to be a forum for advancing intercollegiate legislation with a somewhat different, perhaps more realistic twist to it than the failed Purity Code of 1940.

Aigler's remaining agenda item for that March meeting involved the commissioner's job description. After 22 years of a trial run, it was time to review those responsibilities, especially in the context of the current discussion on financial aid.[41] [42] And a few months later, after extensive debate, the conference administrator would be granted limited powers to enforce revised handbook policies on recruiting and subsidizing.[43] Acknowledging Ken Wilson's inadequacies, Professor Aigler reassured skeptical faculty representatives that with proper mentoring on their part, the new commissioner might prove to be a competent leader after all.

FIELDING YOST had first come up with the idea of hiring a conference manager to assist the Athletic Directors Committee in the spring of 1922. At the time, the Big Ten desperately needed an impartial subordinate to investigate confidential charges of foul play filed by one athletic director against a colleague's program. The jobholder, Yost opined, could turn his findings over to the faculty's Eligibility Committee for ultimate adjudication. In addition to that task, he could perform secretarial duties for the leadership: organize meetings, coordinate biennial scheduling combines, and appoint officials for competitive play among the membership. And perhaps most importantly, the employee could meet with the press—an insufferable task no one else wanted to do.[44]

Desperate for a title to fit the job description, Ralph Aigler, a die-hard professional baseball fan, favored "commissioner." Despite connoting power and influence, the designation proved to be a misnomer. He was effectively impotent.[45] [46]

John Griffith was hired a few weeks later. And as anticipated, he performed the role admirably as the Intercollegiate Conference's first commissioner. With a background in athletic leadership at Drake and later Illinois, he proved to be a very competent manager. The faculty representatives, recognizing some of his additional skills, often sought his input on controversial issues. Advice was shared, but only if requested. With background as a stateside military officer during the Great War, Major Griffith clearly understood the chain of command in the Western Conference.

Somewhat surprisingly, the Council of Ten presidents had no direct say in questions of conference personnel.[47] Original bylaws, as drafted by the founders back in 1896, delegated all matters of governance and operations to their faculty representatives.[48] In short order, the academicians relinquished responsibilities for conference management to the Athletic Directors Committee—men more suited for the task. And since those administrators came up with the idea of a commissioner, it only made sense that they could hire, monitor, and terminate their employee. The Council of Ten's only obligation to the Intercollegiate Conference, by inference, was to ensure that the faculty, directors, and hired staff never compromised the honorable reputations of the institutions sponsoring their athletic association.

During the Western Conference's first 50 years, the presidents had no reason to intervene in any action that placed the prestige of member schools in jeopardy. But by the late fall of 1947, the Council of Nine would finally have reason to break precedence.[49] There was growing concern, at least with one president, that institutional integrity was under threat.[50] And in James Lewis Morrill's opinion, it all had to do with athletic scholarships and an empowered commissioner unwilling to exercise his responsibilities.

DURING THE 1947 spring meetings held in Highland Park, Illinois, the Faculty Representative Committee discussed the current status of the Sanity Code draft permitting dollars, academic scholarships, for qualified student athletes. Anticipating NCAA membership approval of the controversial proposal in seven months, Professor Ralph Aigler moved that his conference adopt a very strict interpretation of the code.[51] Only incoming freshmen graduating in the top 25 percent of their high school class would be eligible for college grants—a requirement far exceeding the proposed NCAA benchmark.[52] The Wolverine wanted the Intercollegiate Conference to remain the standard-bearer for the revised amateur code. Only true scholars should receive scholarships.[53 54] His motion was approved.[55]

Acknowledging that the conference benchmark was a draft—approved only in principle—Aigler still insisted that all conference schools implement academic scholarship programs consistent with that provisional statement before the upcoming fall semester. The law professor was confident that the faculty senates from member institutions would rubber-stamp the final handbook version before the upcoming January NCAA convention. And to emphasize to skeptics outside the conference that the Big Nine fully embraced the Sanity Code, Aigler requested that the commissioner utilize a tool, the "Highland Park Yardstick," to verify member compliance with his proposed draft for the incoming freshman class of 1947-48.[56]

The professor's blueprint for implementing the provisional scholarship rule was well thought out, save for one key feature. He overlooked potential problems in adopting a policy still being re-worded in pencil. The ink version would not be formally approved by the conference until June of 1948![57] Aigler's slip-up would soon place Kenneth Wilson in a humiliating fix, one that would severely damage the commissioner's reputation with a few very powerful members of the Council of Nine.

Despite a past practice of reviewing all conference-meeting summaries, President Lew Morrill had no time to read his copy of the Highland Park minutes in late May. He was far too busy with more pressing administrative concerns.[58] Three months later, after being informed by members of his executive team that "athletic" scholarships were now being granted at a number of conference schools,[59] Morrill suddenly found the time. And what he read greatly disturbed him. Ralph Aigler, it appeared, was a turncoat to the Purity Movement—a cause the Minnesotan, an amateur purist, fully embraced.[60]

BACK IN March of '47, John Hannah had shared with Lew Morrill a copy of an M Club fund-raising letter. Representatives of the University of Michigan had co-signed it. The club, composed of varsity letter winners, was sponsoring a scholarship program for incoming athletes.

Hannah found the plea for dollars hypocritical.[61] On numerous occasions both Ralph Aigler and Fritz Crisler had pointed out to him that the Jenison Awards program was the major reason why Michigan did not support a Spartan application for membership in the Western Conference.[62] [63] The practice was contrary to Intercollegiate Handbook policy.

The Michigan State president pointed out to his close friend that the M Club letterhead included the names of prominent university employees within the athletic department.[64] By implication, the University of Michigan was sponsoring a financial aid program in violation of conference rules.

Morrill appreciated his friend's point. Unsure of what to make of the Wolverine practice, the Minnesota president decided to file the letter away. Perhaps it might come in handy some day.

And now, in late August, after hearing from his staff that most Big Nine schools, including Michigan, were offering athletic scholarships, Morrill rummaged through his file cabinets searching for that M Club letter John Hannah had shared with him five months earlier. He also needed to locate his copy of the Highland Park minutes that he had failed to read back in May.[65] The president had to find out what the faculty representatives approved at the time. Something was amiss.

After glancing over the minutes, the Minnesota leader was convinced that Hannah had stumbled on to something after all. Ralph Aigler couldn't be trusted. His academic scholarship proposal was a ruse: a scheme to ultimately benefit Wolverine football fortunes. Given time and human nature, Morrill was convinced that the financial aid proposal would morph into athletic scholarships, dollars for skills, not brains, by a few conniving coaches and administrators.[66] [67] His reading of the M Club letter substantiated that hunch. The integrity of nine prominent universities now appeared to be at-risk; it was only a matter of time before muckraking press would expose the scheme for what it truly was—a collusive act contrary to conference doctrine.

As it turned out, Morrill (and his staff) misinterpreted Aigler's motion. But the damage had already been done. Although his faculty representative, Professor Henry Rottschaefer, tried in vain to clarify Ralph Aigler's intent,[68] the Minnesota president was unmoved.[69]

And so, having lost respect for Professor Aigler (and most of the ruling Faculty Representatives Committee), Lew Morrill would take matters into his own hands. He would use whatever means necessary to protect the honorable reputation of nine institutions.[70] [71] The most logical course of action, consistent with the bylaws, was to call a special meeting of the Council of Nine and the Faculty Representatives Committee.[72]

IN DECEMBER of 1947, the presidents and academic leadership met to address the Western Conference's revised policy on financial aid to athletes—the Aigler Proposal. Minnesota President James Lewis Morrill, as expected, took the lead. He raised issue with faculty oversight. The academic leadership appeared to be derelict in their bylaws responsibilities. And in his opinion, there was no better example than the recent handbook revision permitting athletic scholarships.

Morrill also took issue with what he perceived as a failure by the faculty to enforce conference rules. The current judiciary process was cumbersome and ineffective. Ken Wilson, now three years into his tenure as commissioner, was not performing well in aiding that process. Big Nine presidents, based on his informal survey, considered him tentative and indecisive. Morrill wanted an empowered officer, one eager to police the conference for violators.[73]

During discussion that followed, the faculty took great pains to reassure the Minnesota president that Professor Aigler's proposal was consistent with the founders' intent. But they were also quick to point out that Morrill had some valid points regarding conference oversight and handbook enforcement. They all agreed to a follow-up meeting; the athletic directors, charged with monitoring the commissioner's job performance, would also be included. [74] [75]

The plenary session finally took place two months later. President Morrill's fundamental concern—safeguarding the integrity of the conference—was addressed to his satisfaction.[76] There was no need for the Council of Nine to assume control; the original bylaws would remain intact. And Ralph Aigler, as passionate about the historical mission of the Intercollegiate Conference as was Lew Morrill, breathed a big sigh of relief. Faculty control would remain in place after all.

The conference leadership also addressed the Council's concerns regarding the commissioner. Morrill and his colleagues were reassured that Kenneth Wilson was the right man for the job. His duties had only recently been expanded. He was now empowered to unilaterally pass judgment and discipline members for mundane violations. It was too soon to judge his performance. Given time, the nine professors were confident that Wilson would prove to be a competent enforcement officer. They noted that he was currently involved with a conference-wide investigation regarding compliance with the new scholarship rule. His report would be forthcoming. They promised to share findings with the presidents.

James Lewis Morrill felt very good after the meeting. He had succeeded in making a statement: the Council of Nine would remain vigilant in its sole responsibility to the conference. He was also more confident that the faculty leadership was truly committed to upholding the Intercollegiate Handbook. But as Morrill knew only too well, the proof was in the pudding. He eagerly awaited the commissioner's unprecedented investigation.[77] [78] [79]

KENNETH WILSON, as recently empowered commissioner of the Intercollegiate Conference, prepared well for his first major presentation before the Faculty Representatives Committee. Four weeks in advance of the spring Big Nine meetings, he prepped the athletic directors on his investigation of compliance with the provisional scholarship rule.[80] And in deference to the man who drafted the historic legislation, he also informed Ralph Aigler of his findings. The chief enforcement officer wanted to be absolutely certain that his upcoming presentation to the conference leadership went without a glitch.

Wilson's report, as it turned out, was surprising and disturbing. Most programs were found in violation of the Highland Park yardstick. Only Ohio State and Minnesota were without blemish.[81]

But of greater concern for the commissioner was what he discovered in West Lafayette. The Purdue administration appeared to have sanctioned a scholarship committee lacking faculty oversight.[82] In essence, this was a major violation of the revised Intercollegiate Conference handbook. The implications for the land-grant university were profound. At the very least, the school could be placed on confidential probation—a hand slap. But the Faculty Representatives Committee could also impose a collective scheduling boycott. The financial repercussions to the institution and damage to the Boilermakers' athletic program, as the State University of Iowa had experienced back in 1929, were profound. Two decades later, the Hawkeyes still struggled from their misdeed. Adding to these potential disciplinary actions against Purdue, the threat of expulsion from the Big Nine for a repeat violation of this magnitude remained a very real prospect.

The commissioner, in attempting to carry out his role as an enforcer, was placing his reputation (and perhaps his job) on the line with this unexpected finding and charge. He had to make a bold statement to skeptics, most notably James Lewis Morrill, that Ken Wilson was the right man for this job after all.

Professor Ralph Aigler, on the other hand, mindful of Purdue's institutional infraction, also wanted to make a bold statement—but to critics of the Purity Movement. Ever since approval of the Sanity Code earlier that year, the Wolverine had been prowling for prey in the underbrush. Aigler needed a member school caught in the act of violating the controversial code. Assuming harsh penalties followed, he planned to trumpet the conference's decisive action to naysayers among the press.[83]

And so, confident that he had his sacrificial lamb, Aigler politicked for disciplinary action far in excess of what was originally recommended for Purdue's wrongdoing.[84] In addition to imposing probation and a scheduling boycott on the school, he insisted the young men that received illegal financial aid, regardless of their awareness of scholarship criteria, should be denied one year of athletic eligibility—ignorance is not defensible in a court of law! And to top it off, all disciplinary actions must be made public knowledge—even the students should be cited in the newspapers. After all, there was no better deterrent than humiliating exposure in newspapers about the country.[85 86]

The Faculty Representatives Committee approved the harsh Aigler motion despite some misgivings.[87 88] They had no choice. The persuasive professor, gifted in forensics, would tolerate nothing less.[89] This was a matter of principle. The reputation of the Intercollegiate Conference of Faculty Representatives—the Wolverine leader's fundamental concern—was at stake.[90] Failure to act with conviction would send the wrong message to a cynical press and its impressionable readership.[91 92 93]

Unfortunately for the legal scholar, Purdue's President Fred Hovde found serious fault with the commissioner's charges after thoroughly reading through his copy of the minutes. The new scholarship policy was still undergoing revision at the time Wilson was performing his investigation. In fact, the faculty leadership had only recently approved a printable version, well after Wilson had completed his survey. The president, in no uncertain terms, threatened to go public with what he considered a "kangaroo court" judicial process.[94]

Having one of the most prominent institutional leaders in the conference angered by Wilson's charges—based on a preliminary draft left to interpretation—did not bode well for the commissioner's approval rating, especially among the Council of Nine. It didn't help matters that Fred Hovde was also a very close friend of Lew Morrill's.

And Ralph Aigler was no better off than his embattled commissioner. President Hovde knew exactly who politicked for more severe and humiliating disciplinary action against his university; the May meeting minutes, which he had carefully reviewed in preparing a defense, were very clear on that point. Needless to say, the chief Boilermaker was still spitting steam a few months later over Aigler's role in the process.[95]

Regardless of his personal feelings about the Michigan faculty representative and the conference commissioner, President Hovde had some valid points about the flawed report and its draconian recommendations; in private, many of the ruling faculty concurred with his assessment.[96][97] Even Professor Aigler expressed concern over the unfortunate course of events for Purdue during private conversation with a colleague.[98]

Desiring to avoid a public airing of Wilson's bungled investigation, the conference leaders caved in to Fred Hovde's threat. There would be no formal censorship of his university. The report would remain confidential; probation was never reported to the press.[99][100][101] They would also cancel plans for a collective boycott. The athletic directors could decide for themselves whether to discipline the Boilermakers.[102][103] As for the four freshmen that unwittingly accepted illegal scholarship dollars from the Boilermakers, all were denied a year of eligibility. It was consistent with the penalty applied to offenders from the other three schools for similar misdemeanors.[104] Their names, however, were not cited in a press release announcing the conference's actions.[105]

The Wilson Report was effectively swept under the rug.[106] The faculty representatives' decision, however, didn't stop Fred Hovde from sharing his frustration with Lew Morrill.[107] Acknowledging his friend's concerns, Morrill felt it was still too soon to render judgment on the fate of the embattled commissioner. But he did take note.

IN HIS first attempt at trying to be an enforcer, Kenneth Wilson essentially blew it. He had Ralph Aigler, in large part, to thank for that. The professor's insistence that the commissioner validate membership compliance with a provisional draft on academic scholarships set him up for failure. It would not be his last. Over the next couple of years, the commissioner would be involved with a few more blunders. The list of skeptics questioning his competency would lengthen.

Ralph Aigler, on the other hand, was undaunted by the course of events. As a seasoned leader, he was well aware that there were always a few bumps in the road in pursuit of an honorable cause. But there was also a lesson learned from this recent experience. Acknowledging that Tug Wilson was not quite the leader in the mold of a Fritz Crisler, he planned to be more proactive in tutoring the commissioner. Over the next few years, he would offer his confidential counsel on questions of leadership and decision-making. But as he soon discovered, mentoring could prove challenging and, at times, very frustrating.[108]

CHAPTER 6

A Commissioner
Under Siege

———

KENNETH WILSON QUICKLY PUT THE Purdue fiasco behind him. Ralph
Aigler would have it no other way. Moving forward, the commissioner's
challenge was to discover another school caught in the act. He needed
a case to prove to skeptics that he was an able enforcer. And his mentor needed a victim to demonstrate to naysayers that the Intercollegiate
Conference was truly committed to the revised law of the land—the
Sanity Code.

Unlike alumni associations, booster clubs lacked official affiliation
with a college or university. Professor Aigler was intrigued with the growing movement. Unfamiliar with the strict Intercollegiate Handbook rules
and regulations, he was confident that some of these organizations, led
by rabid fans eager to aid a winning cause, were offering illegal hand-
outs to athletes counter to the spirit of fair competition. Perhaps there
was an opportunity for the embattled commissioner to demonstrate his
mettle while investigating a few of these unmonitored groups?

Prior to the Second World War, most Western Conference programs
shunned any association with boosters. The State University of Iowa
scandal remained a vivid reminder to Big Ten coaches and athletic directors of the consequences of even a loose relationship with townies.
However, following the end of hostilities in Europe and the Pacific, a

seemingly legitimate role for this type of organization became apparent for conference coaching staffs. Competition for stellar athletes was at an all time high. Constrained by strict handbook rules on interaction with high school recruits, coaches often turned to boosters as a way of marketing their football program.

Ralph Aigler never liked the idea of soliciting alumni assistance, let alone fans unaffiliated with the school.[1] And he had valid reason. During his early years as Michigan's faculty representative, the Alumni Club of Detroit, fully sanctioned by the university, got involved in actively recruiting athletes in an effort at resurrecting Coach Fielding Yost's career.[2] The subsidies scandal proved a black mark on the proud, storied tradition that is Michigan Football.

But now, with booster clubs proliferating in many communities about the Big Ten, the Wolverine faculty representative was suspicious that some schools might be crossing the line. And he was convinced that Ohio State was one of them.[3]

In spring of 1949, Professor Aigler asked the commissioner, in strict confidence, to investigate the Frontliners Club based out of Columbus. He questioned the role that the assistant alumni secretary—a university employee—might be playing in the booster organization.[4] [5] Wilson followed through on his mentor's suggestion. He contacted Ohio State athletic director Richard Larkins. The commissioner wasn't prepared for what followed. The Buckeye department administrator was livid about the inference. In a follow up letter to Wilson, while hurling a few insolent phrases at the conference's chief enforcement officer, he vehemently denied the accusation. The Ohio State University program was without blemish. And to prove his point, he would allow the commissioner access to all departmental records. Confident in his prediction, Larkins copied university President Howard Landis Bevis on the letter.[6] That would prove to be a major mistake.

As it turned out, Larkins was correct. In a follow-up note, Wilson essentially apologized for even raising concern about the university's association with the Frontliners.[7]

The letter, however, was of little consolation. Richard Larkins was now in a heap of trouble with his boss back in Columbus. Apparently President Bevis was not pleased with his director's condescending response to the commissioner's original inquiry. It was unbecoming of a man representing a proud institution; it was also totally uncalled-for and highly unprofessional.[8]

Ken Wilson received a contrite phone call from Larkins shortly after the Buckeye had been taken back to the woodshed adjacent to Bevis's office!

The commissioner of the Intercollegiate Conference made light of the whole matter—it was the surest way to patch things up with a man he considered a good friend. And to help Larkins save face with his boss, Wilson even returned the obnoxious letter. The incident, as far as he was concerned, was past tense; it would remain confidential.[9] (Of course, neither Bevis nor Larkins was aware of a Wolverine's role in this humiliating course of events. Three years later, Ralph Aigler would still question the relationship Ohio State had with the Frontliners.)[10]

Regardless of his gesture of good will towards Ohio State Athletic Director Richard Larkins, this was now the second time in less than a year that Kenneth Wilson had bungled an investigation. And in each instance, his mentor played a role in setting him up for failure.

UNDAUNTED BY the mishandling of both the Purdue and Ohio State investigations, Commissioner Wilson pressed forward. And to assist him, the conference leadership now agreed to provide additional support staff. Perhaps the job was more than any one man could handle? Walter Byers was hired to assist in operations and investigations.[11] Wilson was also offered the professional services of Ed Martin, a former FBI agent skilled in espionage. And if the caseload warranted it, regional private investigators could also be retained.[12]

The revised Intercollegiate Handbook was finally ratified by the faculty senates of all member schools just prior to the 1949-50 academic year. The commissioner could now enforce the rules and regulations of the Big Ten with an official document that even satisfied Boilermaker Fred Hovde.

Wilson immediately charged nine schools, including Michigan State, with minor recruiting infractions. Walt Byers' assistance was greatly appreciated. Eight of those charged—all employees of conference institutions—willingly confessed their sins after re-reading their copies of the revised conference catechism.[13]

The athletic directors were impressed with Wilson's overall handling of this latest investigation. His report was thorough and the recommendations appropriate.[14] The positive feedback was a ray of hope for Professor Aigler. Perhaps his mentee was qualified for this job after all.

Buoyed by the commissioner's recent success, Aigler encouraged him to take on more challenging cases. Wilson was now charged with exploring possible recruiting violations by head coaches in the major revenue sports. Two programs were cited.

A perennial loser in the autumn gridiron battles, Indiana was a safe and easy target. Unlike the case involving Ohio State Athletic Director Richard Larkins—a dominant personality in his own right—little harm could come for implicating Bernie Crimmins, a new member of the coaching fraternity. Wilson had no past relationship with the Hoosier. Crimmins was formally reprimanded for illegal contact with a prospective athlete in violation of the handbook.[15]

But perhaps of greater satisfaction for Ralph Aigler, Michigan State was also fingered for an infraction. This was now the second time in just two years as a conference member that the college was found guilty of violating the handbook. But this misdemeanor, unlike the earlier one, was of greater significance—not just for the Spartans but also for a conference program located in Iowa City.

As it turned out, basketball coach Pete Newell was cited for violating General Regulation (GR) XIV, section 4: "Anything not expressed in the forgoing principles (on recruiting) shall not be permissible."[16] The commissioner, availing himself of this vague, if not bewildering statement, used what he called a "technical" reprimand in charging Newell with a recruiting violation. It was in essence a warning, not just to the Spartan coach but also to his colleagues about the conference. He wanted to send a message: even arcane rules, challenging to read let alone interpret, would be enforced.[17] Unfortunately for Wilson, his concocted penalty would come back to haunt him. And somewhat ironically, the man most upset over the reprimand wasn't even a Spartan. Iowa Faculty Representative Paul Blommers, the man who cast the lone vote opposing Michigan State's admission into the conference a few years earlier, was livid about the unusual decision. He had a valid gripe.

Apparently, back in the spring of 1951, Michigan State Coach Newell and his young assistant, John Benington, watched a high school senior shoot some baskets at Jenison Fieldhouse. In Wilson's opinion, this constituted a "try-out." It allowed the two coaches an opportunity to assess the boy's talent prior to offering him an academic scholarship.

Despite the tactic not being directly mentioned in the Intercollegiate Handbook, Wilson felt compelled to warn Newell and President Hannah that in his opinion this was a recruiting misdemeanor. He failed to press charges however. John Hannah, after all, was a very intimidating personality.

A year later, Newell got caught again. Two high school prospects were reportedly playing one-on-one in the field house. Standing in the upper deck, not too far from his basketball office, the coach observed the action below.

Wilson's decision to impose a technical reprimand on Newell, a minor penalty in the context of a harsher punishment recently imposed on Iowa basketball Coach Frank "Bucky" O'Connor, was the last straw for Professor Blommers. If the decision regarding the Spartan coach accomplished anything, it justified in his mind that the commissioner had to go. The man was incompetent. [18] [19]

Coach O'Connor had briefly visited with the mother of a certain prospect in a restaurant; the discussion centered on financial aid. Later realizing that he may have violated the puzzling GR XIV, section 4 rule in the handbook, O'Connor confessed to Wilson what he considered a minor recruiting violation.[20] The high priest for enforcement was unmoved by the coach's act of contrition. The infraction—talking to a parent without the student being present—was a clear-cut violation of a very vague rule.[21] The penance—no direct contact with high school recruits for one year—was a devastating blow for a new coach trying to build a basketball program in Iowa City.[21]

Disturbed by the surprisingly severe penalty, especially in the context of the Newell verdict, Paul Blommers challenged the commissioner's decision. O'Connor's action, much like Newell's, was not mentioned in the handbook; it was inferred. If Wilson was consistent in his determinations, the Hawkeye coach deserved just a technical reprimand. The Joint Appellate Board, called to review the appeal, was moved by the story and O'Connor's personal admission of guilt—it substantiated his reputation as a man of integrity.[23] But in the end, the faculty representatives on that board "upheld and affirmed" the commissioner's action.[24] They had no choice. As Ralph Aigler reminded his colleagues, this appellate decision was of historic proportions—the constitutional law equivalent to Marbury v. Madison![25] It was the first time that judicial review of a commissioner's action was carried out by the Intercollegiate Conference. It was also a unique opportunity for the academic leadership to remind conference coaches that Ken Wilson was a force to be reckoned with.[26] And for the beleaguered commissioner, still struggling over offending Professor Paul Blommer,[27] the appellate board's conclusion was reassuring.[28] [29]

ONE WEEK following the O'Connor case review, Professor Ralph Aigler, the senior member and presiding chair of the Western Conference appellate board, received a letter postmarked Iowa City. Paul Blommers wanted to raise an issue he had failed to bring up during the recent hearing for fear of embarrassing Commissioner Wilson. In hindsight, he questioned his restraint.

Blommers was upset over what he perceived as Wilson "discriminating against Iowa," especially in the context of the two Newell cases. He felt the commissioner was too soft in dealing with the Spartans and its basketball coach. "I wonder if we had protested—as Michigan State apparently did—that we [also] did not understand the [rule, whether] we too would have received a letter similar to the one sent to Newell. Or was someone simply making things too hot [for the commissioner]?" [30] The Hawkeye was no doubt referring to John Hannah. The college president had a reputation for direct hands-on involvement in his institution's athletic program. [31] By this time, Hannah was also a recognized power among his colleagues on the Council of Ten, in part due to his friendships with Lew Morrill and Fred Hovde.

A number of months earlier, Professor Blommers had added his name to a growing list of faculty representatives and presidents questioning whether Ken Wilson was the right man for the job. [32] This current incident substantiated that earlier doubt. [33]

UNBEKNOWNST TO Faculty Representative Paul Blommers, there was reason for Commissioner Wilson's waffling over what type of penalty to impose on Michigan State Coach Pete Newell. At about the same time that Iowa was appealing the Frank O'Connor verdict, Kenneth Wilson was embroiled in a highly confidential (and very contentious) probe involving Michigan State College and an East Lansing booster club. The 26-month ordeal, drawn out in part due to his procrastination, would emotionally challenge the embattled commissioner forced to periodically confront an intimidating John Hannah. But in the end, with the counsel and support of two Wolverines cleverly hiding in the bush back in Ann Arbor, he would finally succeed in capturing Ralph Aigler's sacrificial lamb. And in so doing, Ken Wilson would profoundly embarrass the professor's long-time adversary and the institution he represented.

CHAPTER 7

Help Wanted

—

THE JOB DESCRIPTION WAS STRAIGHTFORWARD: collaborate with leaders of alumni clubs throughout the state in promoting Michigan State College. Applicants for the position were expected to be bright, personable, hard-working and, above all else, well-recognized Spartan graduates. George Guerre was the ideal candidate—at least in John Hannah's opinion. He was both a decorated athlete and a proven student leader. There was one problem. He didn't want the job.

George Guerre was born and raised in Flint. His father was Italian, his mother Polish. They shared a Catholic faith tradition and a desire to live the American dream. Their two children embraced both convictions.

The family lived in a second floor flat across the street from the A.C. Delco sparkplug plant. His parent's owned a beer garden and din-er downstairs. As far back as George could remember both he and his sister helped out with the family business. Sweeping the floor, busing tables, and washing dishes were routine responsibilities. But there was also time for playground activities. The schoolyard was only a few blocks away. And despite being small for his age, he quickly learned that speed, agility, and a little gutsiness could make up for any physical shortcom-ings. George excelled in most sports; football, however, was his passion.

Following a stellar senior season at Flint Central, "Little Dynamite" was selected honorable mention All-State—quite an accomplishment for a boy who stood no taller than 5-feet 5 and weighed 145 pounds fully dressed in pads and uniform. After graduating from high school, he enrolled at the University of Michigan, located about 35 miles away. George planned to study engineering. He also wanted to play football for Fritz Crisler. But a patriotic call to duty put long-term plans on hold. He enlisted in the Army Air Corps at the end of his freshman year. Three years later, after serving in both Africa and Europe, Lieutenant Guerre, an accomplished B-17 navigator, was honorably discharged.[1]

Mindful of the veteran talent Coach Crisler was re-accumulating back in Ann Arbor, and encouraged by a close friend currently playing football in East Lansing, the diminutive running back transferred to Michigan State in the spring of '46. He also changed his major. George planned to study business. By mid-October, after an incredible back-up performance against Pennsylvania State College, he earned a starting position in Coach Charlie Bachman's outdated "Flying-Z" offense. Little Dynamite would end up exploding for over 1000 yards that season. In recognition of his contribution to the football program, Bachman sub-sequently offered him a Jenison Award, financial aid that supplemented limited college expenses covered under the GI Bill.[2][3][4] It was the first time George had heard about the Spartan subsidy program.

One month later, in mid-December, Biggie Munn was hired to rekin-dle a smoldering football program. President Hannah, who played a ma-jor role in bringing the former Michigan assistant coach to East Lansing, promptly expanded the Jenison program to aid the cause. With that largesse from the administration, Munn and his assistant coaches were able to recruit additional highly skilled athletes from high schools about the country.[5][6] A few years later, loaded with talent, Michigan State was recognized as a legitimate national power. And George Guerre, a one-time Wolverine, became a household name among the Spartan faithful.

Shortly following completion of his final season in a green and white uniform, John Hannah requested a meeting with the star half-back. He wanted the personable senior class president to fill a va-cancy in the Alumni Office. Guerre was six credits shy of graduating with a business degree. In Hannah's opinion, lacking a diploma was irrelevant—a few summer school courses could easily fix that problem. He needed George to help resurrect a number of dormant alumni clubs about the state. His title would be assistant field director for alumni relations.

Guerre was initially noncommittal. At the time, he was contemplating a career in insurance sales following graduation later that spring. During the previous summer he had interned for an agency in Lansing. He found the work intriguing; he also liked being his own boss, a conclusion he arrived at after serving three years in a military steeped in bureaucracy. He envisioned working for Michigan State, a large public institution in its own right, would be no different.

Regardless of George's initial reservations, Hannah prevailed. He began working for the college as of January 1, 1949—just two weeks after Michigan State had been provisionally selected for membership in the Intercollegiate Conference.

Sixteen months later, Guerre resigned. He had had enough. Institutional politics and challenging personalities had taxed his patience. In hindsight, Big Ten Commissioner Kenneth Wilson may have hastened that decision.

In the fall of 1949, only a few months after the ad hoc Committee of Three had found that Michigan State was "as a whole" in compliance with the Intercollegiate Handbook,[7] Guerre was cited for a recruiting violation.[8] General Regulation XIV forbade any university employee from communicating with a prospective student athlete, in this instance, a high school senior attending an alumni club gathering in Muskegon, Michigan. Guerre confessed his wrongdoing even though he never committed one—at least in his mind.[9] He merely greeted the young man. Higher ups at Michigan State, however, determined it best not to challenge the Big Ten commissioner's decision, especially so soon after being officially approved for membership in the conference. His sentence, handed down by Wilson, would be "[no] contact...with any prospective athlete for a period of one year."[10] And for a man convinced of his innocence, it was an insult to his integrity.[11]

The hand-slap by the commissioner, and the way the college handled it, was the last straw. Guerre held on for a few more months. In May, he tendered his resignation to his boss in the Alumni Office. A week later he would begin a long-standing, very successful affiliation with Ohio National Life Insurance Company.[12] George never regretted his decision.

FOREST H. Akers attended Michigan Agricultural College around the turn of the century. He never graduated; he was kicked out after a few years. Poor academic performance was the official reason—a reputation for mischief may have contributed to him getting the boot. Thirty years later, now vice president of the Dodge Division of Chrysler Motor Corporation, the self-made leader and highly successful businessman was elected to the State Board of Agriculture. Akers would serve in that capacity for almost two decades. The school's leadership would one day acknowledge the erstwhile prankster's numerous contributions to Michigan State by naming the college golf course and a huge residence hall complex in his honor.[13]

Akers enthusiastically supported Spartan athletics. A one-time athlete at the college,[14] he created a scholarship and loan fund valued at $45,000, (equivalent to $435,000 in 2013),[15] to aid "worthy male students."[16] The Sanity Code, embraced by John Hannah at the same board meeting that the corporate executive announced his generous gift, would re-define "worthiness" with an emphasis on classroom accomplishments—something Akers failed to appreciate during his foreshortened stay on campus decades earlier!

Prior to generously gifting Michigan State, Akers had assisted student athletes in other ways, namely jobs. As a senior executive at one of the largest manufacturing companies in the country, he found employment for many Spartan graduates that embraced teamwork and a commitment to a common goal: success.[17] Those favorable attributes, gained both on the gridiron and in the lecture hall, could greatly benefit Chrysler's leadership development program.

Jacweir "Jack" Breslin, yeoman Spartan athlete, dedicated college student, and recognized campus life leader exemplified Forest Aker's intent.[18] Following graduation in the spring of 1946, the Dodge Brothers Division hired the three-sport student-athlete. His future was bright with Chrysler. But four years later, Breslin would resign—and with Aker's blessings. John Hannah wanted him back in East Lansing.

JACK BRESLIN dominated the playgrounds while growing up in Battle Creek. Not only a big kid for his age, he also proved to be one of the quickest. By his teens, he excelled in baseball, basketball, and football while attending Battle Creek Lakeview. He also was a good student. However, following graduation in the spring of '38, he decided to forego college. His father had died from a tragic car accident while Jack was a young boy. Mom had no choice but to find work to support her three children during the Depression. As the oldest member of the family, Jack felt an obligation to help out.[19] He took a position unloading box-cars at the W.K. Kellogg Cereal Company a few blocks from home.

Nine months later, Jack quit his job. Long hours of physical labor in the factory undoubtedly contributed to that decision. In late summer of 1939, he enrolled at Michigan State College with plans of becoming a teacher.[20] Seven years later, he would graduate with a degree in education.[21]

Breslin's extended stay in East Lansing, somewhat unusual for a college student back then, was for one reason: money. Higher education, including room and board, was expensive even in those times. Failing to qualify for any academic grants, he took on a full-time off-campus job during his first year at Michigan State. It was the only way he could cover expenses while also assisting his mother back in Battle Creek. He learned very quickly about time management; there would be no room for athletics on his busy calendar.[22] But by Christmas break, Jack realized that a full credit load was too much to handle. There were few hours for study while working evenings and weekends to make ends meet. After completing three quarters of classwork, he dropped out of school.[23] Perhaps in a year or so, after accumulating some cash in the interim, he might be able return to the lecture halls. That decision to become a student in absentia would one day prove providential for Jack Breslin.

In the December of 1940, President Robert Sidey Shaw announced plans to retire from Michigan State College. Six months later, John Hannah would assume Shaw's office in the Administration Building near Circle Drive.

Shortly after his appointment, President Hannah set his sights on improving the weekend culture on campus for both students and faculty. In his opinion, there was no better way to achieve that end than with a successful football program—a conviction gained two decades earlier as a law student at the University of Michigan. But to accomplish his strategic initiative, Hannah knew that Coach Charlie Bachman needed talented athletes. And so, a few weeks following completion of the 1941 football season, the president announced plans to institute the Jenison subsidy program. Named after the man who had bequeathed his entire fortune to the college a year earlier, the Frederick Cowles Jenison Awards were intended for "worthy and deserving students...possessing unusual qualities of leadership and who have demonstrated mental ability and physical strength and vigor."[24] The emphasis was on non-scholarly attributes; in fact, the only real requirement was athleticism.

Not too long after official approval of the Jenison Awards by the State Board, patriotic fervor hit the Red Cedar Campus. Just about every able-bodied male student was signing up for military duty. Jack Breslin, now back in college after a one-year leave, was no different. But a history of childhood asthma would keep him out of the military; he was classified 4-F.[25] As a consequence, he remained in school as a part-time student while continuing to support his mother and two younger siblings back in Battle Creek.

In the late summer of 1943, Michigan State announced plans to sever its contractual relationships with other schools in all sports, football included.[26] [27] As an institution sponsoring an ROTC program, it had no choice. The Army War Department forbade its trainees from competing; there was no time during a busy day of military instruction for intercollegiate athletic practice.[28] However, the Army brass did permit intramural play. As a consequence, Athletic Director Ralph Young organized a gridiron program pitting residence halls against each other, many boarding some proven, highly skilled athletes from colleges about the country.[29] Jack Breslin, despite being a part-time student, was eligible to compete. He eagerly signed up for a club affiliated with one of the campus dormitories.[30] With little if any requirement for practice, he was confident that he could keep up on his studies and maintain that off-campus job. And as luck would have it, Spartan coaches, asked to monitor play on the athletic fields south of the Red Cedar River, took note of the big kid with quick feet from Battle Creek. They encouraged him to try out for the Spartan football team once the war was over.

By the spring of 1944, the Army loosened its grip on college athletic departments assisting its cause. The military training program was a resounding success. Millions of inductees had been deployed. Many were now bivouacked in southern England while awaiting General Dwight Eisenhower's decision on when to commence D-Day. There was no longer a need to use college campuses to prepare additional young men for combat; military bases would suffice.

As a direct consequence of the War Department's announcement, schools like Michigan State, hindered by ROTC contracts, were now allowed to resume intercollegiate competition. Unfortunately for the Spartans, very few varsity-caliber athletes, other than some 4Fs, resided in East Lansing at the time. Football coach Charlie Bachman, desperate for able bodies, issued an urgent plea, publicized in the *State News* and *Lansing State Journal,* for any college students interested in trying out for the team.[31] Jack Breslin took him up on the offer.[32] After an impressive spring practice, the coach awarded him a Jenison grant.[33] [34] Financing his college education with off campus jobs would no longer be a concern.

Over the next two seasons, the bruising fullback and gifted punter would excel on the gridiron and within the classroom. In addition, due to time management skills gained from those challenging early years in East Lansing, he was also able to participate in campus leadership. During his junior year, Jack assumed a seat on the Student Union Board.[35] He was later elected senior class president.[36] While serving in that role, he was obligated to meet with the college president on a periodic basis to discuss student issues. John Hannah got to know him quite well through those encounters. He was impressed with the Battle Creek native—a young man who overcame much adversity before finally gaining success at Michigan State. As their relationship matured during that senior year, Hannah took on a mentoring role. He dissuaded Jack from accepting an outstanding offer from an upstart professional football team. He saw no future in it.[37] Instead, he encouraged him to contact Forest Akers for potential employment opportunities.[38] Breslin heeded the advice. A few weeks following graduation, Jack and Renee, his new bride, packed up and headed for Allentown, Pennsylvania.

Five years later, John Hannah took a chance and contacted Jack Breslin, now a district sales manager for Dodge Motor Division in Allentown. George Guerre had just tendered his resignation. The president needed another prominent Spartan athlete with leadership skills to fill the vacancy in the Office of Alumni Relations. Breslin was the right man for the job.[39] Hannah predicted a very bright future for him at Michigan State.

That encouragement was all Jack needed to hear. The call from President Hannah could not have occurred at a more opportune time. Renee was expecting their second child; they both wanted to be closer to family and friends. Four weeks later, the Breslins arrived back in East Lansing. And by mid-June, Jack would assume his new position as assistant director of alumni relations and field director to Spartan alumni clubs about the state.

SHORTLY AFTER the Sanity Code was enacted in January of 1948, Michigan State revised its financial aid program to be consistent with the law of the land. All athletes would now be eligible for grants but only "if the student meets the academic standards prescribed by the [Faculty Committee on Scholarships]."[40] The board, however, felt a responsibility to those upperclassmen previously promised a free education. That conundrum, not unique to Michigan State's board, prompted the NCAA to amend its code. Acknowledging that these grants were in effect legal contracts, the national organization would not penalize colleges and universities for honoring them.

But all would change one year later. Michigan State College was now a provisional member of the Big Ten. Official membership was predicated on the school disbanding its controversial subsidy program.

After contemplating its limited options, the State Board of Agriculture, based on President John Hannah's recommendations, reluctantly reneged on a promise it had made to a group of athletes one year earlier. Endowment income from the Jenison Trust could no longer be used to finance college educations for approximately 70 upperclassmen.[41] Membership in the Intercollegiate Conference, a strategic initiative dating back to 1936, superseded the well being of students expected to donate well over 30 hours a week to the college's football program each fall.

Karl McDonel, the school's business manager, was given the unenviable task of informing members of the football team of this disappointing news—they were now responsible for all college expenses. He would be meeting with them in about a week over at Jenison Fieldhouse. Athletic department staff planned to be in attendance to answer remaining questions. The board meeting for January of '49 closed on that somber note.

CLAUD ERICKSON first heard about the plans to terminate the Jenison program during a brief visit to the administration building. The engineer had just dropped off his latest invoice to Karl McDonel for oversight services involving a recently completed infrastructure project. Small talk typically followed. McDonel, however, was in no mood for idle conversation. In a few hours he would be meeting with 70 student athletes over at Jenison Fieldhouse. In confidence, he shared with the consultant the reason. The 1922 MAC graduate, recalling his own struggles with financing an education three decades earlier, left the office deeply troubled over the implications for those young men.

A few weeks later, a group of prominent businessmen and professionals from the greater Lansing area were invited by Claud Erickson to meet and discuss the future of Michigan State athletics. During that gathering at a downtown restaurant, the Aggie outlined his vision. He needed their support to aid an honorable cause—assisting a group of students left in the lurch.

The Spartan Foundation was organized that evening. And to cover initial legal expenses for incorporation, those in attendance agreed to ante up $100 each.[42] In recognition of that generosity, donors would become founding members of the Century Club, the fund-raising arm of the foundation.[43] Membership would carry with it special privileges— tickets to games, passes for football practices, and personal contact with coaches and players.[44]

Claud Erickson was selected as president of the organization.[45] Passionate about the foundation, the engineering consultant, a man of modest means, eventually became one of its major contributors. No longer would he confidentially gift the State Board upon completion of any campus project—a tradition he started shortly after then Secretary John Hannah agreed to honor the unusual and highly lucrative Dirks-Erickson Handshake Agreement. Instead, he deposited future rebates to the college in a Century Club bank account in Lansing. Within a few years, his fund-raising organization had accumulated $55,700,[46] equivalent to $478,000 in real dollars.[47] With that endowment in place, the Spartan Foundation was ready to help out a lot of needy students!

Although Michigan State maintained no affiliation with Claud Erickson's foundation,[48] George Guerre of the Alumni Office joined the group in the fall of 1949. The Spartan Foundation had recently been incorporated. Its mission seemed honorable: to raise and disburse scholarship dollars for "talented and ambitious high school students who appear to possess unusual ability for agriculture, engineering, music, home economics, athletics, industry, commerce, journalism, government, science and any other arts or professions in which a course of study (was) offered at Michigan State."[49] [50] Although it was not a legitimate alumni club, Guerre felt it was within his job description to associate with an organization that claimed so many Spartan graduates among its membership.[51] He maintained no relationship, however, with the subsidiary Century Club—the $100 annual dues were out of the question for the recent college graduate!

In theory, as an employee of Michigan State, George Guerre's association with a booster organization disbursing scholarship dollars not monitored by the college was in violation of the Intercollegiate Handbook. But in the end, it didn't really matter. He resigned his position at the school in May of the following year. Four weeks later, Jack Breslin would be hired to sit behind George's desk in the Alumni Office. Within a few months, he too would develop a relationship with the booster club. Unfortunately for Michigan State College, unlike his predecessor, Breslin "made a serious mistake in identifying too closely with the [Spartan] Foundation."[52] His association with the boosters, and the Century Club in particular, would ultimately cast "aspersions" on the institution and greatly embarrass its leadership[53]—and it all had to do with a letter given to him by Claud Robert Erickson.

Ralph W. Aigler

Despite having little interest in athletics during his undergraduate years in Ann Arbor, Professor Aigler would eventually play a critical role in leading the wandering Wolverines back into the Big Ten in 1917. His reward: de facto leadership of one of the most recognized college athletic programs in the country for almost four decades. (Bentley Historical Library, University of Michigan)

Ralph W. Aigler

Availing himself of a 'bully pulpit' gained from his position as Michigan's faculty representative to the Big Ten, Professor Aigler would impose his will on colleagues within the conference and about the country. He quickly became a leading spokesman for the Purity Movement—a group of college leaders opposed to any form of financial aid for the amateur student athlete. (Bentley Historical Library)

Fielding Yost

The UM athletic director's 1932 scheduling agreement with Spartan Athletic Director Ralph Young would assure that the Wolverines controlled the date and venue for all future football contests between the schools. The confidential understanding guaranteed MSC the 'scrimmage game' weekend in perpetuity—a matter of great frustration for new President John Hannah a decade later. (Bentley Historical Library)

Henry Dirks

Unbeknownst to then Secretary of the College John Hannah, Engineering Dean Henry Dirks consummated a very lucrative contract with consultant Claud Erickson without a signature. The "handshake" agreement would indirectly lay the groundwork for Erickson's booster club—one that would greatly embarrass the college years later. (MSU Archives and Historical Collections)

Frederick Cowles Jenison

In 1939, he bequeathed his entire estate to MSC. President Hannah would later use income from that endowment to finance the Jenison Awards. By the early 1950s, in part due to those dollars, the Spartans were a national power and successfully competing against the Michigan Wolverines. (MSU Archives & Historical Collections)

Herbert Orin Crisler

The UM athletic director encouraged his Michigan Moles, living about East Lansing, to continue digging for any evidence that might implicate MSC in some covert, collaborative relationship with the Spartan Foundation. (Bentley Historical Library)

Edgar Harden

As the Spartans' faculty representative, he was deputized by President Hannah to clean up the mess at MSC in the aftermath of the 1953 Spartan Foundation probation. He earned kudos for his exceptional performance. In 1978, MSU's Board of Trustees would call him back home to serve as interim president of the university until a replacement was found. (MSU Archives & Historical Collections)

Claud R. Erickson

His booster club, the Spartan Foundation, was accused of funneling laundered money to former Jenison Award student athletes with residual eligibility, a major violation of Big Ten rules. (Department of Engineering, MSU)

John Hannah (third from left) with military personnel

In February of 1953, President Hannah assumed a temporary job at the Pentagon as assistant secretary of defense. His one-year sabbatical occurred at a most inopportune time for the college leader—the Spartan Foundation probation was announced shortly after his departure for Washington. (MSU Archives & Historical Collections)

Clark Brody

A huge dormitory complex is named for this prominent Aggie alumnus who served on the State Board for over three decades. The 1954 Brody Fumble would profoundly impact President Hannah's first attempt at changing the college's name to Michigan State University. (MSU Archives & Historical Collections)

Howard Remus Smith

The distinguished 1895 graduate of The State Agricultural College played a major role in the first 'name change' battle of '54, in large part due to his friendship with a prominent law professor from Ann Arbor named Aigler. (MSU Archives & Historical Collections)

G. Mennen "Soapy" Williams

The governor's Paul Bunyan Trophy proposal was a political campaign ploy to keep him in the public's eye—and hopefully gain him some votes among loyal MSC/UM graduates. In hindsight, the liberal Democrat probably lost some voter support, at least in Ann Arbor. Most Wolverines vehemently opposed the idea. (Bentley Historical Library)

Mr. Clean

Gerhard Mennen Williams was born into a wealthy East coast family (Mennen Company) that manufactured popular shaving products—hence the nickname "Soapy." *Mr. Clean* is an unrelated household cleanser manufactured by Proctor & Gamble Company. The trademark is used with permission.

Harlan Henthorne Hatcher (L)

The one-time Buckeye would experience his baptism by fire into the intense relationship that defined the UM-MSC series with the Paul Bunyan Trophy escapade of '53. A few months later, matters would really heat up—the Board of Regents expected him to spearhead opposition to MSC's 'name change' legislation. (Bentley Historical Library)

Paul Bunyan Trophy

The Paul Bunyan Trophy proposal cropped up just prior to MSC's first official conference game with UM. The Wolverines, unlike the Spartans, wanted nothing to do with a trophy intended to elevate the series to rivalry status!

John Hannah (L) and G. Mennen Williams (R)

Michigan State's 1955 Centennial Celebration kick-off: Another photo-op for a governor always campaigning (due to two-year term limits). His track record spoke for itself, six November victories in 12 years. (MSU Archives & Historical Collections)

Claud Lamar Brattin

A Wolverine turncoat, the MSC engineering professor shared a document with his friend, John Hannah, which would prove critical to the college winning the decisive 'name change' battle of 1955. (MSU Archives & Special Collections)

John Hannah (front row, third from right) and Howard Remus Smith (front row, second from right)

Smith would be honored with Michigan State College of Agriculture and Applied Science's Centennial Award at the June 1955 commencement ceremony. Unlike the old Aggie, who accepted his honor that day, the graduating seniors chose to receive their diplomas by mail two weeks later. By that time, the 'name change' would become official state law. Their sheepskins would include the school's newest title, Michigan State University of Agriculture and Applied Science in Old English font at the top—much to the frustration of Howard Remus Smith! (MSU Archives & Historical Collections)

E. Blythe Stason

The UM Law School dean maintained a pivotal role in the name change battles of '54 and '55. His wise counsel to President Hatcher ultimately led to armistice—and a rare defeat for the Wolverines in a contest far removed from the gridiron. (Bentley Historical Library)

Arthur Brandon

The UM Director of Public Relations was charged with improving the institution's haughty reputation where it really mattered—the state legislature. As the Paul Bunyan Trophy and the 'name change' incidents bore out, it was a formidable task. (Bentley Historical Library)

Kenneth "Tug" Wilson

The one-time Northwestern athletic director successfully politicked for leadership of the Big Ten following Commissioner John Griffith's death. Within a few years, Wilson probably questioned why he ever left Evanston. (The Big Ten Conference)

Marvin Niehuss

The UM vice president, with Arthur Brandon's assistance, drafted the successful strategy during the first 'name change' battle of 1954. (Bentley Historical Library)

CHAPTER 8

Michigan Moles

——

"...The real problem is not in the enforcement machinery after the data have been gathered but in *getting* the necessary data."

PROFESSOR RALPH W. AIGLER, 3 MARCH 1948[1]

FRITZ CRISLER FIRST HEARD ABOUT the Spartan Foundation somewhat serendipitously. It was mid-winter of 1951.[2] A University of Michigan graduate living in East Lansing clued him in on the booster club during an alumni gathering near town. Apparently he was under pressure to join the organization—it was understood that all members were required to annually donate to the foundation. Endowment income would be used to aid worthy students attending Michigan State. Crisler shared the little bit of espionage with his boss. Ralph Aigler instructed his athletic director to look into the matter and keep him updated on any developments.

MICHIGAN MOLES were certain alumni and fans of the university that happened to live in the greater Lansing area. Many were well-known civic leaders, businessmen, or professionals. Allegiance to Ann Arbor, for all intents and purposes, was kept in confidence; it was not politically or financially in their best interest. And because of their prominent roles within the community, many of these Wolverine loyalists happened to be friend or acquaintance of high-ranking Spartans—administrators, faculty, or head coaches. Ralph Aigler and Fielding Yost knew who they were. Quite often they relied on them for insider information about the college's athletic department practices.

Professor Aigler first hinted at the existence of an informal underground network shortly after the Spartans hired Jim Crowley in the summer of 1929. Within months of his arrival on campus, the Michigan faculty representative was aware of questionable recruiting and subsidizing practices in East Lansing—rumors that could only have been spread by a loyal undercover agent.[3] Years later, Aigler would hear about Biggie Munn's Kiwanis Club outburst—fingering Michigan for unfounded subsidy violations—well before the press could report it; a Wolverine in attendance placed an urgent long-distance phone call to Ann Arbor right after the tirade.[4] And a few weeks following Michigan State's provisional admission into the conference, Aigler revealed confidential information with a few conference colleagues that suggested the presence of an insider on campus—in this instance, someone with access to the registrar's office.[5][6]

Edward Vandervoort was a Michigan Mole—and, as it turned out, a somewhat reluctant one. In early February of 1951, Fritz Crisler, on orders from Ralph Aigler, placed a call to him. He requested a private meeting. He was vague about the reason. A few days later, Ed met up with the Wolverine administrator.

Crisler was not one for small talk. A Michigan alumnus living in Lansing had been solicited to join a new Michigan State booster club operating in the area—the Spartan Foundation. His source declined the invitation; he later shared the scoop with Crisler. Apparently the organization had a subsidiary—the Century Club—charged with raising money for the foundation.[7][8] Crisler knew that Ed was well connected with prominent people about Lansing. Perhaps he had some additional information to share?

Vandervoort was surprised by Crisler's curiosity. The foundation was no secret. Many prominent businessmen and professionals claimed membership. The Michigan letterman even volunteered, somewhat sheepishly, that he too was a card-carrying member.[9] In fact, there were quite a few Wolverines in the club—it was the expedient thing to do in a town dominated by Spartan faithful.[10]

The foundation was legally incorporated in the early spring of 1949; by November, it was up and running.[11] Its mission was to disburse scholarship grants to needy college students attending Michigan State.[12] The Century Club raised money for the foundation in line with state laws on tax-exempt status. Its name was chosen to evoke a sense of "glamour" or exclusivity, ultimately to promote membership.[13] In return for an annual contribution of $100, special privileges were assured the member.[14] Ed didn't go into details. As far as he was aware, the club was similar to those in operation in Ann Arbor, Columbus, Madison, and Iowa City.[15] The only difference—the Spartan Foundation was incorporated.[16]

Crisler thanked him for the scoop. But he needed more information. Acknowledging Ed's affiliation with the foundation and its subsidiary, would he be willing to offer the names of members? He was particularly interested in whoever managed the books for the Century Club.

The questions were now hitting a little too close to home for Vandervoort. He was comfortable with providing Fritz with the name of Hugo Lundberg.[17] After all, it was public record that the industrialist was secretary-treasurer of the foundation. But to reveal a closely guarded list of the membership—that was troublesome. Many of these donors were business associates; others members, like Ed, were quite active in the chamber of commerce. Vandervoort's Hardware and Sporting Goods, the family-owned business, was highly regarded throughout Michigan. Its reputation, gained over five decades, might be compromised if word ever leaked that he had collaborated in an investigation of an organization promoting Michigan State College.

Fritz appreciated Ed's predicament. He was merely trying to find out a little more information about the group for Ralph. The Michigan faculty representative was suspicious that the foundation might be up to no good. Vandervoort needed no explanation. He was well aware of booster practices. Thirty years earlier, just before he moved to Ann Arbor to play football for Coach Yost, the *Detroit News* broke a story about over-indulgent recruiting practices on the part of a few fervent Wolverine graduates affiliated with the Detroit Alumni Club.[18] And what made it even more memorable for Ed was that one of the athletes involved in the subsidy scheme was his old high school buddy, Harry Kipke.[19] But Vandervoort was confident that the Spartan Foundation was legitimate. He declined to provide any additional names to the athletic director.

Fritz decided to back off on his questioning. But he informed Big Ed that Ken Wilson would be clued in on the Spartan Foundation during the upcoming February conference meetings. As chief compliance officer for the Big Ten, it was the commissioner's job to stay on top of these booster clubs. Tug could decide for himself whether there was enough dirt to justify sending a conference spy up to East Lansing to poke around. In the meantime, should Ed become aware of any questionable payments to athletes, he was encouraged to contact either him or Tug.

ALBERT VANDERVOORT was an avid outdoorsman. He loved to hunt and fish. His four sons shared his passion. But the younger two boys were also interested in competitive sport, football in particular. Del graduated from Lansing Central High School after excelling as a big, quick-footed lineman. He attended Michigan Agricultural College where he earned three varsity letters as an Aggie. Following graduation, he joined his father and brother Tom in the family hardware business located two miles west of campus in downtown Lansing. Recognizing the important role his college affiliation had in business development, Del became quite active in alumni affairs. Within ten years, he would play a major role in organizing a booster organization—the Downtown Coaches Club—to promote Spartan athletic programs and a new head coach named Jim Crowley.[20] The Notre Dame legend would soon use the club's membership to assist him in luring talented recruits to East Lansing with dollar bills.[21]

"Big Ed" played football at Lansing Central a few years later with Michigan high school legend Harry Kipke. Vandervoort eventually followed his teammate to Ann Arbor. Over the next three years, while competing at Ferry Field, the two friends would help Coach Fielding Yost regain his winning ways. Following graduation, Ed took a job as teacher and coach at a high school in California. After a brief stint out west, he landed a similar position in Menominee, Michigan. The opportunity to hunt and fish year-round in the Upper Peninsula was too good to pass up. But with the untimely death of his father, Del and Tom called him back to Lansing. They desperately needed his help in managing the family hardware business. Ed reluctantly conceded.[22]

At around the same time Vandervoort returned to mid-Michigan, his old buddy was hired to coach Michigan State. Mindful that Ed was now back in town, Harry Kipke asked the former Wolverine tackle to assist him in coaching the Spartan linemen. He eagerly accepted. Vandervoort's brothers supported the decision. After all, Ed's affiliation with the college might benefit the family business some day. And so, in the early fall of 1928 Vandervoort would assume a part-time position in the athletic department at Michigan State. With an affable personality, he quickly made friends about campus. And with Del's encouragement, he also joined the Downtown Coaches Club. In short order, Ed Vandervoort would become an adopted member of the Spartan family.

Kipke's first year in East Lansing was a success—at least in the opinion of his bosses. Despite a 3-4 record, the team waged a valiant battle with the coach's alma mater. Michigan athletic director Fielding Yost was impressed with his protégé's overall accomplishments with so limited a talent pool. Following that season, without President Robert Shaw's approval, he quietly negotiated Kipke's return to Ann Arbor in late spring.[23] [24]

Big Ed opted to stay in Lansing rather than join his friend on the sidelines in Michigan Stadium; he planned to focus on promoting a new business line for the hardware store—sporting goods. Colleges and high schools were expanding their athletic programs to meet student demand. Equipment and uniforms were direly needed for various sports. It proved a wise decision. Within a few years, Vandervoort's Hardware would supply athletic gear to just about every high school in the state. And with Del's green blood, in combination with Ed's Wolverine (and Spartan) connections, the family business could claim the two state universities as major clients as well.

Coach Kipke won a lot of football games during his first few seasons in Ann Arbor. But unscrupulous recruiting and subsidizing practices eventually cost him his job. A few years later, Yost would retire. At risk of losing the Michigan account, Ed made it a point to befriend the new head coach and future athletic director Herbert Crisler.[25] The contract with Vandervoort's Hardware was never in doubt.

IN LATE February of 1951, as promised Ed Vandervoort, Fritz Crisler met up with Ken Wilson between conference meetings at the Chicago LaSalle Hotel.[26] The Wolverine athletic leader shared with the commissioner information he had gleaned about a booster organization based in Lansing. Crisler gave Wilson the name of the secretary-treasurer. He encouraged him to contact the club officer and, at the very least, keep Ralph Aigler updated. The Michigan faculty representative, he reminded Wilson, had a personal interest in this matter.

Six months later, Professor Aigler realized that Wilson, his mentee, had yet to follow up on Crisler's request. Embarrassed by the oversight, the commissioner promised to get right to it. Unfortunately, he had misplaced the name of the booster club officer he was asked to interrogate. But recalling a recommendation made by Crisler at the time, he did contact Ed Vandervoort. A week later, he met with the hardware vendor in Lansing to learn of any new developments since February.

Wilson started out by sharing with Vandervoort what little he knew about the Spartan Foundation. He quickly cut to the chase. Ralph and Fritz were suspicious that the organization might be nothing more than a front for funneling dollars to students no longer receiving Jenison grants. Was Ed aware of any unusual practices? Ralph was particularly interested in the relationship between the club and Michigan State. Were any Spartan administrators involved in the foundation?

Big Ed was stunned.[27] And for a seemingly interminable moment, he was speechless while thoughts of recent events raced through his mind.

Back in February, Fritz had raised the question of malfeasance. Were any of Ed's buddies handing out money under the table? Vandervoort was confident in his denial. But Crisler had never mentioned the possibility of a covert relationship between the Spartan Foundation and the college. And now, in the context of a recent letter he had received from Jack Breslin, an employee of Michigan State, he wondered if there might be something to Ralph's conjecture after all. The assistant alumni association director, a prominent and quite active member of the Century Club, had mailed out a note reminding fellow boosters of special privileges associated with membership; in that same letter he also subtly reminded them of responsibilities inherent in club affiliation, namely fund raising.[28] [29]

Vandervoort knew most of the leadership and coaching staff at Michigan State. President Hannah was a trusted friend. In fact, John and Sarah often asked Ed's daughter Nan to babysit their children.[30] The college administrator was a man of integrity and deep-seated convictions. There is no way John would tolerate any practice contrary to the spirit of the conference mission. Biggie Munn was an old fishing buddy. Ed had known him since he arrived in Ann Arbor back in 1938 to assist Fritz in coaching the Wolverines. He shared Hannah's character traits—in fact that was a major reason why John hired him. Biggie would never condone any scheme to funnel money to athletes in violation of Big Ten rules. And Ralph Young was one of the nicest, most honorable men he had ever met in college sport; the two had maintained a wonderful business relationship. Although not quite in touch with the daily operations of the athletic department as of late,[31] [32] Ralph ran a clean operation in Ed's opinion.

But his thoughts kept returning to that "Breslin Letter." Could there be a connection between the foundation and the school that he was not aware of? Were some members with college administrative ties, such as Jack, actually working behind the scenes to aid the Spartan athletic program? Had club leaders duped him into joining a rogue organization? And what were the potential consequences of quietly collaborating with the commissioner? If word ever leaked that he was the principal informant for an investigation into a foundation with a seemingly honorable mission, the family business might suffer irreparable damages.

Vandervoort finally responded to Wilson's question. He would prefer not to offer any further comments.[33] Acknowledging the businessman's predicament, Tug could only encourage Ed to contact the conference office should he come across any suspicious activities. As chief compliance officer, it was his duty to enforce the Intercollegiate Handbook. Monitoring ten schools proved to be a daunting task.[34] Any input Ed might offer would be greatly appreciated.

IN ADDITION to being a member of the Spartan Foundation, Ed Vandervoort was also very active in the M Club, an exclusive booster group of Michigan varsity letter winners. In fact, within a few months he would assume its presidency.[35] The club's mission was noteworthy: raise money for academic scholarships. All proceeds, consistent with Big Ten rules, were turned over to the university's general scholarship fund to subsidize qualified student athletes.[36] Booster buddies about East Lansing had sold him on the idea that the Spartan Foundation shared a similar, yet expanded mission. All students, not just athletes, were eligible for scholarship dollars. But now, based on conjecture raised by Ken Wilson earlier that afternoon, he questioned that sales pitch. Ed slept poorly throughout the night.

A few days later Fritz Crisler received copy of a letter signed by the assistant director of alumni relations at Michigan State College.[37] There was no accompanying note. The envelope was postmarked Lansing, Michigan. It lacked a return address. It didn't matter. The Michigan athletic director knew the source.

Dear Century Club Member: Through the compliments of Biggie Munn, we would like to present you with this secret practice pass. This pass will admit you to all Spartan football sessions during the fall, with the exception of Saturday afternoon, Sept. 15. This practice will be closed to all.

Biggie also has asked me to extend to you his thanks for your interest in the foundation.

Just a word from the writer—we need 100 more Century Club men. If you will get just one more yourself, we will get the additional 100 easily for at this writing we have 136 Century Club men. Give it a try!

Cordially yours,
Jack Breslin.[38]

Recognizing the implications of the mimeograph, Crisler immediately contacted the occupant of Room 320 Hutchins Hall over in the Law Quadrangle. Professor Ralph Aigler was ecstatic. He planned to meet with his athletic director later that afternoon to read the letter and discuss strategy.

AS IT turned out, the assistant director of alumni relations never drafted the Century Club letter. Claud Erickson did. The one-time consultant to Michigan State had hand delivered the template to Jack Breslin in early September.[39] As president of the Spartan Foundation,[40] the Aggie felt Breslin's name and status would carry greater weight—especially with the football season just around the corner.[41]

Jacweir Breslin was 31 years of age. After five years of working as a mid-level manager for Dodge Motor Corporation, he was quite comfortable in making decisions within the context of a large bureaucracy.

His job description as assistant alumni director appeared to permit that license. The note handed to him by Erickson was innocuous. The enclosed gift was nothing special; just about anyone could contact the athletic department and request a practice pass—you didn't have to be a person of influence, let alone a member of an exclusive booster club.[42] [43] And the comments attributed to Biggie seemed genuine. There was no reason to validate them.

He accepted Erickson's draft, lacking an official college letterhead, as transcribed. [44] One hundred and thirty six letters, passes included, would be personally signed and mailed out the following day. Breslin's boss, Alumni Director Tom King, was never informed of the plan.[45]

RALPH AIGLER and Fritz Crisler met in the director's office later that afternoon. The lawyer agreed with his director. The Breslin Letter did appear to directly link Michigan State College with boosters—groups notorious for sidestepping handbook rules and regulations. The challenge now was to find further evidence to substantiate that hunch.[46]

Aigler wanted Crisler to contact a few additional moles living in Lansing. If Ed Vandervoort would no longer cooperate, surely there were other Michigan alumni affiliated with the club that might be willing to share insider information? Find out what they knew about the foundation and its leadership. Who was its president? What about financial records? The foundation was incorporated; there had to be an annual filing with the State of Michigan. And what about the secretary-treasurer—no doubt he maintained documents on donations and disbursements? Aigler needed his name. He should also provide Ken Wilson with a copy of the letter. Inform him to hold off on any formal inquiry until more evidence was gathered.

And for his part, the lawyer would continue to oversee the preliminary investigation from his office in Hutchins Hall.[47] Aigler reminded Crisler that he had been waiting 20 years for this opportunity. He was not going to let anyone, including the commissioner, screw it up now.

Wilson's mismanagement of the Boilermaker probation of '48 and the Buckeye-Frontliners relationship of '49 were still fresh in his mind.

The 1951 season-opener with Michigan State College was only a week away. The Scrimmage Game with the Spartans would mark the beginning of a very busy few months for Michigan's athletic director. Regardless of official job responsibilities, Fritz Crisler would find the time to periodically meet with his moles back in East Lansing. Hopefully, by the end of the football season, there would be enough evidence in hand for the commissioner to serve notice to Michigan State.

WILLIAM REED first heard about the Breslin Letter back in early October. He had just assumed a job with the Big Ten as assistant commissioner.[48] The position, recently vacated by Walter Byers, was created a few years earlier to assist Tug Wilson in carrying out his expanded duties.[49] [50] [51] It would now be Reed's responsibility, as deputized chief enforcement officer, to coordinate and monitor all investigations. The Michigan State-Spartan Foundation investigation, although not yet an official inquiry, was top on Byers' list. But eight months later, despite gaining Ralph Aigler's nod to proceed with a formal investigation in the interim, Wilson had yet to serve notice to Spartan administrators. Bill Reed was frustrated—and he had good reason. Ken Wilson was incapable of making a decision.[52]

Prior to departing the Big Ten for the NCAA,[53] Walt Byers had briefed Reed on the significance of the Michigan State case. If found complicit in a rogue boosters scheme, the college could be charged with a major violation of the conference handbook—loss of faculty control over intercollegiate athletics. Public censure would be a certainty. Adding to that humiliation, the Spartans could face at least a two-year scheduling boycott by the membership—collective discipline with profound financial repercussions.[54] But of greater concern, a repeat offense of this magnitude could place the college at risk of expulsion from the Intercollegiate Conference.[55]

Recalling that earlier conversation with Byers, Reed was surprised by Wilson's current procrastination. Back in December of '51, during the annual Big Ten meetings held in Chicago, the commissioner was asked to deliver a "state of the conference" address before a joint session of faculty representatives and athletic directors. He talked tough. The recently empowered conference administrator shared with attendees his plans for upholding the Intercollegiate Handbook. He would have zero tolerance for any practice contrary to written law. Top on his list was illegal booster support for athletes. The phenomenon was spreading like a plague within conferences. The Big Ten was not immune. But Wilson vowed to work tirelessly to stem the contagion, at least within the Western Conference. With Bill Reed assisting him, while retaining one of J. Edgar Hoover's retired G-Men, Ed Martin, to aid in espionage, he planned to impose harsh penalties on offenders.[56][57]

Shortly after that talk tough address, Wilson and Reed had met with the leadership of the Spartan Foundation. Claud Erickson, its founder and president, claimed no wrongdoing.[58] He had willingly shared with Ed Martin his financial books a few weeks earlier. But he adamantly refused to provide the agent with a list of contributors. [59] Erickson wanted to avoid embarrassing prominent members, many of whom were graduates of other conference schools, most notably the University of Michigan.[60][61] He also refused to divulge how dollars were disbursed.[62]

Frustrated with Erickson's defiance, Wilson then made a phone call to John Hannah. The college president reassured the commissioner that his institution was not complicit in a booster scheme.[63] And wishing to avoid any embarrassing publicity, he promised full cooperation in the investigation.[64][65]

Hannah visited with Claud Erickson a few days later. [66] He was well aware of the booster club president. They had first met back in June of 1940. At the time, the college secretary was reviewing an unusual handshake agreement Erickson had consummated with Dean Henry Dirks of the engineering department. The fee arrangement was not consistent with historical business practice for retained consultants. But after seeking legal counsel, Hannah realized he had no recourse. He would continue to honor the handshake. And in appreciation, Erickson took it upon himself to rebate Michigan State a portion of all future invoices. It would come to a halt, however, in mid-summer of 1950. And it all had to do with a State Board member's curiosity about that unusual contract.

FREDERICK MUELLER was a very successful Grand Rapids businessman. He was also an Aggie. "Fritz" graduated from Michigan Agricultural College in 1914 with a degree in mechanical engineering. Three decades later, in mid-summer of '45, he was asked by John Hannah to serve on the school's governing board.

A few months in advance of Mueller's return to campus as a trustee, President Hannah had announced plans to resume a contractual relationship with Claud Erickson.[67] He predicted massive infrastructure growth over the next decade. Millions of dollars of surplus state revenue, accumulated since 1942, would soon be available to fund that construction, thanks in large part to Governor Harry Kelly's Victory Building Program. A proven talent prior to the war, Erickson was now needed to oversee building projects on both sides of the Red Cedar River. The consultant eagerly accepted the offer to again serve his alma mater—and make a few bucks on the side as well.

Mueller first came across the unusual boilerplate statement while reading through his board packet mailed out in advance of the January 1946 meeting. "Acceptance of a check for $1,000 from Claud R. Erickson, Consulting Engineer, to be used as the College Administration desires. Mr. Erickson requests no publicity concerning this gift." [68] The donation coincided with a $6000 invoice from the consultant for monitoring construction of the married veterans' trailer court on campus. Mueller thought nothing of the "miscellaneous" announcement. Three months later, in April, he noted a similar statement included in the same section of the minutes. And once again, it correlated with an invoice for services rendered, this time for work on a water and sewage project.[69] But by July, the savvy businessman began to notice a pattern, one that would continue over the next few years.

Finally, in June of 1950, Fritz Mueller raised the question no long-serving trustee had ever before asked. It followed discussion on a proposal by Claud Erickson to convert the North Campus power plant to an alternative fossil fuel. Projected costs and oversight fees seemed out of line. Curious about Michigan State's relationship with the consultant, Mueller requested additional information about his contract with the college. John Hannah assumed center stage; five minutes later, the board was fully aware of the history behind the Dirks-Erickson Handshake agreement consummated ten years earlier. Acknowledging Erickson's practice of generously donating back a portion of his invoice to his alma mater, the consultant fees, based on a percentage of total construction costs, still seemed excessive in Mueller's opinion.[70] Four weeks later, in large part due to the board member's concerns, the college severed its relationship with Claud Erickson. Michigan State would now contract with Commonwealth Associates of Jackson—and for a flat fee.[71][72]

Regardless of that board decision made one year earlier, John Hannah now had to confront his former consultant about the Spartan Foundation's relationship with Michigan State. While expressing appreciation for Erickson's role in creating a privately endowed scholarship fund for worthy students, he was concerned with how the booster club might be disseminating dollars to athletes. He reminded the Aggie that conference rules forbade the practice.

Hannah requested that Erickson fully cooperate with the commissioner's office. Ken Wilson needed the names of donors and recipients in order to carry out his investigation. Erickson politely declined. He had already shared financial documents with a retired FBI agent retained by the conference; but he was not going to reveal any names.[73] And Hannah, a man known for his persuasive tongue, somewhat uncharacteristically, had no response to the alumnus' recalcitrance. A year earlier, while Erickson was still under contract with Michigan State, the president might have used a "carrot and stick" approach to force compliance. But the Dirks-Erickson Handshake Contract was now past tense.

Hannah's final request was that Erickson turn all contributions to the Spartan Foundation over to Michigan State. And somewhat to his surprise, the defiant alumnus agreed—at least in part. Future donations to the Century Club would be given to the college's general scholarship fund.[74] [75] [76] But current assets, well in excess of $33,000, would remain in a Lansing bank, with all donor names protected by federal banking rules.

Shortly following that meeting with Claud Erickson, Hannah contacted Ken Wilson. He shared mixed results of his encounter with the foundation leader. Although disappointed with the president's "failure to secure access to records of the Foundation," Wilson expressed appreciation for his involvement in the probe. [77] He was now satisfied that Michigan State College had been fully cooperative in aiding his investigation.[78]

Ralph Aigler failed to share Ken Wilson's sentiments. When informed by the commissioner of Hannah's report a few days later, he effectively blew a gasket. [79] In his opinion, the president of Michigan State College wasn't trying hard enough. He could have invoked certain privileges of his office, including legal recourse, to gain that critical information. Lacking a list of all contributors to the Century Club, the conference investigation was certain to fizzle out—a matter Aigler was not going to permit.[80] He advised Wilson to use powers granted to the office of commissioner and effectively indict the college for obstruction of justice. By imposing probation on Michigan State, the lawyer was certain Wilson would finally gain the upper hand—complete cooperation from John Hannah.

With that mandate from his mentor,[81] the indecisive commissioner of the Intercollegiate Conference suddenly found himself caught in the crossfire between two very powerful and intimidating combatants.

Seven years earlier, Ken Wilson was an athletic director. He was also bored. The vacated commissioner's seat, brought on by John Griffith's untimely death, was an unparalleled opportunity to advance his career. He was fully confident that he was the right man for the job. But now

he questioned that decision to leave Evanston. Expanded handbook enforcement responsibility, an obligation not required of his predecessor,
was causing him great anguish if not a funk.[82]

In hindsight, it was apparent why Ken Wilson was derelict in filing
formal charges against Michigan State College. He may have been swim-
ming in waters way over his head. Acknowledging his inadequacies as
a decisive leader, it appeared that his only option, short of resigning,
was understandable: procrastinate. He would hold up the proceeding
against Michigan State while hoping for irrefutable evidence that might
surface in the meantime.[83]

CONFERENCE ENFORCEMENT Officer Bill Reed was well aware of
Ralph Aigler's latest demand to impose probation on John Hannah's
college. He had been included in the recent conversation Ken Wilson
had with the Michigan law professor. But after two weeks of waiting for
a decision from the commissioner about whether to proceed, Reed was
beside himself. The delay had cost them considerable leverage in the
case against Michigan State.

Reed's solution to Wilson's procrastination was straightforward:
transient insubordination. He confronted his boss and demanded action.[84] And much to his surprise, it actually worked. A few days later, John
Hannah received a letter from the commissioner of the Intercollegiate
Conference requesting a formal hearing. His reason was purposely
vague: "'a violation may exist' of such a nature as possibly to incur penal
action against Michigan State College under the Conference rules governing unearned aid to athletes."[85]

Five days later, after consulting the college attorney, President
Hannah responded. In a wordy statement, he questioned the ambiguous
charge. Wilson's administrative staff had found no evidence to implicate
Michigan State in any wrongdoing. Was there really a need for a hearing? But in the spirit of cooperating with the office of the commissioner,
he begrudgingly expressed a willingness to meet if necessary. Hannah's
only request was that the hearing take place quickly. He was a very busy

man; upcoming obligations overseas required that he be gone throughout June.[86]

Ken Wilson had misread John Hannah's letter. He assumed that the president had neither interest in nor time for a hearing. With that in mind, and consistent with Professor Aigler's confidential recommendation of three weeks earlier, he felt compelled to move forward with his threat—a one-year probation for obstruction of justice. A lengthy Western Union note from Chicago summarized the reasons. The "Telegram Indictment" had just one condition for termination of the embarrassing penalty: full "disclosure of the operations of the Spartan Foundation as they affect the eligibility of athletes at Michigan State College."[87]

Hannah was livid. He immediately sought out Ken Wilson—and, of all places, he located the commissioner in Ann Arbor.[88] After clarifying the misunderstanding, prompted by letters rather than telephone communication, they agreed to move forward with a formal hearing after all.

THE OFFICIAL gathering to address the charge of handbook rules violations—offering financial aid to unqualified student athletes—took place on June 4, 1952.

The college administration requested that its attorney, former governor Kim Sigler, represent the school. The practice broke with conference tradition. The implications of the hearing, especially in the context of Michigan State's evolving national reputation, were of such gravity that John Hannah felt he had no choice.[89] [90]

The commissioner presented his case. In essence, it was based on hearsay, all in the context of the Breslin Letter. Not a single claim of malfeasance was filed against the college. No student athlete was cited for receiving aid from the Spartan Foundation. The college was not charged with undermining Rule 7—the handbook verbiage on scholarships—by collaborating with a rogue group of alumni and fans. In fact, "there was only the inference that there must have been some violation of Conference regulations."[91] Regardless of these major holes in his argument, the commissioner insisted that the accused—Michigan State College—must prove its innocence.[92] It would be placed under probation until fulfilling that unusual requirement.[93]

Faced with the formidable task of trying to defend itself against "rumor, gossip, and inference," the Spartan attorney asked that John Hannah testify.[94] The president pointed out that the college had made every effort, short of legal recourse (a matter he wished to avoid due to embarrassing public exposure), to force the Spartan Foundation to reveal all of its activities, including financial, to the commissioner. It also requested that all future funds raised by the booster group be turned over to the institution's scholarship committee. He had even offered to use the influence of his office to force dissolution of the foundation and its subsidiary Century Club if so requested.

The hearing closed on that note. A decision by the commissioner on whether to uphold his earlier Telegram Indictment (and its one-year probation) would be forthcoming, most likely within a few weeks, after he reviewed the college's argument.

Three months passed; there was still no word from Chicago. Michigan State Faculty Representative Lloyd Emmons finally decided to send a letter to Wilson, reminding him of his promise. There was no reply. Emmons penned another note a few weeks later. Once again, there was no response from the conference office in the LaSalle Hotel.

As it turned out, there was reason for the commissioner's slight of common courtesy to Lloyd Emmons. His mentor, Ralph Aigler, was sensitive to Kim Sigler's earlier arguments for the defense. Aigler knew darn well that the case against the Spartans violated all concepts of a fair trial. But consistent with his past, behind-the-scenes, scrutiny of Michigan State practices,[95] he saw no reason to terminate this investigation. Let the threat of probation remain in force—it served a purpose. Sooner or later there had to be a break in this case; somebody would come forward with the truth; a legitimate indictment and appropriate sentence could then follow.

RALPH AIGLER'S delay tactic against the Hannah administration had no impact on the athletic fortunes of Michigan State. The Spartans continued their ascent to national football prominence. Biggie Munn's team, still unable to compete for a Big Ten crown, would go undefeated. It was the second year in a row for the juggernaut of talent previously financed with Jenison dollars. The Associated Press eventually proclaimed the college its mythical national champions for the 1952 season.[96]

The Michigan law professor's strategy also had little impact on the administrative operations of Michigan State College. In June, John Hannah alerted the State Board of the charges filed by Commissioner Wilson against the land-grant institution. He shared all that he knew about the Spartan Foundation and its subsidiary Century Club, the Telegram Indictment, the threat of probation, and the current status of the conference investigation. The board was impressed; it commended Hannah and his officers "for the manner in which the matter (had) been handled to date."[97] The confidential motion further stated that the administration should "use every possible means to protect the best interests of Michigan State College."[98]

Six months later, while acknowledging "the increasing responsibilities involved with administering the affairs of Michigan State College," the State Board of Agriculture unanimously voted to increase President Hannah's salary to $20,000 per year.[99] The December motion was a vote of confidence. It substantiated a previous resolution that had commended him on ten years of exemplary service to Michigan State as a leader, visionary, and educational statesman.[100]

Shortly after that pay raise was approved, an urgent gathering of the board took place in East Lansing. President-elect Dwight Eisenhower requested that John Hannah join his administration and serve as assistant secretary of defense for manpower and personnel. Mindful of the prestige associated with the prominent appointment, not just for Hannah but for the college as well, the State Board approved a one-year sabbatical while he served in Washington.[101]

THE FUTURE was indeed very bright for Michigan State College of Agriculture and Applied Science as 1952 came to a close. Its academic house was finally in order. Two confidential surveys from the mid-1940s, one noting graduate school deficiencies, the other pointing out substandard undergraduate classroom instruction, had both been satisfactorily addressed with the assistance of University of Chicago consultant Floyd Reeves and Michigan State Professor William Combs.[102] [103]

And the college's athletic programs were performing beyond expectations. Hannah's obsession with Big Ten affiliation proved to be a brilliant strategy. In only four years as a member of the Intercollegiate Conference, non-revenue sports were gaining respectability. The glass trophy cases at Jenison Fieldhouse were filled with numerous examples to support that claim.

The crowning moment for the pioneer land-grant college, however, still lay ahead. With the New Year about to unfold, Michigan State would finally be allowed to compete for conference football titles. Since all Jenison athletes had either graduated or exhausted remaining years of eligibility, the Crisler Asterisk Motion would no longer apply to gridiron victories over conference foes.[104] [105]

Unfortunately for Spartan fans, all that excitement would quite suddenly come to a halt in mid-February of 1953. The commissioner of the Intercollegiate Conference of Faculty Representatives, after seven months of fretful rumination, was finally ready to act on a threat dating back to early June of the previous year.

CHAPTER 9

An Act of Contrition

"All of us, whether legally trained or not, are rather steeped
in the notion that a man should not be punished without
proof of his guilt and that it is unfair to the individual to
throw the burden upon him to establish his innocence."

PROFESSOR RALPH W. AIGLER, 17 FEBRUARY 1932[1]

IN LATE JANUARY OF 1953, shortly after the inauguration of Dwight
Eisenhower, John Hannah assumed secondary residency in Washington.
As assistant secretary of defense for manpower and personnel, the col-
lege president would be charged with formulating policy to effectively
dismantle a military that had ballooned to over five million employees.[2]
It was quite a task—he was given one year to accomplish it.

The State Board of Agriculture agreed to loan Hannah to the
Department of Defense with one stipulation: he must continue to serve
the college as president in absentia. In order to carry out that obligation, Hannah devised a game plan for the next 12 months. A five-mem-
ber administrative board would run the school on a day-to-day basis; he
would be available for conference calls if needed. The college leader also
planned to fly home every Friday evening to spend the weekend with his
wife and children. But on Saturday mornings, he would meet with his five
deputies to address challenging operational matters. And finally, Hannah

agreed to attend all monthly State Board meetings; he would return to East Lansing one day earlier to fulfill that Friday morning commitment.[3]

It appeared to be a rock solid plan. Unfortunately, in all the excitement of preparing for his tour of duty, he had overlooked one lingering issue—a matter that would haunt him throughout his sabbatical in Washington.

AT ABOUT the same time Secretary Hannah was acclimating to his temporary job at the Pentagon, Commissioner Kenneth Wilson was contemplating how to respond to a letter he had received from the college president six weeks earlier, back in late December. Reading between the lines, Hannah was clearly annoyed. Faculty Representative Lloyd Emmons had written three notes to the commissioner requesting closure on an obstruction of justice charge filed against the Spartan administration dating back to early June. Almost six months later, there was still no response from Chicago. Adding to Hannah's frustration, just about everyone involved in conference leadership and oversight, including his colleagues on the Council of Ten, was now aware of what was supposedly a highly confidential investigation. Michigan State had been "thoroughly embarrassed" and "cast in an unfavorable light" due to this drawn out affair. All Hannah wanted now was a decision, some direction from the commissioner's office, on what was the next step.[4] Any further delay placed the college at-risk for leaks to the press—embarrassing publicity that was not in the grand plans for his institution.

Mindful of his latest slight, however, one to a respected member of the Council of Ten, Wilson contacted Aigler and requested advice in how to respond to Hannah. A few days later, the lawyer met up with the commissioner and his associate, Bill Reed, at the Big Ten offices in Chicago.

Unlike the commissioner, Aigler was not the least bit intimidated by Hannah's letter. He reminded the conference enforcement officers that the University of Michigan had filed its confidential complaint against Michigan State College in the late fall of 1951. A little over a year and a half after the fact, the commissioner's office was still struggling to gain possession of financial documents and names from the Spartan Foundation's Century Club—evidence deemed critical to the investigation.

Wilson's probe, in Aigler's opinion, had dragged on, in large part, due to lack of institutional cooperation on the part of Michigan State. It was implicit in membership that all conference schools collaborate with the commissioner's office in aiding any investigation. The newest member of the club was clearly not living up to that responsibility.

The Wolverine law professor, now mindful of President Hannah's greatest fear, embarrassing publicity about his college, recommended moving forward with the stalled probation. Wilson should compose a formal letter clearly spelling out the terms to Hannah.[5] He was certain that his old nemesis would exercise his appellate rights. Assuming that appeal was over-ruled, the commissioner could then approach Hannah about plea-bargaining. And if that failed, he could finally issue a press release announcing the year of probation.

FOLLOWING HIS first week of duty at the Pentagon, Assistant Secretary of Defense John Hannah returned home to East Lansing and a weekend of planned promises. Arising early Saturday morning, well before Sarah and the children were awake, he departed Cowles House and walked over to his office in the nearby administration building. He wanted to get through some paperwork before his five administrative deputies arrived a few hours later.

The stack of mail was as expected—notes from parents, alumni, politicians, and reporters; everyone had a special request or an axe to grind; the standard fare for the leader of a major academic institution. What was not anticipated in that pile, however, was a letter postmarked Chicago and dated February 3, 1953. After a five-week delay, Commissioner Kenneth Wilson had finally responded to a note dictated by Hannah just a few days prior to Christmas.

The president quickly scanned the three-page communiqué. Eight months after first alerting Michigan State of his plans to impose probation on the school for unfounded charges, Wilson had decided to finally follow through with his threat. Hannah immediately tried to telephone the commissioner at his home in Evanston. There was no answer. He then called the conference office, but again, no response. Recognizing the importance of timing, he sent off an urgent telegram to the conference office in Chicago. Hannah was irate over Wilson's use of the term 'probation;' he promised a formal reply.

Secretary Hannah's official response arrived at the LaSalle Hotel a few days later.

> The action you propose would be a serious blow to Michigan State College. We feel it is very unfair. You are doing now substantially what you proposed to do summarily eight months ago without granting us the right of a hearing or an opportunity to be heard. At that [eventual] hearing [in June] you produced no evidence of any kind or nature in any way connecting this College with the Spartan Foundation. You had only suspicions that the Spartan Foundation was doing something in violation of Rule Seven...
>
> Now, in the light of that suspicion and belief on your part, we are to be convicted in the eyes of the nation of some offense. You propose to put us on probation.
>
> It requires no stretch of the imagination to realize what this means. First, there will be a blast in the newspapers from one end of the country to the other, and from then on every activity of this college will be under suspicion.[6]

Hannah, a poultry scientist by training, appeared to have suddenly developed an interest in linguistic form, etymology in particular![7] While citing *Webster's Unabridged Dictionary*, he provided the commissioner with his favored definition of probation: "The method of treating a delinquent convicted of an offense, whereby he is not imprisoned but is released on a suspended sentence under supervision and upon special conditions."[8]

Based on his reading of the Intercollegiate Handbook, Hannah felt the commissioner lacked that power to tether a member school.

But what really troubled him was the connotation of that one word: probation. The president was willing to accept any other term—warning, reprimand, or censure—whether deserved or not. But probation implied conviction, and Hannah was adamant that his school had been found guilty of no wrongdoing.

The president was on a roll by now. "The wording of the second condition in your proposal we feel is harsh and unfair—'it shall be incumbent on Michigan State College to secure or exhaust every possible remedy in an effort to secure detailed and complete information concerning all financial disbursements of the Spartan Foundation to the time of its dissolution.'"[9]

What does this mean? How are we to exhaust every possible remedy? Is it your intention that we must go to court and take legal action to compel the Spartan Foundation to turn over to you something that you have in mind?

Again we ask that you put yourself in our place with that kind of a club continuously hanging over our head. I am sure you would feel that same as we do.[10]

Hannah, now more composed after venting his anger in written format, decided to close on a positive note. It was his "earnest hope" that the question could be quietly resolved without the need of an appeal—an embarrassing ordeal that would not be in the best interest of Big Ten, let alone Michigan State, once the probation became public knowledge. He requested that the commissioner "reframe" his position in light of comments shared and "accept this letter in the spirit in which it is written."[11]

Unfortunately for John Hannah, Ralph Aigler didn't share in that "spirit." He wanted publicity—the more, the better. After receiving word of Hannah's petition for reconsideration, the lawyer advised Ken Wilson to stay the course. But first, as they had previously discussed, he owed the president a reply spelling out in detail his formal charge, effectively an update of his earlier Telegram Indictment, and the latest evidence supporting Michigan State's collusion with the Spartan Foundation.

KEN WILSON'S follow-up letter to John Hannah, unlike recent practice, was much more timely; it took only four days. He didn't deviate from the script drawn-up by his mentor.

The emboldened Wilson suggested that it was highly unlikely that Michigan State officials were not aware of the Spartan Foundation. The size of the organization and its assets were too large to go unnoticed. He considered it a responsibility of all member schools to be "fully acquainted with funds they know or have reason to believe are being used in their behalf, or at least when they are potentially in behalf of athletes." In addition, he pointed out that he had "positive testimony," no doubt from a Michigan Mole, that when solicitations were made, "they were stated to be used for the purpose of assisting athletes at Michigan State College."[12]

Mindful of the foundation's significant assets of $33,500 at the time the leadership dissolved the controversial scholarship fund, he then referenced a "highly pertinent disclosure." Apparently Claud Erickson had recently revealed to the commissioner that approximately $3,800 had been "loaned" to student athletes after exhausting their eligibility. "The fact that we have been able to establish to this extent direct aid to students outside institutional channels leads me to believe that additional amounts could well have been disbursed to students, including [current] athletes, in like manner."[13]

Adding to this surprising disclosure, Wilson's sources pointed out that no former student athlete involved in those loans had yet to make a payment on any obligation.

He concluded his argument by noting that the Spartan Foundation, in his opinion, had operated in violation of handbook rules regarding unqualified financial aid to student athletes. "The [booster club] fund could well have contributed to many more students, and to a greater extent, than you or I have been able to ascertain."[14]

Lacking cooperation from Michigan State in gathering critical information from loyal alumni and friends of the foundation, he felt compelled to issue a public probation. Three conditions had to be fulfilled for faithful discharge of that notoriety. In addition to ensuring full institutional compliance with handbook rules regarding all future scholarships for student, the school was also asked "to secure, or exhaust every possible remedy in an effort to secure, detailed and complete information concerning all financial disbursements of the Spartan Foundation to the time of its dissolution."[15] And finally, Michigan State was obligated to fully assist the commissioner's office in examining the operation of all other alumni or booster clubs affiliated with the college.

The commissioner closed by offering an olive branch. Should the college expeditiously fulfill all three provisions to his satisfaction, probation could be lifted in advance of the one-year sentence.[16]

As anticipated by Ralph Aigler, President Hannah chose to appeal the penalty.[17] [18] [19] He disputed two points in the indictment:

- The commissioner's charge that Michigan State had an inherent responsibility to monitor the activities of all unaffiliated booster operations.
- The commissioner's authority to impose a penalty, (which was probation), not mentioned in the handbook.[20]

The assistant secretary of defense, now with a battle plan in mind, effectively declared war on the Office of the Commissioner. The confrontation in Chicago, as it turned out, would prove short-lived. It lasted no more than eight hours.

THE INTERCOLLEGIATE Handbook appellate process became conference law in the fall of 1951. The State University of Iowa was the first school to take advantage of it while challenging a decision by Commissioner Wilson; it involved a recruiting violation charged to Hawkeye basketball coach Frank O'Connor. Wilson's action was sustained. The Faculty Representatives Committee stood behind their empowered, yet harried commissioner when he desperately needed some moral support.

Unlike the O'Connor petition, the current appeal by President Hannah was quite different. An institution, rather than an individual, was under indictment. In Professor Aigler's opinion, this case was of greater historic and legal significance.[21] Michigan State, as a member school, was challenging the right of the commissioner, an employee of the conference it sponsored, to enforce the handbook in a way not quite to its liking.[22] And to ensure this appeal remained case law for years to come, the lawyer personally instructed Ken Wilson and his associate, Bill Reed, in how to carry out the hearing. He wanted to minimize any risk for overturning the commissioner's action due to procedural mishap.[23] [24] After all, Hannah had set precedent by including his college's attorney in the original Telegram Indictment hearing almost nine months earlier. No doubt he would have legal counsel present for this gathering too.

The appellate board met on Sunday, February 22, in Chicago to hear an appeal by Michigan State College regarding disciplinary actions imposed on it by the commissioner. The meeting consumed most of the day.[25] In the end, the faculty representatives unanimously ruled that it was within the implicit power of that office to impose probation on the college, "particularly as a device for getting a member to take action which under its implied obligation of membership it is duty bound to take."[26] In effect, it upheld all provisions of Wilson's original Telegram Indictment.

As luck would have it, Ralph Aigler happened to be chairman of the Faculty Representatives Committee that year. His responsibilities included presiding over all meetings—including appellate proceedings. Recognizing the legal and political implications of his position as chief justice of this supreme court should the proceedings ever be leaked, he decided to call for a verbal tally. And so, "when the motion to dismiss the appeal was put to a vote, there was a chorus of 'ayes' and no 'nays.'" Unanimity among his eight peers obviated the need for the Wolverine leader to expose his position.[27] It was a brilliant maneuver—he effectively recused himself from the final tally. Allan Aigler, a savvy Ohio politician in his own right, was no doubt pleased with his kid brother's parliamentary ploy to save face.

Following that decision, Dean Emmons, sitting on the opposite side of the bench, was allowed to rejoin his colleagues. Mindful of President Hannah's aversion to any negative publicity, he immediately requested that a formal vote be taken on the question of whether to reveal to the press the commissioner's plan of action. Much to the satisfaction of the Michigan law professor, no one seconded the motion.[28] The following day, sports writers around the country reported the embarrassing details of probation imposed on Michigan State College by the commissioner of the Intercollegiate Conference.[29] And back in Ann Arbor, Ralph William Aigler, an avid reader of metropolitan Detroit newspapers, was pleased with what was reported.

DESPITE THE circumstantial evidence cited by the commissioner in his official report to John Hannah following the appellate process, there was still no proof that any student with residual athletic eligibility had ever received dollars from the Spartan Foundation. There was also no evidence that Michigan State was even remotely complicit in the operations of the rogue organization. The probation, at least in the opinion of Spartan leaders, was intended for one reason: force the college to comply in an investigation without merit.[30] And the Appellate Board's conclusion, if it accomplished anything, substantiated Hannah's long-held contention: Michigan State was guilty until it proved itself innocent.

Aigler recognized the injustice being served the college with this latest legal maneuver. But he had no choice. At least now, with the appellate decision in hand, Michigan State must cooperate with the commissioner—and it had 12 months to do so before a final determination on its fate was made by the Faculty Representatives Committee. The carrot for the Spartans—if any—was that the order could be rescinded prematurely once all three counts were addressed to the satisfaction of the commissioner.[31]

In the meantime, the law professor from Ann Arbor would leave nothing to chance. Michigan Moles were encouraged to continue searching for new evidence. One source noted a changed attitude among administrators since the disciplinary action was upheld. Aigler shared the observation with Bill Reed. "The people at the College have concluded [that]...their earlier attitude of belligerency was not in their best interest...their primary consideration now is, 'what can we do to clear ourselves?'"[32]

During an official visit to Lansing, Michigan President Alexander Ruthven engaged in some small talk with a prominent local contractor, apparently with maize and blue bloodlines. The businessman was under significant pressure to contribute to an upstart organization called the Gridiron Club. Ruthven, now privy to probation imposed on the Spartans, notified Athletic Director Fritz Crisler. Shortly thereafter, a mole popped-up at the contractor's office to gather further details; apparently the businessman "had the bite put on him for $10,000."[33] The accusation was later refuted by the commissioner's office.[34]

Another Wolverine living underground informed Crisler that a Lansing bank executive was willing to "make available...microfilm copies of any checks" involving Spartan Foundation transactions.[35] The banker agreed to meet with the commissioner under the guise of strict confidentiality. Nothing further came from the offer.

THE IMPACT of probation began to sink in for a few Spartan leaders shortly after the embarrassing public announcement. Ralph Young was the first to take note.

In early March, the conference athletic directors gathered for another stab at finalizing schedules for the 1955-56 seasons. Their first attempt, almost a year earlier, ended in a draw[36]—a small faction was holding out for an alternative, more equitable format for contracting with each other.[37] They decided to meet again in December of 1952. But by that time, the directors were privy to an investigation involving the Spartan program. For various reasons, they decided to table scheduling plans for another three months.[38] Despite no mention in the minutes, certain members of the fraternity may have also wanted to know the outcome of that investigation before arranging contracts for that two-year span. Boycotting, after all, was on their minds—and there was no better way to send a message to the upstarts, clearly a football power by that time, than by quietly denying Athletic Director Ralph Young lucrative scheduling agreements.[39]

And as it turned out, a core group of three schools did just that. In order to qualify for football titles during the 1955 and 1956 academic years, Ralph Young had to sign up a minimum of six conference teams for each season.[40] He was ultimately successful, but it required a lot of work on his part. Although never revealed to the press due to a conference understanding steeped in secrecy, it appeared that Ohio State, Iowa, and Northwestern decided to impose their brand of vigilante justice. As will be seen, those two-year boycotts eventually morphed to four years when the conference directors gathered almost a year later to draft schedules through the 1958 football season.[41]

Putting aside Ralph Young's challenges with drafting future football schedules in February of '53, the real blow for the college's leadership took place a few months later. In mid-May, the NCAA Subcommittee on Infractions reviewed the Big Ten's case against the Spartans. Unfortunately for Michigan State, Professor Ralph Aigler sat on that committee. And if that wasn't enough, Walt Byers, the executive director of the NCAA, also attended those meetings. As former assistant commissioner of the Western Conference, he was well aware of past Spartan shenanigans, including the recent booster club controversy; that investigation was heating up just prior to his assuming administrative leadership of the NCAA.

In a letter to the subcommittee, Chief Enforcement Officer Ken Wilson summarized the reasons for his conference's disciplinary action. He recommended that the NCAA not penalize Michigan State—at least for the time being. Committee member Ralph Aigler, privy to Wilson's frustrations in dealing with a defiant Spartan administration, recommended that Walt Byers compose a letter to the Big Ten commissioner acknowledging the probation; the NCAA would refrain from passing judgment on the college until the Intercollegiate Conference had completed its investigation. Michigan State's Lloyd Emmons would be copied on Byers' letter—a subtle reminder that the NCAA was also looking over the Spartans' shoulders.[42]

In a follow-up communiqué to Wilson, Professor Aigler pointed out yet another reason for having Byers mail out a mimeograph copy to the somewhat pugnacious Spartan faculty representative. "I wanted Emmons to realize that the interest on the part of the NCAA was in accordance with a general plan, otherwise, he no doubt would think that it is another instance of malicious conduct on my part!"[43]

Walt Byers did send that letter to Commissioner Wilson, just as Ralph Aigler had recommended it. But by August, his organization felt the waiting game was over. The NCAA imposed a formal, well-publicized censure of Michigan State.[44] It was yet another humiliation for President Hannah and his college.

TWO WEEKS following Ralph Aigler's successful ploy to subtly strike back at John Hannah's right hand-man Lloyd Emmons, the Big Ten held its annual spring meetings. A motion was put forth by the University of Illinois: "BE IT RESOLVED, that this joint meeting [of faculty and athletic directors]...express its regrets that an association with Dean [Lloyd] Emmons draws to an end, and desires to extend to him the hearty good wishes of all for many years of well earned leisure...."[45] It was unanimously approved.

During that same weekend gathering, the conference leaders approved plans to explore "legislative recommendations representing a 'loosening' approach to the recruiting regulation and the rules on earned and unearned financial aid." [46] The Big Ten was struggling with how to remain competitive with non-conference foes freely offering dollars to non-scholar athletes in the aftermath of the Sanity Code. [47] Iowa's athletic director Paul Brechler proposed the motion—the same man who fervently opposed a Spartan membership five years earlier for those very reasons. And in one final, perhaps defiant act before he would end his relationship with the Intercollegiate Conference, Lloyd Emmons actually seconded the motion. No doubt, the subtle irony was not lost on those in attendance—the Big Ten might soon adopt the one-time recruiting and subsidizing practices of the very college it now held in check!

UNLIKE HIS predecessor, Lloyd Emmons, Professor Edgar Harden was an athlete. Baseball was his passion. While attending Iowa State Teachers College, he was good enough to have been offered a professional contract with the St. Louis Cardinals. But common sense prevailed. He turned it down. After graduating from college, he taught for a few years while pursuing a doctorate in education.

Shortly after the end of hostilities overseas, Michigan State College hired Harden as an associate professor in its Institute for Counseling, Testing and Guidance. He later became director of the Continuing Education Service. With a recognized gift for leadership, John Hannah promoted him to dean of the school within a few years.[48]

Harden was well liked among his peers at Michigan State. Mindful of his interest in athletics, he was selected by the faculty senate to assume the position left vacant by Dean Emmons in June of 1953. And as will be seen, no more worthy man could have been chosen for the unenviable task that lay ahead.

Ed Harden met with his boss shortly after accepting his latest assignment. President Hannah brought his rookie faculty representative up to date on the current investigation of the college. Due to his commitments in Washington, he needed a man he could trust to act on his behalf. Hannah would grant Harden complete "responsibility and authority...

to use every means" available to devise a corrective action plan, a self-directed penance, to atone for the college's past sinful ways—whatever they were.[49] And if that task wasn't challenging enough, the president wanted the probation lifted within 12 weeks, coinciding with the start of the 1953 football campaign.

John Hannah reminded Harden that this was Michigan State's inaugural season in conference gridiron competition. The Spartans had just been crowned the mythical national champions in December. Biggie Munn's team currently owned a 24-game winning streak. Sportswriters from around the country would be descending on East Lansing within the next few months looking for topics to write about. Hannah wanted only positive articles penned about his school. A nagging probation posed a threat to that plan.

THE FIRST order of business for Ed Harden was to earn some trust among the Big Ten leadership—the faculty representatives and athletic directors. He was cordially received at every stop during his travels about the Midwest. He also visited just about every college-affiliated alumni club in Michigan. Compliance with the Intercollegiate Handbook was his oft-repeated message; all Spartan faithful were expected to abide by its rules and regulations on recruiting and subsidizing student athletes.[50]

Harden also made an obligatory visit to Chicago and the conference office in the LaSalle Hotel. Commissioner Kenneth Wilson was impressed with the candid Harden—the encounter was unlike recent interactions with college representatives.[51] The dean clearly spelled out his intention: to have a corrective action plan in hand within three months. And if all remaining terms of probation were fulfilled as well, it was Harden's fervent desire to have the notoriety lifted at that time.[52][53][54]

Six weeks later, Professor Harden sent notice to the commissioner that all requirements spelled out in the February probation had been accomplished. Mindful of Michigan State's defiant "catch us if you can" attitude towards Wilson over the past few years,[55][56] the Spartan expressed sincere regret. Those individuals had been quietly reprimanded. He then confessed what amounted to a few venial sins—minor institutional violations of the conference catechism. Clearly Michigan State had "ignored the activities of the Spartan Foundation...but as a result of this experience...we are now prepared to act as quickly and forcefully as any member of the Intercollegiate Conference."[57]

Harden acknowledged the college's "negligence in developing an educational program designed to make alumni and friends of the institution aware of the policies and procedures" of the conference. He emphasized that a program was now in place to fix that oversight.[58]

The faculty representative then went into great detail about his accomplishments to date. Employee collaboration with the rogue organization was top on his list. Other than Jack Breslin's association with the Century Club, Harden had discovered no other improper relationships among school officials and coaches. "[The alumni field representative] obviously made a serious mistake in judgment in identifying too closely with the Foundation.... That the College has realized this is best indicated by the fact that Mr. Breslin has been transferred to another office on campus and will no longer be identified with the Alumni activities."[59] [60]

Harden also addressed matters of dollar disbursement by the Spartan Foundation. He first approached Claud Erickson, the president of the booster club. After devoting countless hours trying to cajole him into disclosing financial records, he concluded that it was hopeless.[61] "I am firmly convinced that we have gone much too far in satisfying his ego and encouraging him to feel that he is the 'key figure' in this matter. Surely a great institution and a great Conference should never allow any individual to use either of them as a means of gratifying an insatiable thirst for publicity."[62]

Stymied by the defiant Erickson, Harden then approached the two men responsible for writing checks to "qualified" recipients, Gilbert Haley and Jordan Jenkins. The boosters acknowledged that a few of those students were athletes—second and third quarter seniors no longer eligible for gridiron competition. The "loans" never exceeded $500 in any term and were only offered to those with demonstrable financial hardship.[63] But Jenkins, a local attorney, sheepishly admitted that there was no obligation for payback.[64] Unfortunately, all recipients were away from campus at the time. Harden had no way to contact them.

Armed with that indirect, somewhat incriminating evidence, the Spartan faculty representative then considered interviewing athletes still on campus for summer school. Perhaps they might be aware of any misguided dollars being offered to current student athletes? But only one letterman was in school during the month of July; the dean decided to pursue that option at a later date if necessary.[65]

And with admission of that lone impropriety, perhaps the only major revelation in an ordeal dating back almost two years, Edgar Harden closed his case. In four weeks on the job, he had interviewed all parties involved and pursued all leads. There was nothing more that he could add. Despite failing to divulge any egregious wrongdoing, he was confident that the school's examination of conscience had been successful beyond expectations. Michigan State was the better for this soul-cleansing experience.

Harden concluded his written remarks by reminding the conference commissioner that the college's probation, dating back to February, had two objectives in mind. The first was punitive—"This part...was certainly satisfied when the front page of every major newspaper in the United States told the story of our censure by the Intercollegiate Conference." The second was corrective—devise an action plan focused on educating Spartan faithful on the rules of the Intercollegiate Handbook. Harden noted that he had "dedicated my efforts of the past 30 days" and will continue to "devote my efforts during the time I am representing M.S.C." to this matter.[66]

The new faculty representative expressed appreciation to Wilson for his counsel and support during the previous month while he sought to fulfill the terms of probation. Effectively begging forgiveness, he then pleaded that the yearlong penalty now be prematurely lifted.

The commissioner was not moved by this act of contrition. After reviewing Harden's report, he concluded that a promise to be a compliant member would not fulfill the terms of this conference penance.

The Spartan faculty representative failed to accomplish what was ultimately demanded of him—discover evidence to prove that the college conspired with the Spartan Foundation in financially subsidizing non-qualified student athletes. Recognizing the legal absurdity of that demand, however, Wilson promised Harden that a good faith effort in reconciling any admitted major offense "would mitigate the liability [the school] could otherwise confront" in February when the Faculty Representatives Committee would review his final report on the Spartans' year under house arrest.[67]

Michigan State's first attempt at foreshortening its probation ended on that note. Despite Professor Harden's commendable efforts, Commissioner Wilson wanted something more than admission of a few minor wrongs. The Spartan Foundation had raised $55,700 over three years of operation. Harden accounted for all but $5,200. The commissioner expected a full explanation for those remaining dollars.[68] The faculty representative was advised to report back when he had answers. Until that time, the one-year penalty would remain in force.

FRUSTRATED WITH the resistance he had encountered from Claud Erickson, the only man capable of explaining all dollar disbursements, and mindful that it was now only four weeks before the season opener, Edgar Harden contemplated other means to resolve the $5,200 question. Legal recourse was recommended but President Hannah overruled it.[69] Challenging a small group of alumni[70] with misguided yet honorable intentions in a court of law would send the wrong message to thousands of loyal graduates.[71]

Harden's thoughts returned to an earlier option: student interviews. With the entire football team now back on campus for preseason practice, he would find the time to meet with every varsity letter winner. All athletes sign affidavits; all denied receipt of any assistance from the booster club.[72]

And so, confident that he had pursued just about "every possible remedy in an attempt to secure detailed and complete information concerning all financial disbursements to the time of [the Spartan Foundation's] dissolution," Harden again petitioned Kenneth Wilson on the 10th of September.[73] The season opener was just 16 days away.

In his latest argument to cut short probation, Dean Harden noted, "the fact that we have not been able to account for the comparatively small amount of $5,400 [sic] is due to no lack of diligence on our part. We have tried every means of persuasion, including threat of legal action, to get Mr. Erickson to reveal whatever records he has which will clear the picture completely. There are no reasonable grounds for his failure to provide the accounting, which we are as earnest in seeking, as are you. We cannot conceive such disclosure revealing anything damaging to Michigan State College—certainly nothing as embarrassing and humiliating as the public censure to which we have been exposed during the past nine months."[74]

He closed by again pleading leniency while borrowing from his earlier presentation to Wilson. The college was placed on probation for one reason: failure to aid an investigation. He argued that the action was designed to be both punitive and corrective. The "subsequent censure in the press of the nation [was] <u>more</u> than <u>sufficient</u> to meet the punitive [intent]."[75]

Harden's latest act of contrition was acknowledged but once again ignored by Ken Wilson. Groveling would get him nowhere. The penalty would remain in force until full accounting for all dollars disbursed was made.[76] And realizing that this was the second time Harden raised concern over embarrassing publicity associated with the punitive tag, Wilson decided to issue a press release.[77] A nation of college sports enthusiasts was reminded in newspapers the following morning that Michigan State College, the reigning mythical national champions, was still under house arrest. Wilson also informed inquiring reporters that an update on probationary status of the college would be provided the faculty leaders during the annual December Big Ten meetings.[78]

KEN WILSON shared with his mentor Edgar Harden's concerns over the ongoing notoriety attached to the current probation. Needless to say, Ralph Aigler was pleased. This was just as he had predicted. Public exposure of an offense—even one not yet proven—should be disconcerting for any institution charged with a higher purpose, the education of future leaders in industry, government, and the professions. Putting aside all complex conference rules on enforcement, embarrassing press remained the only truly effective tool to ensure compliance with the Intercollegiate Handbook.[79]

The mastermind behind the investigation of the Spartan Foundation remained resolute: the school must be held accountable for all outstanding dollars. There would be no leniency.[80] [81] Professor Aigler, the son of a banker and civic leader, simply could not believe that responsible businessmen and attorneys "acting in a trustee capacity" could be derelict in documenting the whereabouts of a few thousand dollars.[82]

Edgar Harden was frustrated. There was literally nothing more he could do to bring premature closure on this ordeal. Lacking the willingness to pursue legal recourse against Claud Erickson, Michigan State had no choice but to complete its one-year sentence—unless, of course, some mitigating circumstance might arise!

CHAPTER 10

Mr. Clean

———

"Dear Mr. Crisler: I can see no particular reason why any
trophy should be set up for the games to be played between
the University [of Michigan] and Michigan State. To do so
would relegate the University to an importance on level
with the Lansing school.... It would be my recommendation
that the proposed trophy be ignored by the University
and that no further attention be given either to its
location or its adoption or recognition as a trophy."

JUDGE HIRAM R. SMITH, UM '09 LITERATURE,
'11 LAW; 20 JANUARY 1955[1]

"Dear Judge Smith: I, personally, concur in your sentiments
about the football trophy to which you refer.... Because of
political overtones, it is rather a delicate matter but I do hope
we can [eventually] find a way to discontinue the whole idea."

ATHLETIC DIRECTOR HERBERT ORIN CRISLER; 1 FEBRUARY 1955[2]

TWO WEEKS FOLLOWING COMMISSIONER KEN Wilson's decision to deny leniency in his sentence imposed on Michigan State, the Spartans opened
their 1953 football campaign in Iowa City. The land-grant college

soundly defeated the State University of Iowa, 21-7. It marked the first official gridiron victory for the school as a member of the Big Ten. The 1948 Crisler Asterisk Motion—effectively a collective boycott imposed on an unwanted newbie—was finally past tense.[3] [4]

The successful outcome gained at Iowa Stadium was significant for another reason as well. Biggie Munn's reigning national champions had just extended their three-year winning streak to 25 games. Sportswriters were finally giving the Spartans' their due.[5]

The prolonged winning streak and the inherent national renown may have been gratifying for long-suffering Spartan alumni and fans, but for John Hannah, it was reason to worry. Charged with protecting the integrity of his institution, extended success, in his opinion, could only lead to trouble: "unpleasant and undesirable" over-emphasis on winning at all costs.[6] In confidence, Hannah was actually hoping that some conference team would put an end to the streak and the sooner the better. His only request, as shared with Purdue's President Fred Hovde, was that it not be the University of Michigan![7] The Wolverines didn't need any additional bragging rights in an intrastate series they had dominated since its inception.

IN OCTOBER of 1946, Michigan State College consummated the "Spaghetti and Meatballs Contract" with the University of Notre Dame.[8] The unprecedented long-term agreement would resurrect an old home-and-home-series between the two schools. John Hannah was looking for publicity—no other program could guarantee it like Notre Dame. Father John Cavanaugh was looking for competitors—most Big Nine schools shunned the small private university; its de facto national recruiting network of urban Catholic high school coaches, parish priests, and loyal laity was one major reason.[9] [10]

With that contract in hand, President Hannah was now assured two national powers on his college's football schedule each season. The other school was Michigan. Unlike the mutual agreement with Notre Dame, state politicians had a major say in the biennial contract with the

Wolverines. Dates and venues, however, were left to the athletic directors to work out.

Traditionally, the Michigan-Michigan State game was held in Ann Arbor. And following an understanding between Athletic Directors Fielding Yost and Ralph Young back in the early 1930s, it would always take place the opening weekend of the gridiron season—the Scrimmage Game.[11] [12]

The reason for contesting the intrastate series in Ann Arbor was straightforward: money. Seating capacity at College Field paled in comparison to Michigan Stadium. And for Ralph Young, that added revenue, especially during the Depression, was critical to balancing his athletic budget. Reserving the season opener for the Spartans was another matter. The complexities of Big Ten scheduling limited the non-conference dates Fielding Yost could offer his colleague from East Lansing. And since he wanted to keep mid-season Saturday afternoons available for more desirable East and West coast competitors, the only date left for the wannabe Spartans was the last weekend in September, the traditional season opener for the Intercollegiate Conference. Fielding Yost's scheduling excuse was tenable in Ralph Young's opinion. But the Michigan State athletic director also understood who maintained the upper hand in these biennial negotiations. Young, after all, desperately needed those dollars, and Yost knew it too.

Unaware of the secret Yost-Young agreement, one of John Hannah's first initiatives as president of Michigan State was to try to rectify the inherently unfair competitive advantage the Wolverines held over his Spartans.[13] [14] The win-loss record spoke for itself. Over the next eight years he would seek remedy on numerous occasions. Realizing that his athletic director was incapable of accomplishing what he sought—contests later in the season and on occasion in East Lansing—he eventually turned to his loyal and feisty lieutenant, Faculty Representative Lloyd Emmons, for redress. And by mid-January of 1949, Hannah had his prize, a limited package deal.

The Wolverines, somewhat begrudgingly, agreed to visit the recently expanded Macklin Stadium in 1953.[15] [16] [17] State politics undoubtedly played a role. The intrastate contest that year would celebrate Michigan State's inaugural season in Big Ten gridiron play. There was no way Crisler and his Board in Control could decline that Spartan invitation. After all, other than three visits to East Lansing during Michigan's Decade of Defiance (1908-1917), the Wolverines had made it a tradition to cross the Red Cedar River only for major Aggie/Spartan events—the 1924 College Field dedication and the 1948 Macklin Stadium expansion.

Having achieved the venue concession, at least for one game, Lloyd Emmons then brazenly requested that it be played later in the season.[18] His boss wanted a more appropriate date for the intrastate contest; Hannah also wanted to transition the long-running series into a bona fide rivalry now that the college was a conference member.[19] Once again, after some heated debate, Crisler conceded to the Spartans a mid-November weekend.[20] The Saturday contest would close out Michigan State's first official season of Big Ten play.[21]

At the time he agreed to Emmons' demands, Fritz Crisler, of course, had no idea that four years later, on a balmy Saturday afternoon in November, Biggie Munn's team would be a national powerhouse, let alone tied with Illinois and Wisconsin for first place in the conference race. The game with the Wolverines would gain headline coverage in just about every metropolitan market. Despite sloppy play, sportswriters were hailing the victors—they just happened to be dressed in green and white that afternoon.

GERHARD MENNEN Williams was elected governor of the State of Michigan in November of 1948. The heir to a personal grooming products fortune, "Soapy" attended a prep school out East before graduating from Princeton. A few years later, he earned a law degree from the University of Michigan. During his years in Ann Arbor, he deviated from family tradition and became affiliated with the Democratic

Party. A little over a decade later, Williams would run a successful campaign for governor. He would ultimately serve as chief executive for 12 years.

Williams never stopped campaigning for re-election during his long tenure in office.[22] He had no choice. Two-year term limits effectively mandated the practice. And so, on October 1, 1953, one week following Michigan State's successful season opener against the State University of Iowa, an unexpected telephone call from the governor's office in Lansing should have come as no surprise to the athletic director of the University of Michigan.[23]

Williams suggested that a trophy be awarded to the winner of the annual intrastate contest. The fact that the State of Michigan could now proudly claim two taxpayer-supported schools as members of the highly regarded Intercollegiate Conference supported his argument.[24] Mindful of the popularity of the series among the voting public, the man who occupied the corner office in the Capitol Building also proposed that he present the award, his "Governor's Trophy," to the winners following conclusion of that historically significant game.

Fritz Crisler was reticent. It remained a matter for his Board in Control of Intercollegiate Athletics to determine. Despite being chair of that policy-making body, he had no power to unilaterally make a decision with so many political implications. The board met on a monthly basis; the next meeting was scheduled in a few weeks. Crisler promised to get back with the governor following debate. Williams voiced approval of the plan; his only request was that their discussion remained in confidence—no leaks to the press.

Ralph Young, Michigan State's athletic director, received his call from Governor Williams a few minutes later. He anticipated no problems—any proposal that might elevate the intrastate series to rivalry status was desirable from his perspective. It was consistent with John Hannah's strategic plan dating back at least a decade. Young would run it past his Athletic Council and get back with Williams within a few days.

Less than 24 hours later, the governor had his answer—at least from East Lansing. A quorum of council members, urgently gathered by Ralph Young, fully supported the idea.[25] He also reminded the state's chief executive that President Hannah would be back on campus for his weekend furlough from Washington within a few days. Young was confident that his boss would stand behind the council's hasty decision.

The Spartan athletic director's enthusiastic reply was all Williams needed to hear. The governor decided to press ahead with plans. After all, the game was only six weeks away. A trophy had to be designed and constructed in short order.

Needless to say, Herbert Orin Crisler was a bit peeved when he received word from Williams' secretary later that afternoon. After mulling over Soapy's latest move, he decided to contact the governor the following morning. Clearly the crafty politician had no respect for university protocol. Crisler would now try a different tactic—a history lesson. Williams was lectured on the role trophies played in unique intercollegiate rivalries. He seemed to imply that one commemorating a lopsided series with the Spartans didn't merit that distinction. After all, since 1898, Michigan State could claim only six victories. Other than a few ties, the final score in all remaining games favored the Wolverines.

In Crisler's opinion, "it (was also) customary and a matter of precedent and tradition that for the most part a team has only one trophy" to contest with a bona fide rival. Multiple trophies "would tend to dilute one another."

Over the years, the University of Michigan had received several requests "to enter into trophy arrangements with other institutions." It opted out. The Little Brown Jug, an earthenware water container misplaced by a Wolverine manager following an unexpected Minnesota victory over Michigan in 1906, remained the school's only coveted prize.

Even Ohio State, which had assumed rivalry status with Michigan following its third straight win over the Maize and Blue in 1921, was turned down. Fielding Yost and his head coach, Fritz Crisler, in collaboration with the Board in Control, had decided that "the rivalry between the two institutions [in the late 1930s] was rather intense…and that a trophy that did not come about naturally or as the result of some little incident, [like the Little Brown Jug]…was never very successful."

And to add to his argument, Crisler pointed out that Northwestern, lacking a true rival at the time, petitioned the Wolverine Board in Control in June of 1948. The Wildcats proposed a trophy be awarded to the winner of their game with Michigan. The request was politely turned down for lack of student initiative.

Unfortunately for Fritz Crisler, Soapy Williams chose to not take notes on that history lecture. After all, he was running for re-election— even though the official campaign was still a year away. Any publicity stunt originating from his office, such as a shared trophy, was good political strategy for an incumbent with ambitions for higher office.[26] Williams was only 42 years of age. A landslide victory could very well catapult him into the national limelight and ultimately gain him residence in the White House.[27]

Shortly after his second telephone conversation with the governor, a newspaper reporter from Lansing called Crisler. So much for confidentiality! Comments from an unidentified source suggested that Fritz was opposed to the plan. Would he like to respond? The Wolverine athletic department leader cautiously sidestepped the question—the Board in Control had yet to make a decision.

The following day, another member of the press contacted the director. Apparently the Michigan State Athletic Council had met the afternoon before; a reliable source indicated that the Spartans unanimously approved Ralph Young's motion.[28] Did Crisler have any comment?

The media barrage was relentless by now—even the Detroit papers were getting into the act. A day later, Governor Williams' secretary called and asked if Crisler would like to meet with the project manager charged with carrying out Soapy's plan. Perhaps the athletic director could offer some suggestions on the design of the trophy or its inscription? She pointed out that the governor wanted the mythical Paul

Bunyan astride the State of Michigan. The statue would be 5-feet high and carved out from a tree cut from up north. The massive, disproportionate base would have ample room for a prominent plaque commemorating Williams' pivotal role in the project. The names of succeeding governors and annual game scores could easily be etched in as well.

By now, the Wolverine athletic director was really frustrated. But he kept his composure. He encouraged the secretary to remind Soapy that this was not yet a done deal. Unlike the Athletic Council in East Lansing, he could not gather a quorum to discuss the proposal until the 16th of October. Period. Scheduling conflicts precluded any time sooner; many board members had full-time job commitments in cities far removed from Ann Arbor.

Despite maintaining his unwavering stance, Crisler did meet with the governor's project coordinator later that day. Rough sketches of the trophy and a proposed inscription were shared. Crisler pointed out to the staffer that Michigan, with all due respects to the head of state, could not approve of any plans until the Board in Control fully reviewed the proposal. Regardless of university protocol, Soapy's political aide reminded the athletic director that the sculptor needed adequate time to complete the large carving—and that deadline was now!

The following day, a telegram dated October 14, 1953 was placed on Fritz Crisler's desk. The governor was moving forward with plans and would value any final comments on the design or inscription.[29] The Wolverine athletic director immediately wired a Western Union note back to Williams: "am running into some trophy complications here; have called special board meeting this weekend to resolve the question; suggest processing of trophy be held in abeyance until first of week; best regards—Fritz Crisler." The governor relented.[30]

AT THE same time Michigan Athletic Director Herbert Crisler was pleading with G. Mennen Williams to delay action on the Governor's Trophy proposal, Professor Ralph Aigler was monitoring progress in Commissioner Ken Wilson's investigation of the Spartan Foundation.

Confidential updates from the Big Ten offices indicated that it remained a standstill. Despite Edgar Harden's valiant efforts at swaying ringleader Claud Erickson to come clean and reveal the whereabouts of $5,200, no breakthrough was anticipated. And therein lay the problem for the law professor. With only four months remaining on the one-year sentence imposed on Michigan State, time was running out. A golden opportunity to make a national statement about his conference's unwavering stance on financial aid for student athletes—and nab an old nemesis in the process—was passing him by. Aigler's retirement was less than a year away.

The terms of probation were very clear. Michigan State was given one year to clean up its house. Ed Harden's corrective action plan, in place since early September, accomplished as much. The college was also obligated to "secure, or exhaust every possible remedy" in explaining the whereabouts of all financial disbursements from the booster club.[31] Harden did a commendable job on this account too; even Ralph Aigler would agree. But had he truly exhausted all remedies? What about legal recourse, a court order?

Regardless of Aigler's frustration with the impasse, it was becoming apparent that his commissioner would have no option but to announce that Michigan State had faithfully fulfilled the terms of probation as of February 1954. His press release would report that no significant violation was found; no direct collaboration between college and Century Club was discovered; almost all dollars dispensed by the Spartan Foundation were accountable. Ken Wilson would conclude by declaring that Michigan State College was once again a member in good standing.

That anticipated announcement by the commissioner—in essence, that the Spartans got off scot-free—no doubt troubled Fritz Crisler as well. He was certain there was an employee at Michigan State College, perhaps an assistant coach, with very dirty hands. Confident in that conviction, the athletic director currently wanted nothing to do with a politically motivated trophy acknowledging the winner of an annual intrastate contest—a mandated series but by no means a true rivalry.[32] And he wasn't the only Wolverine with that feeling.

Michigan alumni were up in arms over G. Mennen Williams' proposal.[33] [34] Students about Ann Arbor were equally irate. The collective opinion was that the Wolverine athletic leadership had been placed in an awkward position. With media darling Michigan State clearly in favor of the trophy,[35] any reported Michigan opposition would substantiate long-held opinions among certain politicians and news reporters that the institution was a self-righteous, egocentric bully, especially in its relationship with the land-grant college.[36]

THE BOARD in Control of Intercollegiate Athletics finally met on Friday, October 16th—a little over two weeks after first being informed of the governor's plan. Just about the entire meeting, held at the Michigan Union, involved the controversy.[37]

Fritz Crisler summarized the course of events to date. Following his comments, Board Member John Hibbard shared some gossip. Frederick Mueller, who sat on the State Board of Agriculture, was a close friend of the Grand Rapids insurance agent.[38] The two met for lunch three days earlier. Mueller, an ardent Republican and future Commerce Secretary in the Eisenhower administration, was livid over the entire matter. He wanted nothing to do with aiding the perpetual re-election campaign of the state's liberal governor. He informed Hibbard that he had spoken with a member of the Spartan Athletic Council regarding the behind-scenes decision to support Soapy Williams' politically motivated ploy. That individual assured the influential State Board member that the council, contrary to press reports, had not acted on the matter.

Fritz Mueller then contacted Faculty Representative Edgar Harden. The man charged with cleaning up the current probation mess in East Lansing offered a different version. The Athletic Council had approved of the trophy "providing it (was) a Governor's trophy and not a Williams' trophy."[39]

Hibbard also mentioned that a representative of the Michigan Student Legislature had recently visited with him. Plans were in store for a demonstration opposing Soapy's slippery scheme. There was no desire on the part of the students to "enter into a trophy arrangement with Michigan State College until (it was) off probation."[40]

It was now Professor Aigler's turn to offer comment. He had just communicated with Ed Harden about the Paul Bunyan matter. Harden seemed to have changed his story since the earlier conversation he had with Fritz Mueller. He now claimed that the Athletic Council had taken no action on the governor's proposal.

The Spartan athletic leader then questioned the law professor about "his reaction to the trophy." Aigler informed him that he personally objected to it. The "rivalry between the two institutions [had become] so intense now that it almost approached bitterness." He felt that anything that might "increase that [tension] should be avoided at all costs."[41]

Mindful of Aigler's position on the politically sensitive issue, Harden apparently felt at ease sharing his. Contrary to President John Hannah, the rookie faculty representative opposed the governor's plan. He disliked the fact that a "political element" had entered into the creation of a trophy being offered for an athletic event between two state-supported schools.

In closing, Harden agreed to "sit on the lid over at East Lansing." He would contact Tom King, one of Hannah's key deputies running the school while the president was on sabbatical, and "tell him that this [trophy matter] must be held in complete abeyance and that he would bend every effort to persuade [the Athletic Council] to go along [with this latest plan]." He agreed with Aigler that ultimately any trophy proposal should be a matter worked out between the two institutions—devoid of political gamesmanship.[42]

Aigler then shared with fellow board members a recent conversation he had had with one of his third-year law students. David Bellin substantiated John Hibbard's comments: the student body was very much opposed to any trophy. Acknowledging the embarrassing political predicament Governor Williams had placed the university leadership in, Bellin suggested that the question be placed before the students; poll them for their opinion. In so doing, Aigler, Crisler, the Board in Control, the administration, and the Regents would all be off the hook—the student action would assure the institution of no political backlash from a resourceful head of state back in Lansing.

Arthur Brandon, the director of university relations, was invited to the special athletic board meeting. His counsel was eagerly sought. Brandon concurred with the law student's assessment: the proposal had to be "divorced from Governor Williams." The university lobbyist recommended that the faculty representatives and athletic directors from the two institutions meet to draft a joint statement that the Board in Control and the Athletic Council could embrace. And if Michigan State opposed this plan, he suggested an alternative strategy: have the two schools "share it" regardless of the outcome of the annual football contest. The trophy would become meaningless over time and ultimately forgotten. It was an intriguing suggestion. The meeting closed on that note.[43]

TWO WEEKS later, with only nine days remaining before kick-off in Macklin Stadium, representatives of both Michigan State's Athletic Council and Michigan's Board in Control secretly met in Detroit to discuss the trophy controversy, far removed from inquiring press.[44]

Fritz Crisler took control of the meeting. The former coach and his faculty representative flawlessly carried out Arthur Brandon's game plan.

Perhaps in the interest of currying Ralph Aigler's favor, Michigan State's Edgar Harden and Athletic Council Chairman Tom King supported the Wolverine proposal that "the establishment of any trophy should be held in abeyance to permit...further discussion and consultation."[45] Both Spartans were well aware that in February, now just three months away, the fate of Michigan State could very well lay in the hands of the influential dean of faculty representatives. If the powerful

Aigler was satisfied that Michigan State had faithfully fulfilled all terms of probation, any rumored residual disciplinary action—scheduling boycotts—against the college by certain skeptical conference athletic directors might be headed off.[46]

The four men carefully crafted the press release. The intent was to save face for the beleaguered Wolverines who had been hammered by reporters for appearing to oppose the governor's very popular proposal. The joint statement would acknowledge the Spartans' original support for the idea had waned. It would also note that Michigan's Board in Control of Intercollegiate Athletics had delayed taking action on Williams' idea in part "because of doubts as to the appropriateness of the proposed design...."[47] In effect, the governor's plans were being held in check because the Wolverines' didn't like the way Paul Bunyan looked! The real reason for opposing the trophy, of course, was never mentioned: to block any action that might facilitate transition of the intrastate series to rivalry status.[48] [49] The press release would mention that Michigan State's athletic leaders also thought the trophy was ugly; in point of fact, they could have cared less about the lumberjack's appearance—they just wanted to remain in Ralph Aigler's good graces.

The Wolverine faculty representative then suggested that the student bodies from both schools should have final say in the creation of any trophy honoring the winner of the annual intrastate contest. Lacking interest among that core constituency, there was no reason for administrators to promote it now.[50] Harden and King supported Aigler's amendment to the press release. (The Spartan representatives failed to mention that Michigan State students were overwhelmingly in favor of the trophy.[51] [52] [53] But that reminder would serve no purpose at the moment, let alone in February.)

Fritz Crisler was greatly relieved after proofreading the draft—mission accomplished.

G. MENNEN Williams first learned of the press release the following day.[54] After consulting with his political advisers, he decided to defiantly move forward with his plan. After all, most polls demonstrated surprisingly strong public support for a trophy commemorating the "traditional rivalry between the [schools]."[55]

A letter to the presidents of both institutions was mailed out that afternoon.[56] And befitting a man with a law degree from the University of Michigan, the governor's note was masterfully worded. There was no mention of the recent joint press release from Ann Arbor and East Lansing.

> Some time ago I announced my intention of establishing a rotating "Governor's Trophy" emblematic of the football rivalry between the University of Michigan and Michigan State College. At that time I also indicated that suggestions from both…schools would be solicited, and I very much appreciate the attention that representatives of the two schools concerned have given to the matter.
>
> Because of the time element, we found it necessary to commence preparation of the trophy nearly a week ago and as a consequence we are, unfortunately, unable to take full advantage of any further suggestions offered.
>
> It is requested that suitable arrangements be made for the presentation of the trophy during half-time ceremonies and later to the winner of this year's game.
>
> Sincerely,
> GMW
> Governor[57]

Perhaps in deference to his old professor, Williams also copied Ralph Aigler.

As expected, John Hannah took no issue with the letter; President Harlan Henthorne Hatcher did.

Unfortunately for the Michigan leader, there was little time to respond. No doubt, the director of university relations, Arthur Brandon, was urgently called to Hatcher's office. Together, they had to find a way to clean up what was proving to be a very sticky mess. The following morning, just eight days before kick-off, a letter addressed to the Honorable G. Mennen Williams, Governor of the State of Michigan, was mailed from Ann Arbor. Prior to sealing that envelope, Brandon made darn sure there was no institutional self-conceit interposed between lines. The university, after all, depended on legislative appropriations from Lansing—and the governor, as the lobbyist knew only too well, had the final say on those bills.

Dear Governor Williams:

Thank you for your letter of November 5, informing me of your plan to present the trophy "emblematic of the football rivalry between the University of Michigan and Michigan State College." Prior to receiving your letter I was asked by the press to comment on the announced trophy. A copy of that statement is enclosed.[58]

Hatcher essentially reiterated what he had shared with reporters just prior to receiving his mail from Lansing.[59] It was consistent with the athletic department's party line.

My personal opinion is that a football trophy should be primarily a team or student matter. Any ceremonies connected with the presentation of a trophy should have the teams or their representatives as participants.[60]

Judging from the phrasing, Ralph Aigler was also invited to the president's office. The conservative Republican wanted nothing to do with turning a nationally televised football game into a campaign stop for a liberal Democrat with aspirations for higher office.

Essentially acknowledging defeat at the hands of the governor, Hatcher then changed course and focused on the proposed halftime presentation involving Soapy Williams at mid-field.

> I understand that the football captains are usually quite busy between the halves, and for this reason it would seem desirable to have the trophy unveiling prior to the game.[61]

That suggestion was clearly an Aigler ploy to minimize the role of party politics in the event. It proved to be Hatcher's only recommendation regarding the trophy ceremony. Since John Hannah was the host, it remained his decision on how to carry out the presentation. Despite their differences over the years, the professor was comforted in knowing that Hannah, an acknowledged Republican, shared similar political feelings regarding the current liberal head of state.

ON NOVEMBER 14, 1953, Michigan State College defeated the University of Michigan in East Lansing. The final score was 14-6. Following the game, the Spartans were awarded the Paul Bunyan Trophy—an inaugural ceremony that effectively redefined the series as a bona fide rivalry, much to the frustration of loyal Michigan Wolverines. Governor G. Mennen Williams stood nearby Coach Biggie Munn while newspaper cameras captured the moment inside the locker room.[62]

As it turned out, the University of Michigan (and Ralph Aigler) experienced an additional loss that day. During pregame ceremonies at mid-field in Macklin Stadium, the public address system inadvertently broke down. The governor, while making the presentation of his trophy to both team captains, was silenced to all but those within earshot.[63] Denigrating catcalls—most coming from 10,000 angry fans decked out in maize and blue in the north end zone—assumed precedence. The press, sympathetic to the governor's desire to transition the series to rivalry status, wrote favorably of the pregame event the following morning.[64] The campaign stop on the 50-yard line was a success after all.

The trophy was proudly placed in a large glass case over at Jenison Fieldhouse a few days later. The following year, the University of Michigan defeated Michigan State in Ann Arbor. The final score was 33-7. Coach Bennie Oosterbaan was presented the Governor's Trophy at mid-field shortly after time ran out. After the ceremony, Fritz Crisler helped carry Paul Bunyan back to the Wolverine locker room. And on behalf of loyal Michigan alumni about the country, he irreverently placed it in a broom closet. The trophy remained there, collecting dust, until the following year.[65] [66] [67]

Six decades later, Michigan football players fervently compete for the right to house Paul Bunyan inside Schembechler Hall for the next 12 months, alongside numerous Big Ten and national championship trophies. If successful in a contest that has rotated between Ann Arbor and East Lansing every year since 1958, the valiant Victors now proudly hoist the unsightly trophy and parade it about the stadium. Oblivious to its early history, exuberant students and alumni press forward to take smart phone snapshots of the carved caricature with their gridiron heroes.

IN MID-OCTOBER of 1953, Professor Ralph Aigler had expressed concerns to Board in Control members over the authenticity of an award borne out of political expediency. A trophy commemorating a series, let alone a rivalry, between the two schools must originate among the students. Lacking that fundamental requirement, he was confident that the Paul Bunyan Award would become a passing fancy.[68] Based on a third-year law student's suggestion, Aigler proposed a student body poll to decide the fate of the governor's proposal. The vote never took place.

CHAPTER 11

Decisions

———

"Remember always that no player, no team, no
coach, no sport is ever more important than the
good name of Michigan State College."

PRESIDENT ROBERT SIDEY SHAW[1]

DEAN EDGAR HARDEN WAS WELL aware of the rumors. A core group
of athletic directors planned to discipline Michigan State. The college
administration's "catch us if you can" defiance towards conference officials was unacceptable for any member of the conference undergoing
an investigation, let alone a brash newbie.[2][3][4] Regardless of the commissioner's final report to the Faculty Representatives Committee due
out in February of 1954, perhaps four directors were contemplating
boycott extensions beyond 1955-56.[5][6][7][8][9] And what made their plan so
intriguing—Michigan State would be ineligible for title competition
during those two years. Lacking a quorum of six conference competitors, the college, based on handbook rules, could make no claim to a
Big Ten crown for the 1957-58 seasons—a continual reminder of its
misconduct towards the commissioner and his staff.[10] Vigilante justice.

SHORTLY AFTER his June appointment as faculty representative to
the Intercollegiate Conference, Ed Harden struck up an inconspicuous

working relationship with Ralph Aigler; even President Hannah was un-aware of Harden fraternizing with the enemy.[11] The Michigan law pro-fessor, with a plethora of experience in Big Ten politics, was more than willing to offer counsel to his rookie colleague, especially regarding a corrective action plan certain to pass muster with the commissioner.[12] Harden eagerly accepted the generous offer. At the very least, the good will engendered from interaction with the influential veteran could serve him well in accomplishing a more daunting task—early termina-tion of the college's probation.

Aigler's proposal was no doubt sincere. But the Michigan faculty rep-resentative was also obsessed with that unaccountable $5,200.[13] Some college employee must have disbursed laundered money to a handful of Jenison athletes no longer eligible for financial aid. Interacting with Harden might provide him some valuable insider information. As an undercover agent, he could cautiously share findings with the belea-guered commissioner—a man desperately needing a jump-start in his stalled investigation of the Spartan Foundation.

Unfortunately for Ralph Aigler, a mythical lumberjack took prece-dence in private conversations with Ed Harden. During the six weeks leading up to the mid-November football contest in East Lansing, there was little time to discuss anything else. Aigler needed a collaborative strategy to hold Soapy Williams in check on this trophy matter. The two professors would eventually join up with Fritz Crisler and Spartan administrator Tom King in Detroit, all undercover, to arrive at a joint statement on the governor's politically motivated ploy.[14]

The Michigan tactic, orchestrated by Fritz Crisler to put a noose around Paul Bunyan's neck, ultimately failed. But Dean Harden earned kudos for his role in steering King, John Hannah's dependable right hand man, in the Wolverines' direction on this controversial issue. His promise to Aigler, in advance of that Detroit meeting, helped the uni-versity save face and avoid some embarrassing press.[15] Perhaps his short-term collaboration with the two influential Michigan leaders might pay dividends in ten weeks when those four angry athletic directors would gather with their colleagues to contract schedules for the 1957-58 football seasons? [16]

THROUGHOUT OCTOBER and into early November, while Paul Bunyan dominated conversation back in Ann Arbor and East Lansing, the commissioner's office in Chicago remained focused on any new leads in its Spartan Foundation investigation. Unfortunately, there were none. Even secret agent Ralph Aigler could offer little additional information. It appeared that Ed Harden was correct—lacking any cooperation from an obstinate Claud Erickson, there would be no further breakthrough.

Ken Wilson was frustrated. As commissioner, this probe into suspect Spartan activities was to have been a golden opportunity for him to finally demonstrate his mettle as chief enforcement officer of the Big Ten, especially to his skeptics among the conference leadership. But now, due to this impasse imposed by Erickson, all he could possibly do was save face—make sure his February presentation before the faculty leaders, just a few months away, went without a glitch. It was critical that he appeared in control of the entire investigation, something he had lacked on three previous occasions: Purdue in '48; Ohio State in '49; and Iowa in '52.

Fortunately for Wilson, the plan was already in place for a final visit to East Lansing scheduled for early February of 1954—this was included in the original indictment that announced a year of probation. He would meet with Dean Harden sometime in late January for an update on the Spartan faculty representative's internal investigation since their last meeting in mid-September. Wilson would emphasize his great disappointment in the college leadership's inability to explain the whereabouts of that remaining $5,200. His formal report on whether Michigan State had satisfactorily fulfilled all terms of probation would then be shared with the Faculty Representatives Committee one week later. That group could then decide the college's fate—absolution or further penalties. (Scheduling boycotts were another matter—that was a decision left for the men drafting schedules. Anticipating the commissioner's

February report, the athletic directors had tabled earlier plans to sign contracts for the next few seasons until they could collectively review Wilson's conclusions.)

Regardless of the outcome of that Faculty Committee debate, Ken Wilson would finally appear in control of a major investigation. His report, drafted with the assistance of associate Bill Reed, would be shared with the Council of Ten presidents—Lew Morrill included. The commissioner had reasons to feel smug.

THE BUILD-UP for the 1953 intrastate contest exceeded expectations. Biggie Munn's success over the past three years at Michigan State, in combination with the storied tradition of Michigan Football, contributed to the hype for a lopsided regional series that dated back to 1898. NBC Television announced plans to carry the game over its national network of stations; at least 43 million viewers were anticipated. Sports information director Fred Stabley honored requests for press box or field passes from 400 sportswriters about the country. Thirty-seven radio stations planned live broadcasts from Macklin Stadium.[17] It was an athletic event unlike any other sponsored by the pioneer land-grant college.

The Big Ten horse race was into its final stretch. Illinois, Wisconsin, and Michigan State were in a dead heat by the second weekend in November. Coach Munn's powerhouse had one loss to Purdue marring its record.[18] Other than a tie to Nebraska earlier in the season, the talented Illini were without a blemish. They had soundly defeated the University of Michigan the previous Saturday in Champagne. The reigning conference champion Badgers had just one loss to Ohio State. And to add further excitement in this sprint to the finish line, Wisconsin and Illinois would be competing against each other in Madison. The outcome of that game, in combination with the one in East Lansing, could very well decide which school should book airline tickets to Pasadena in four weeks.

The official conference gridiron campaign would end the following week—traditionally the last Saturday before Thanksgiving. Due to a scheduling boycott imposed on it four years earlier by Illinois, Northwestern, and Wisconsin (shortly after its official admission into the Big Ten), Michigan State was unable to negotiate a season closer with a conference member. That snub forced Ralph Young to sign a contract with Marquette University instead.[19] The game with the Hilltoppers would hold little significance in determining the winner of the Big Ten crown.

For mid-November, the weather was surprisingly balmy in East Lansing. The skies were clear and the temperature was 67 degrees.[20] During the one-minute Governor's Trophy ceremony just prior to kick-off, NBC opted to break for commercials.[21] The producers wanted nothing to do with the slick political gambit staged by Soapy Williams, much to Professor Ralph Aigler's relief.

As ballyhooed gridiron contests often go, this one also proved to be no classic. Both teams played poorly. Despite dry conditions, there were eight fumbles; a 20-mile per hour breeze from the southwest hampered passing and contributed to three interceptions.

Following a scoreless first quarter, the college took the lead during the second 15-minutes of play with a sustained drive ending in a touchdown. The half ended with the Spartans leading 7-0. Michigan State's offense crossed the goal line once again during third quarter. The final 15 minutes of action, however, were ugly—at least for fans decked out in green. A Spartan punt return, marred by yet another fumble, gave the Wolverines a first and goal at the Michigan State four-yard line. Three plays later Michigan had six points on the scoreboard. The point-after was wide to the left.

During the next series, Michigan State fumbled two handoffs but recovered both of them. A Wolverine interception, aided by that stiff breeze gusting from the south end of Macklin Stadium, ended the drive. With great field position, Michigan needed just 25 yards to score. Two plays later, the Maize and Blue were once again faced with first and goal at the Spartan four-yard line. Munn's defense quite suddenly rose to the occasion. Four downs later, the Wolverines returned to their sideline

with no additional points for Coach Bennie Oosterbaan. The game ended shortly thereafter. The final score: 14-6.[22]

The celebration inside the locker room included players, coaches, some college administrators, and the governor of the State of
Michigan.[23] [24]

Shortly following Soapy Williams' presentation of his uncomely trophy, excitement inside the Spartan locker room turned to hysteria with
word that Wisconsin had trounced the Illini in Madison, 34-7. Michigan
State remained in a three-way tie for the conference lead. But with the
Badgers unable to represent the Big Ten in the Rose Bowl due to handbook regulations forbidding back-to-back visits to Pasadena, Ralph
Young was suddenly faced with the possibility of booking chartered
flights to southern California for New Years Day.

The following week, Michigan State eked out a win against the pesky
Hilltoppers. Wisconsin, after beating Illinois seven days earlier, struggled in its contest with the Golden Gophers. The game ended in a tie.
Regardless of the Big Ten rules on post-season play, the Badgers were
out of the race for a conference crown in 1953

At about the same time the Wisconsin-Minnesota game in
Minneapolis was being contested, Illinois was competing against
Northwestern in Champaign. As expected, the Illini soundly defeated the Wildcats. The win guaranteed them a share of the Big Ten title. It also assured them a principal role in a prolonged drama, one
that would take place on center stage at the LaSalle Hotel later that
evening.[25]

PARTICIPATION IN post-season bowl contests was forbidden for
Intercollegiate Conference members since the early 1900s. The ruling academic leadership felt the games were not in the best interest of
the participants. The Big Ten ended its football season on the weekend prior to Thanksgiving for a reason. Student athletes, just like all
other undergraduates on campus, needed time to focus on studies prior
to December final exams. Preparation for a New Years Day bowl game

might prove a distraction for young men seeking a greater purpose—a college degree.[26] [27]

That honorable Western Conference tradition would come to an end in the late fall of 1946. The Faculty Representatives Committee, after much soul-searching, signed a five-year contract with the Pacific Coast Conference to compete in the Rose Bowl.[28] Somewhat surprisingly, Professor Ralph Aigler's athletic director played a major role in that decision.

In late December of 1939, Herbert Crisler was invited to attend a Rose Bowl contest with a few of his coaching colleagues from out West. It was a first for an amateur purist opposed to any post-season play. He begrudgingly accepted the offer.

The game pitted the host school Southern California against the University of Tennessee. And what angered Crisler, while sitting in the stands prior to kick-off, was why the Pacific Coast Conference leadership ever invited a representative from the Southeastern Conference to visit Pasadena? After all, the Volunteers were a part of the "southern menace"—Deep South schools openly recruiting and subsidizing athletes. The invitation was sending the wrong message, especially for an event garnering so much national interest. Midway through the game, however, the Wolverine assistant athletic director had his epiphany.[29]

The Tournament of Roses Committee had recently turned over administrative responsibilities for the New Years game to the Pacific Coast Conference. The organizers wanted to focus on the gala leading up to the grand event—a civic enterprise more suited for it to manage. As a consequence, the faculty representatives of the Pacific Coast were thrust in the unenviable position of finding a suitable opponent for the annual contest. Mindful of that task, it suddenly "dawned" upon Crisler that he might have been unfair in "silently censuring" the host leadership.

> The Faculty Committee of the Pacific Coast Conference has two choices; one to accept the management of the game, the other to relinquish it to others who would be delighted to receive it

but whose athletic ideals and practices are not to be especially envied. Undoubtedly the more wholesome effect on football will result if the first choice is exercised, but since we refuse to become identified with the game, we compel the people out there to take the Tennessees, the Alabamas, Tulanes and Dukes. We force them to give institutions $120,000 to take back and lavishly spend, to recruit and subsidize another team to go out and get the melon. Then we scream to the high heavens when those institutions come up in our territory and take away boys who otherwise would remain in our Conference. Rather than blame the Pacific Coast people we should censure ourselves for not cooperating with them.[30]

Crisler's solution to the quandary faced by the Pacific Coast faculty leadership was simple: contractually guarantee a long-term relationship with the Western Conference in the annual Rose Bowl game.[31]

A few years later, with the help of the influential Ralph Aigler,[32] the Big Nine announced its plans to the press—it would break with hallowed tradition. But there were certain conditions tied to that controversial decision: to de-emphasize winning at all costs, a member school could only visit southern California every three years;[33] to downplay any focus on dollars, profits from the post-season contest would be equally shared among all conference schools; and to point out its commitment to student athletes, the impact of post-season play on academic performance would be reviewed periodically during the five-year experiment.[34]

The University of Illinois was chosen by the Faculty Representatives Committee to be its first Big Nine emissary. The mythical 1947 National Champion Michigan Wolverines followed the Illini path to Pasadena in January of '48. In his annual report to the University Regents a few weeks later, somewhat prematurely, Crisler declared the post-season experiment a resounding success. He had data demonstrating that Coach Bennie Oosterbaan's athletes actually fared better in the classroom compared with one year earlier, despite all the December distractions.[85] [36]

A few years later, mindful of Fritz Crisler's research, the faculty leadership voted to renew the contract.[37] [38] They also effectively granted the Athletic Directors Committee the task of choosing a representative team, a responsibility more appropriate for it to decide.[39] The faculty would merely rubber-stamp the directors' recommendation. That decision, to delegate selection responsibilities to administrators not charged with overseeing the integrity of the Intercollegiate Conference of Faculty Representatives, would ultimately come back to haunt the academic leadership a few years later.

RALPH AIGLER had no say in how Fritz Crisler might vote. But based on his opinion, shared in confidence with a close friend, Illinois deserved to go to Pasadena should it end up in a tie with Michigan State. Unlike the Spartans, who just barely defeated Michigan in an error-prone game held in East Lansing, the Illini dominated his Wolverines down in Champaign.[40]

Aigler posed a valid, yet somewhat skewed, point. In fact, the final score of the Michigan State game might have been quite different had it been contested in Ann Arbor—as had been tradition. Michigan won all six home games that season; its three losses occurred on road trips to Minneapolis, Champaign, and East Lansing.

Fritz Crisler didn't need Professor Ralph Aigler's unqualified spectator advice to decide which school was the better gridiron representative for the conference. As a former coach, he could easily evaluate the performances of both Michigan opponents. And in his opinion, Illinois was the better team. The decision on which school to represent the Intercollegiate Conference in the 1954 Rose Bowl, however, was much more complicated than comparing team proficiency on the football field against his Wolverines on back-to-back weekends.

Since first receiving a copy of the Breslin Letter from one of his Michigan Moles two years earlier, Crisler had been covertly involved in the Spartan Foundation investigation. He was well aware of the terms of the one-year probation. Michigan State could compete for a conference title in football—but there was no mention of post-season play in Pasadena. The possibility never crossed the minds of those involved in drafting the statement: Ken Wilson, Bill Reed, and Ralph Aigler. But by inference, the Spartans, still under house arrest, should not be granted bail.

Shortly after Michigan State defeated the University of Michigan, articles appeared in newspapers suggesting this possible predicament for the Western Conference. Sportswriters speculated about how eight athletic directors, including Fritz Crisler, might cast their votes should Illinois and Michigan State end up in a dead heat.[41] And as expected, everyone had an opinion—including one prominent state politician.[42]

A few days after those articles appeared in the papers, State Representative Haskell Nichols felt obligated to pen a note to the Wolverine athletic director. The powerful first-district representative from Jackson reminded Crisler just how important this potential vote was for the state. Michiganders took great pride in both of their Big Ten schools. Having either institution participate in the "Rose Bowl [was noteworthy and] would bring great credit to the State of Michigan."[43] And if that wasn't enough reason to support the Spartans, Ralph Aigler's former law student, in no uncertain terms, reminded Crisler that $30 million was appropriated by the state legislature for both schools during the current fiscal year![44][45] It was now payback time.

And so, mindful of the political ramifications, not only for him, but also for his employer, should there be a tie-breaker tally, Fritz Crisler would cast his vote in favor of the sister-state institution located only two miles from the Capitol. Michigan State, he would proclaim to anyone with press credentials, was clearly the better team.[46]

COMMISSIONER KEN Wilson contacted all ten conference athletic directors by telephone Saturday evening, shortly after Illinois defeated Northwestern. It was their duty now to decide which school—Michigan State or Illinois—would represent the Big Ten in the Rose Bowl on New Years Day. The newspaper reporters, he reminded them, were eager for an answer. They had deadlines to meet—Sunday morning editions would begin rolling off the press within a few hours. He planned to use a round robin polling method to arrive at a decision.

Based on recent newspaper accounts, Michigan State's probation would play no role in how Western Conference athletic directors might cast votes should there be need for a tiebreaker. All men queried insisted that gridiron performances trumped probation politics.[47] [48] They were lying. As it turned out, on Saturday evening, November 21, 1953, a defiant faction of directors opposed sending a parolee to southern California. Four deadlock tallies later, an exhausted commissioner decided to call it quits for the night. It was close to midnight.[49]

Wilson proposed a meeting of all members the following afternoon in Chicago. Perhaps a face-to-face discussion might lead to compromise— and a conference representative for the extravaganza in Pasadena.[50]

Amazingly, despite challenging travel logistics and inclement weather, nine athletic directors showed up for the LaSalle Hotel lock-in 12 hours later. The lone absentee was stranded at Willow Run Airport near Ann Arbor;[51] there was no way Fritz Crisler could attend the meeting.[52] [53]

Ken Wilson was suddenly in a real bind. He needed Crisler to help sway some votes and break the deadlock. Lacking his commanding presence in Chicago, the commissioner proposed that the Wolverine leader remain available back in Ann Arbor for conference calls.

Based on the commissioner's late Saturday evening survey, Minnesota, Purdue, and Indiana were not going to budge. Lew Morrill, Fred Hovde, and Herman Wells were all good friends of John Hannah— and their faculty representatives knew it! [54] And assuming his promise to the people of the state of Michigan was sincere, Crisler would maintain his support for the Spartans regardless of private reservations.[55] Four solid votes for Michigan State.

An old scheduling boycott against the college may have impacted decisions by the athletic directors from Northwestern and Wisconsin. Back in December of 1949, when contracts for the current 1953 season were being drafted, the two programs chose to impose vigilante justice on Michigan

State for past antics prior to gaining membership in the exclusive club. As a consequence of their decision to discipline the college's athletic program, neither the Wildcats nor Badgers had waged battle against a Munn-coached team during the past few seasons. The directors, respecting their football coach's opinions, would line up behind the Illini.

The other school opposing a Spartan trip to Pasadena was the State University of Iowa. As it turned out, Athletic Director Paul Brechler was no friend of Michigan State College. In large part due to his staunch convictions about the program in East Lansing, Iowa cast the one defiant vote opposing the Spartans' application for conference membership back in December of 1948.[56] Six months later, during scheduling contract meetings for the 1950-53 football campaigns, he declined to negotiate with the reprobates. His three-year scheduling boycott concluded on the 26th of September when his Hawkeyes hosted Michigan State in Iowa City. The Spartans crushed the State University during their first official weekend of conference competition. But that outcome had nothing to do with revenge—Coach Biggie Munn just happened to field a far better football team.

Brechler ignored competitor performance, however, in casting his vote the previous evening. Despite the Hawkeyes having no gridiron relationship with Illinois that season, the athletic director sided with the Illini. The current Spartan probation was undoubtedly a major factor; it substantiated his past convictions about the program and its lax leadership.

That left Ohio State. Richard Larkins undoubtedly polled his head coach, a passionate military historian, about his preference. Wayne Woodrow "Woody" Hayes, in his third year directing combat troops in Ohio Stadium, was soundly defeated by Illinois and Michigan State—both battles took place in Columbus. But the Illini were far more decisive, at least based on the final score. With Buckeye support for Coach Ray Eliot's infantry, Ken Wilson could count four commitments for Illinois.

AS ANTICIPATED by Commissioner Wilson, the meeting at the LaSalle Hotel proved to be quite contentious. However, after five hours and one very expensive long-distance phone call to Ann Arbor, the deadlock was finally broken. Michigan State, by a 5-3 tally, would represent the Big Ten in the Rose Bowl.[57]

With a 'gag rule' imposed by the commissioner on all members in attendance, the press could only speculate on how school representatives had voted.[58] Unaware of Paul Brechler's deep-seated convictions about Michigan State, some sportswriters assumed Iowa had lined up with the college. They argued that the Spartans' definitive victory over the Hawkeyes early in the season sealed that vote.[59] But of greater intrigue for press pundits, especially those back in Michigan, was how Wolverine Athletic Director Fritz Crisler sided in the final tally.[60]

Shortly after the decision was announced, Michigan State spokesmen Ralph Young and Edgar Harden expressed fawning appreciation to Crisler for his support throughout the drawn-out ordeal.[61] [62] But back in East Lansing, John Hannah and Biggie Munn maintained different sentiments. Apparently the Spartans had a few spies in that room. Their reports indicated that the Wolverine director favored the Illini throughout most of the afternoon.[63] [64]

Despite Hannah's private feelings about Michigan's purported duplicity, he had to act presidential to the media. A prepared statement from East Lansing followed Wilson's announcement. On behalf of all Spartans, he expressed great appreciation at being selected to represent the Big Ten in the Rose Bowl. It was justly deserved.

But then, somewhat surprisingly, the president borrowed a phrase from a press release five years earlier. At that time, Michigan State had just been officially welcomed into the Intercollegiate Conference after the Committee of Three verified reasonable (but not complete) compliance with four mandatory stipulations laid out by the Faculty Representatives Committee.

We promised the other members of the Western Conference when Michigan State was admitted to membership [a few years ago], that we would do everything in our power to be worthy members. We will do our best to prove ourselves deserving of the additional honor the conference has now bestowed upon our university.[65]

Needless to say, as the Spartan Foundation investigation bore out, that promise to "do everything in our power to be worthy members" was broken shortly after Michigan State was selected to replace the University of Chicago. Hannah's athletic administration would prove derelict in monitoring handbook compliance both on and off campus.[66] His failure to revamp the Athletic Council to reflect true faculty control and to address leadership problems within the department contributed greatly to an embarrassing chapter in Michigan State's storied athletic history.[67] [68]

RALPH AIGLER first heard about the decision shortly after the directors' meeting was adjourned late Sunday afternoon. Fritz Crisler had filled him in.

The following day, he dictated a letter to the commissioner of the Intercollegiate Conference. Reading between the lines, the powerful dean of faculty representatives was a little peeved.

> Well, I see the die is cast. I am not brash enough to question the conclusion of a majority of the Athletic Directors that Michigan State is our most "representative" team...Certainly, the action in selecting Michigan State, [however]...will be interpreted by the country at large, as meaning that Michigan State is virtually in good standing with the Conference.[69]

Just in case he had forgotten, Aigler reminded Wilson that the college was still under house arrest: it had yet to account for that $5,200. Ed Harden's September report on the school's corrective action was commendable. But until he could divulge the whereabouts of those remaining dollars, Aigler's understanding was that there would be no early termination of probation.

That plan was now past tense. The Faculty Representatives Committee must find a way to explain itself out of this humiliating predicament, one that sportswriters and editorialist had predicted a few weeks back. Rubber-stamping a decision by the directors to allow a member on probation to represent the conference in the Rose Bowl would send the wrong message—the Big Ten didn't practice what it preached when it really mattered on game day.

There was only one obvious solution to this dilemma. The commissioner must announce plans to visit East Lansing before the annual December conference meetings in Chicago. Remind the press that his intentions were consistent with the terms of probation. Downplay any correlation with the recent decision by the athletic directors.[70] [71]

His meeting with Harden should be brief: review the current status of the Spartan faculty representative's internal investigation. Regardless of Harden's failure to divulge anything further concerning the missing $5,200, Wilson must conclude that Michigan State had fulfilled all terms of probation. There was no longer reason to enforce the penalty until February.[72]

Two weeks later, on the second day of the conference meetings held in the LaSalle Hotel, the commissioner of the Big Ten submitted his "Report on Michigan State College."[73]

Ken Wilson, while appearing fully in control, started out by reminding the faculty leaders that the probation was a one-year sentence. There remained an option for early rescission of the penalty should all conditions of the sentence be fulfilled to his satisfaction.[74] And now, after reviewing Dean Edgar Harden's accomplishments since July, Wilson concluded that Michigan State College had "impressively demonstrated its intention to faithfully discharge the purposes of probation as imposed upon [it], and that, as of the present time, [it] had [also] satisfactorily discharged the conditions of probation."[75] Wilson brushed over any query regarding the unaccountable dollars. (Six decades later, the mystery remains unsolved.)

Wilson recommended that the penalty be immediately lifted. A motion was tendered, supported, and approved. There was no comment on how the nine faculty leaders voted.[76] It didn't matter. Ralph William Aigler got what he wanted.

But the commissioner of the Intercollegiate Conference of Faculty Representatives was still not done with his assignment. The press release had to be drafted in such a way as to avoid any pretense of manipulating a recent, poorly managed decision by the athletic directors.

Later that Friday evening, well after all conference meetings had concluded, Ken Wilson met with a tired group of reporters. His statement was brief. Michigan State, by a "unanimous" decision, had been granted absolution.[77] The school administration, in less than a year, had fulfilled all conditions for premature termination of probation. The institution was once again a member in good standing.

There was little need for questioning the commissioner about the faculty leaders' reasons for commuting the sentence only a few weeks in advance of Michigan State's departure for Pasadena. Wilson's well-contrived spin of events seemed credible for members of the press. The following morning, newspapers gave little notice to the announcement.

ASSISTANT SECRETARY of Defense John Hannah first heard about the good news later that evening. He had just arrived back in Lansing after spending the week in Washington, D.C.

The college president had mixed emotions about the commissioner's announcement. Ten months earlier, while on a two-day furlough in East Lansing, he had opened a letter from Ken Wilson informing him of plans to impose probation on Michigan State. And a few hours later, Hannah would learn that his father-in-law had been found unresponsive outside his Harrison Road residence on the north side of town. Robert Shaw was pruning trees at the time of his stroke.[78] He passed away later that evening in a Lansing hospital. John and Sarah kept vigil at the bedside.

Robert Sidey Shaw had preceded John Hannah as president of Michigan State. A stoic, soft-spoken leader, Shaw maintained one obsession throughout his four decades in service to the institution—protecting the upstanding reputation of Michigan State College. No athlete, coach, team or sport was ever more important than the good and honorable name of the pioneer land-grant school. "Shaw's Law" was first announced to a young reporter interviewing for a new public relations position in the college's athletic department.[79] The president would continue to share his mantra with anyone affiliated with the athletic program on campus: coaches, athletes, and administrative support staff. [80] John Hannah, his secretary of the college at the time, was no exception.

President Hannah began micromanaging the athletic department in December of 1941 shortly after assuming Shaw's mantle. At the time, he was pressing his director, Ralph Young, to gain some concessions from his counterpart in Ann Arbor. Frustrated with Young's inability to sway a recalcitrant Fritz Crisler on dates and venues for the annual intrastate gridiron contest, Hannah effectively demoted him while continuing to meddle in management matters more appropriate for a trusted athletic director. As a consequence, over the next decade, the department lacked an empowered and respected administrator and compliance officer—a critical oversight following admission of the college into the Intercollegiate Conference.[81]

Hannah's obsession with promoting a successful athletic program, while inappropriately involving himself in daily operations, ultimately laid the groundwork for an errant booster club that would eventually come back to haunt him. A disengaged Ralph Young, only a few years away from retirement, was quite understandably oblivious to the antics of the Spartan Foundation directors.[82]

The faculty leaderships' decision to impose probation was well deserved. Edgar Harden's validation of many Spartan offenses was sobering. His corrective action plan, after performing root-cause analysis, was admirable. A contrite Michigan State would now adopt policies certain to ensure compliance with conference rules and regulations. And John

Hannah, humbled by an internal investigation that cast shame on him and a proud institution, would do his part by resurrecting his father-in-law's old practice. Whenever the opportunity availed itself, he would remind anyone associated with Spartan athletics, including proud alumni, of some very wise words—Shaw's Law.[83]

PROFESSOR RALPH Aigler and his wife Eileen had made it a practice to visit Pasadena in late December of just about every year since 1946.[84] As dean of the Western Conference faculty representatives, it was important that he mingle with Rose Bowl officials, dignitaries, politicians, and sportswriters involved in the highly publicized extravaganza. The original decision to participate in the annual event, after all, was politically motivated. As Fritz Crisler had pointed out a few years prior to the Big Nine consummating its controversial contract with the Pacific Coast Conference, there was no better pulpit to preach the gospel of pure amateur play than during that week out in Pasadena. And it was absolutely essential that Ralph William Aigler be present to deliver that message.[85] [86]

Shortly after Commissioner Kenneth Wilson announced that Michigan State, and not Illinois, would be representing the Big Ten in the Rose Bowl, Ralph and Eileen Aigler decided to celebrate New Years in Ann Arbor rather than southern California.[87] He gave no reason for breaking with a holiday tradition.

MICHIGAN STATE represented the Intercollegiate Conference of Faculty Representatives well in Pasadena. As anticipated by the conference athletic directors, Biggie Munn's talented team dominated play on the gridiron against the University of California at Los Angeles.

But more importantly for President John Hannah, the coaching staff and student athletes had made quite an impression on the Rose Bowl Committee, various dignitaries, and members of the press during their weeklong stay near Los Angeles.[88] [89] [90] [91] A few days following the Spartans' victory over the Bruins, his office was inundated with highly complimentary comments about the team's performance away from the football field.[92] It reaffirmed for Hannah a long held conviction—competitive sports offered student athletes a learning experience unlike any they might receive in the lecture hall or laboratory.[93]

A few weeks following Biggie Munn's success in Pasadena, the State Board of Agriculture met in East Lansing for its January gathering. One agenda item, in particular, required extensive discussion.

In December, Ralph Young had announced plans to retire by the end of the current academic year.[94] [95] Edgar Harden played no small part in that decision; it was a critical component of his comprehensive corrective action plan. The school needed an empowered leader—a man of highest integrity and resolve, gifted in managerial skills—to clean up the tarnished athletic department.[96] And by early January, shortly after the Spartans successful venture out west, Harden was convinced that Clarence Munn was the right man for the job. President Hannah, despite expressing concern over Munn's departure from coaching while still at the summit, accepted his faculty representative's recommendation.[97] He informed the board a week later that the coach would resign to take on the new challenge.[98] They endorsed the action.

Unlike the Munn announcement, which shared front-page headlines with Joe DiMaggio and Marilyn Monroe's hasty decision to marry at City Hall in San Francisco, the final act of the State Board that Friday afternoon merited little press.[99] In fact, the story garnered no more than a couple lines hidden inside a few newspapers about the state.[100]

A motion to change the name of the school "from Michigan State College of Agriculture and Applied Science to Michigan State University" was unanimously approved by the board.[101] That seemingly inconsequential resolution would soon set off a powder keg in Ann Arbor.

CHAPTER 12

The Brody Fumble

——

"Dear Marv: Since I sent you last week a copy of the
letter [sic] which my friend Howard Smith had written
to Mr. Brody, together with a copy of my reply to
Smith, I am now enclosing two more copies. One of
these is a copy of Brody's reply to Smith.... I dare say
you will find Brody's letter to Smith interesting."

PROFESSOR RALPH W. AIGLER; 25 JANUARY 1954[1]

BY LEGISLATIVE ACT OF THE United States Congress, Catholepistemiad
of Michigania was founded in 1817 by Justice Augustus Woodward. A
few years later, the name of the secondary school, located in the small
trading town of Detroit, was changed to the University of Michigan. The
original title, incorporating both Latin and Greek in a somewhat concocted manner by the founder, was felt to be "pedantic and uncouth"
by certain political leaders within the Michigan Territory.[2] It was also
difficult to pronounce!

Twenty years later, the federal territory transitioned to statehood. In
that same year, the school was relocated to Ann Arbor.

The new state's first constitution of 1837 clearly defined the role of
higher education for its citizens. The university, born out of federal law,

would be effectively adopted by Michigan as a center for the advancement of knowledge and intellectual exploration. Branches of the institution, serving as preparatory schools, would fall under its auspices. Agricultural studies, as a department of the university, were included in that mandate.

Ten years later, the University of Michigan abandoned its responsibilities for coordinating the state's complex system of higher education. That decision would incense the powerful and influential agrarian movement—a dominant economic force at the time. Lacking an institution willing to service their needs, the farmers politicked the legislature in Lansing for an agricultural school. Their wish was soon granted in a revised 1850 constitution. The Agricultural College of the State of Michigan was founded five years later.

The state college, located in East Lansing, went through a number of name changes over the decades as it continually redefined itself. In 1861, while facing bankruptcy, the administrators applied for congressional grants made available in the recently passed Morrill Act. Each state was now eligible for 250,000 acres of federal land that could be sold off to finance an institution willing to adopt Justin Morrill's philosophy on higher education. Michigan was the first in line—Pennsylvania and many other states quickly followed.

In accepting those terms, the agricultural school was required to expand its curricula to include mechanics (engineering) and military science. And to reflect its new mission as an institution promoting utilitarian/practical studies, the school was renamed The State Agricultural College by the legislature in Lansing.[3]

Five decades later, the Michigan constitution was again rewritten. The State Board of Agriculture was now charged with oversight responsibilities for the institution. In acknowledging the change in governance, the legislature also modified the name of the school: Michigan Agricultural College. It was a poor choice of words. The college was a full-fledged university by that time, offering advanced degrees in many disciplines unrelated to agriculture.

Aggie graduates generally took great pride in their alma mater, despite its ongoing struggles with an identity. If there was a problem with the latest name change, it lay with what was printed in Old English font at the top of their diplomas. Simply stated, a degree from an agriculture college hindered employment opportunities for young men and women with interests unrelated to agrarian science or practice.[4] As a consequence, the state legislature once again renamed the school. Michigan State College of Agriculture and Applied Science was crafted to reflect the true character of the institution.[5] Regardless of its latest appellation, most people referred to it simply as "Michigan State." And for the next 28 years, just about everyone, including President John Hannah, was happy with the official name and its vernacular. That would all change in mid-January of 1954.

IN THE spring of 1951, following an extensive national search, the University of Michigan announced plans to hire an Ohio State professor to replace its retiring president. Six weeks later, Harlan Henthorne Hatcher assumed the office previously occupied by Alexander Ruthven.

That decision by the Board of Regents was surprising for one man: James Lewis Morrill of the University of Minnesota. John Hannah's good friend, also a Buckeye by birth and diploma, knew Hatcher quite well from their earlier years serving together on the faculty in Columbus.[6] While acknowledging him as a "wonderful chap, delightful to know," Morrill questioned his leadership capabilities. "You can relax...the gauge of comparative administrative strength, acumen, and effectiveness slants distinctly northwestward...."[7] [8] He was confident that the politically savvy Spartan president would suffer little, especially in the annual competition for legislative appropriations, while Harlan Hatcher was in Ann Arbor.

President Hatcher's first year in office was quite uneventful. All that would change in October of 1953. The Paul Bunyan escapade proved to be a rude awakening for the Ohioan. No one with Wolverine blood, other than the governor, was pleased with the outcome. The new president's office was inundated with letters from alumni upset over a political ploy that effectively elevated the annual grudge match with the Spartans into a legitimate rivalry worthy of national press. The inferred message was not subtle—Hatcher should have done more to fend off the advance from Lansing.

But it was a little noticed announcement by the State Board of Agriculture, two months later, which would prove to be Harlan Hatcher's formal introduction into the emotionally charged politics that defined the relationship between the two large public institutions. And by early spring of 1954, the Buckeye turncoat probably questioned why he ever applied for the job in Ann Arbor.

MICHIGAN STATE College of Agriculture and Applied Science was a misnomer. In point of fact, the school was much more than an undergraduate institution focused on the practical sciences. And with its centennial year rapidly approaching, John Hannah felt it critical that the name more accurately reflect the transition of The Agricultural College of the State of Michigan into a major academic center for research educating graduate students from around the world in studies unrelated to agriculture or the applied sciences.[9] There was no more appropriate and concise title than "Michigan State University."

The State Board's resolution was sent through usual channels to the halls of government within the Capitol. Board members predicted little political resistance. After all, the governor, legislature, and citizenry were fully supportive of the measure. What they failed to anticipate, especially in the immediate aftermath of the recent trophy controversy, was the fierce resolve of some very passionate Wolverines. And it all had to do with steadfast respect for an institution and its storied tradition.

THE MICHIGAN Board of Regents didn't have much time. Based on the press release from East Lansing, the State Board of Agriculture planned to petition the legislature for a name change in the very near future. And in the aftermath of Michigan State's recent Rose Bowl victory, the

Wolverine leadership was certain that the bill would pass through the House and Senate chambers without significant opposition. Favorable press regarding the school and its patriotic leader, currently on sabbatical in Washington, was at a feverish pitch. Soapy Williams would undoubtedly sign the bill into law. The photo-op, with prominent Spartans and politicians strategically placed about him, was certain to make the front-page of every newspaper within the state.

The regents had no issue with Hannah's board promoting a change in the college's title. Michigan State was clearly a university by their definition: it maintained nine undergraduate colleges; it offered graduate studies in many disciplines dating back decades. In fact, the land-grant college's graduate school was one of the largest in the country.[10] They also had no issue with petitioning the state legislature—precedence had been set long ago with its three previous name changes.[11] What did trouble the regents was the proposed title: Michigan State University; it was too similar to the name embossed on diplomas earned in Ann Arbor. "In conversations, in articles and news references, in legislative bills, in acts already on the statute books, in student transcripts and other records, there would be endless opportunities for mistakes."[12] Confusion was inevitable.

But on a higher level for the proud members of the Board of Regents, Michigan was not going to share its reputation as one of the most highly regarded academic research centers in the world with a sister-state school due to political cronyism. The proposed change, using "the combination of words *Michigan* and *State* and *University* [was] an infringement upon the name of the University of Michigan."[13]

Charged with protecting the honorable reputation of an institution that had its origin dating back to 1817, the regents' assigned President Harlan Hatcher the task of ensuring the defeat of House Bill No. 75.

Hatcher immediately met with his vice president, Marvin Niehuss. It would be the one-time law professor's job to coordinate the school's strategy. And Niehuss, in turn, made a quick phone call to Arthur Brandon. This was clearly a matter requiring the manipulation of public perception—something the renowned university, with a reputation for haughtiness, had struggled with over the past few decades.[14] [15] If Michigan was going to succeed in crushing this State Board of Agriculture initiative, Niehuss needed to deftly control debate in the taverns, the newspapers, and ultimately, the State Capitol. And there was no better man for that job than his director of university relations.

The Niehuss-Brandon strategy was straightforward. After thoroughly researching the subject, they would draft a brief on why the name of the college should not be changed to Michigan State University. And to support the regents' concern that two state-supported schools with similar names might lead to unnecessary confusion, Brandon would solicit responses from other publically funded schools having recently undergone name changes. He needed evidence to support that assertion. The duo also planned to ghostwrite a press release for President Hatcher that would clearly spell out why the university opposed the State Board proposal.[16] The carefully worded statement must effectively educate the uninitiated—the common folk, the ones who cast votes in November elections. Finally, they would need a legal opinion supporting the Wolverine stance to share with legislators—a matter left for the president to address.

Harlan Hatcher spent little time mulling over his assignment. Rather than retain outside counsel, he would avail himself of internal talent under his employ. He contacted E. Blythe Stason, dean of the highly regarded Michigan Law School. And one week later, after gathering in Hutchins Hall with two fellow scholars, both experts in Michigan constitutional law, Stason provided a response.

The three law professors thoroughly reviewed the 1908 Michigan Constitution. They discovered a few critical points favoring the regents' defiant stance: there was "clear intent on the part of the Constitutional Convention that there shall be just one university in [the] state;" in addition, "the State Board of Agriculture [was to] have jurisdiction over 'the agricultural college.'" They also noted "the Constitutional Convention contemplated two separate constitutional educational corporations, but only one [state] university." And to support their points, the state document even went so far as to spell out what institutions of higher learning would be funded with public dollars: "the legislature shall maintain the university, the college of mines, the state agricultural college, the state normal college, and such state normal schools and other educational institutions as may be established by law."[17]

In commenting on legislative financial support, the professors speculated on whether the framers of the constitution might have also been concerned about economies of scale. Duplication of services, most notably at the graduate level, would prove more costly and less effective with two universities subsidized by the state of Michigan. But Hatcher knew that side argument would get him nowhere in a debate with John Hannah in 1954. Colleges and universities were rapidly expanding to meet the educational needs of a society in transition following the Second World War. In addition, graduate programs had been in place at the Michigan State dating back decades.

But what really caught President Hatcher's eye as he glanced through the legal brief was a comment on the third page. No doubt Stason's expertise in administrative law prompted the closing remark.[18] "A very practical statutory question is bound to arise if the legislature establishes another institution called a state university." Hundreds of laws involving the various state-supported schools would have to be "examined and clarified to indicate precisely which institution is involved."[19] The take home message, at least for Harlan Hatcher, was clear as day: changing the official title of the college was far more complicated than hastily passing a bill and having the governor sign it into law.[20]

Bolstered by Stason's legal brief, the president of the University of Michigan went to work. Within a few days, friendly legislators about Ann Arbor and southeast Michigan were contacted. And by late January, those senators and representatives were tuned-in to the Wolverine strategy.

DESPITE THE Board of Regents' concerns over the proposed name change, most Wolverines remained in hibernation as of early February.

Very few were even aware of the issue. Mindful of this fact, as well as the invaluable role prominent, well-informed alumni might have in educating their state representatives, Director of University Relations Arthur Brandon decided to spend some unbudgeted department dollars and mail out an addendum to the quarterly *Letter to Michigan Alumni*. The communiqué, intended to keep graduates updated on issues and events involving their alma mater, had just been sent out prior to Michigan State's announced name change plans.

The glossy printout, a succinct four pages, defined the problem and spelled out the regent's position. *Postscript: Letter to Michigan Alumni* cautiously appealed to the Wolverine faithful.[21] It was critical, however, that the statement be devoid of notorious Michigan self-conceit, a matter of ongoing concern for the university's front man in the state legislature.[22] Unfortunately, Brandon's attempt at educating the slumbering faithful backfired. The governor and legislative leaders were soon inundated with notes from, shall we say, extremely proud graduates demonstrating an attitude Brandon wanted to avoid.

Two letters to Governor G. Mennen Williams best demonstrated that point. The first came from Edward A. Kuich, class of 1950. The Menominee stockbroker minced no words in his opening paragraph. He questioned why an institution of one hundred years was still struggling to discover a "name of which it can be justly and jealously proud." Kuich cut to the chase.[23]

Traditionally and historically Michigan State College has none of the aspects of a university. The mediocre scholastic caliber of Michigan State College is well known throughout the mid-west. This school should be concentrating on ways and means of raising its scholastic standards, rather than changing names.[24]

He then offered a few reasons, straight from Brandon's manifesto, for why the governor should oppose House Bill No. 75. While thumping his chest, the feisty Wolverine closed by professing allegiance to his alma mater.

Our State of Michigan can be proud to possess the most outstanding university in the world today. This is the opinion of
leading educators everywhere in the world. The University of
Michigan has a scholastic standard that is the marvel of the
world of higher education and the jealous pride of over 160,000
living alumni. Let us not decimate the University of Michigan's
outstanding 117 years of proud history by such devious means
of infringement, and confusion, and outright coldly calculated
fraud...Speak out and preserve our outstanding system of higher education.[25]

The governor provided his standard, politically correct response. If the
bill passed muster in the House and Senate, he would give it serious
consideration.[26] Translated, Soapy would do the most expedient thing.
After all, he was up for re-election in November.

Eugene D. Mossner '52 was in his first year of law school at Wayne
State University when he wrote to Governor Williams. He too borrowed
from Brandon's *Postscript: Letter to Michigan Alumni.*

But unlike Kuich's "in your face," flag-waving approach, the law
student decided to use semantics in trying to sway the head of state.
Availing himself of a number of dictionaries and encyclopedias, he
claimed that a university, by tradition, must have both a law and medical school. Michigan State had neither. The school also lacked graduate
studies in other important disciplines such as dentistry and pharmacy.
"It would seem more in keeping with their make-up then, that MSC remain a college." [27] He concluded by reiterating a common theme shared
by other Wolverines petitioning for the governor's allegiance: the name
change was merely a ploy on Michigan State's part to capitalize on the
prestige and renown of the University of Michigan.

Despite rearing up an institutional repute he wanted to avoid,
Arthur Brandon's *Postscript: Letter to Michigan Alumni* accomplished just
what Harlan Hatcher had wanted—arousing Wolverines eager to aid the
cause.

Many years earlier, while interacting with a colleague, Professor Ralph Aigler commented on the unique loyalty and enthusiasm Michigan alumni held for their alma mater.[28] It was based on a tradition of excellence in academics, research, and athletics. Call it pride or decry it arrogance—graduates knew their place in the hierarchy of higher education, especially within the state. And in the opinion of most Wolverines, now fully informed of the latest controversy, there was no way a wannabe was going to upstage the University of Michigan.

JUST PRIOR to completing his 12-month tour of duty in Washington, John Hannah received an urgent plea from the White House. President Eisenhower wanted his assistant secretary of defense to remain at the Pentagon through June. Legislation that he had played a key role in drafting during his sabbatical year was now up for debate. Hannah's presence at congressional hearings was critical if those bills were to gain approval by Congress. The State Board relented; it had no choice.[29]

Regardless of his commitment to the federal government over the next six months, in mid-January President Hannah was confident that the proposed name change legislation drafted by college attorney (and Michigan law school graduate) Leland Carr ('06 LLM) would pose no problems for state legislators. He expected little debate—his administration, after all, was well prepared for just about any rebuttal from Ann Arbor. The savvy Hannah even anticipated the administrative law nightmare associated with amending existing legislation to reflect the college's new name—a practical concern Dean Stason would later raise in his confidential legal brief to Harlan Hatcher. "We [should] start from scratch with [a] new, simple one-paragraph [proposal]" announcing, "hereafter [that the school] be known and designated as the Michigan State University." [30] [31] And any past statutory reference to the college "shall be construed to mean [the same]." [32]

President Hannah also had drafted a few documents to support his board's resolution just prior to his departure for Washington: a truncated history of the college as well as a simple survey of all land-grant schools and their current titles. (Most were designated 'university' by the early 1950s.) He planned to include these attachments in a mailing to prominent state politicians and leaders announcing the State Board's desire for a name change. The ghostwriter, no doubt Hannah's dependable right-hand man James Denison, pointed out in the president's standard cover letter that "all of this serves to emphasize the undoubted fact that the name Michigan State College is no longer distinctive—as it was in times when 'State College' and 'land-grant college' were almost synonymous—nor is it appropriate, in view of the undoubted fact that Michigan State College is a university in every sense of the word."[33]

And if that wasn't enough, President Hannah had included one final reminder: "It might be added gratuitously that Feb. 12, 1955, when Michigan State College begins the celebration of its centennial, would be a most appropriate time at which to recognize the stature and prestige the institution has achieved in its 100 years of development from a pioneering agricultural college to the eighth largest university in the United States."[34]

President Hannah had every reason to feel good about his initiative. He planned to check up on the progress of this simple, seemingly straightforward proposal over the next few weekends when he would return to campus and his family at Cowles House. Within four weeks, he was confident that Governor Williams would sign the bill into law. What Hannah failed to anticipate, however, was the major role a proud old Aggie would play in some backroom politicking soon to take place in Lansing.

THERE WAS really no reason for Professor Ralph Aigler to attend the late Friday afternoon roundtable called by Blythe Stason. The law school dean needed to draft a brief for President Hatcher challenging the constitutionality of a name change for Michigan State College. Aigler's legal interests lay in contracts and real estate. He had no expertise in state constitutional law. Other more qualified faculty scholars deserved a seat at that table.

As it turned out, despite not participating in that January 22ⁿᵈ meeting at Hutchins Hall, Ralph Aigler was already deeply involved in the political controversy. And by happenstance, it all came about due to an old friend who had recently moved back to southern Michigan.

Howard Remus Smith was born in 1872, near Somerset Township in Hillsdale County. At the age of 23 he graduated with honors from The State Agricultural College. His interest lay in animal husbandry. A few years later, he earned a master's degree from the University of Wisconsin. An opportunity to instruct students at the University of Missouri followed. Critical references from renowned professors back in East Lansing clinched the deal.

One year later, Smith applied for a position at the University of Nebraska. And once again, it was those letters from nationally regarded researchers at The State Agricultural College that got him the job. As a professor of agriculture in Lincoln, he began work on what would prove to be the definitive college text on animal feeding. Soon recognized as an expert in his field, the University of Minnesota recruited Smith to lead its department of animal husbandry. The researcher resigned a few years later to assume a position in private industry. In short order, he became commissioner of the Chicago Livestock Exchange. During that tenure, he was asked to coordinate a national response to the growing problem of bovine tuberculosis—a financially devastating disease for ranchers and dairy farmers. Smith would ultimately serve as general manager of the National Livestock Sanitary Committee, later referred to as the Livestock Conservation, an organization collaborating with the U.S. Department of Agriculture to eradicate deadly and costly farm contagion.[35]

After a remarkable career in academics, research, and utilitarian service to farmers, Howard Smith retired in 1951 and returned to Michigan.[36] One year later, Michigan State College of Agriculture and Applied Science would honor him with its Alumni Award for Distinguished Service.[37]

That experience, returning to campus during spring commencement ceremonies, reminded Smith of the profound role The State

Agricultural College and some renowned professors had played in jump-starting his career. It rekindled pride in being an Aggie. Shortly after returning to Somerset with his Alumni Award in hand, he vowed to get more involved with his alma mater. He agreed to serve as secretary for the Class of 1895. And as might be expected, Smith soon developed a keen interest in campus activities and events. After all, it was now his duty to keep former classmates updated on what was going on in East Lansing.

SHORTLY AFTER assuming his voluntary position as class secretary, Howard Smith discovered the inconspicuous press release while paging through a local newspaper. Michigan State was proposing another name change, the third time since he had graduated in 1895. The college leadership felt that "Michigan State University" more accurately reflected its "nature and position as an educational institution of [the] State."[38]

Smith was troubled. He immediately penned a note to Clark Brody, chairman of the State Board of Agriculture. They had briefly met one year earlier during spring commencement. The distinguished alumnus objected to the administration's proposal for various reasons, the most significant being plans to abandon a proud tradition. The school's "reputation as the oldest [agricultural] college in the U.S. has been made as a college and not a [university]."[39] And to emphasize his concern, Smith copied his political representatives, Senator Haskell Nichols and Representative Frederic Marshall.[40] What he failed to mention in the letter, however, was that a distinguished professor of law at the University of Michigan would also receive a mimeograph![41] Ralph Aigler expressed appreciation for his copy. He encouraged his friend to share any additional communiqués with him.

Clark Brody responded a few days later. The chairman of the State Board was surprisingly candid with the old Aggie. Reading between the lines, he too questioned the wisdom of Hannah's initiative.

Dear Mr. Smith:

I appreciate your letter of January 18 outlining your objections to changing the name of Michigan State College to Michigan State University. Personally, I shall be glad to abide by the decision of the alumni and the people [should there be a great opposition to the proposal]. We seem to be thriving under the present label. Also I can imagine that there is a possibility of considerable confusion of the two institutions in the minds of some people [if this is to take place].[42]

Brody, the long-serving executive director of the Michigan Farm Bureau, then acknowledged the "integral part" Smith had played in "agricultural progress" and the contribution he had made "(as) a highlight of agricultural history."[43] His opinion, as a distinguished graduate, did matter. He planned to forward the old Aggie's letter to President Hannah.

A few days later, Ralph Aigler would receive a copy of Clark Brody's response. Recognizing the damning implications of the State Board chairman's comments, the professor immediately shared the letter with his boss, Harlan Hatcher.[44][45][46] It appeared that Dean E. Blythe Stason's legal opinion on the constitutionality of a name change wasn't needed after all!

Howard Remis Smith was on a mission. The sentimentalist-graduate of the pioneer land-grant college wrote a follow-up letter to his friend in Ann Arbor a couple of days later. He informed Aigler that he had now offered his services to Representative Frederic Marshall, a member of the House Judiciary Subcommittee charged with reviewing the proposed legislation. If requested, he was even willing to appear before the committee. Unaware of Aigler's long-standing feud with John Hannah, Smith described his great admiration for the college president. But on this one issue, he respectfully disagreed with the visionary leader. He reminded Aigler that Michigan State gained its reputation as an agricultural college—not a university.[47] As expected, Smith's friend shared this latest communiqué with President Hatcher and Vice President Niehuss.[48] It might come in handy for Wolverine lobbyists back in Lansing.

A little over two weeks after John Hannah had first proposed the name change to his board, Representative Frederic Marshall penned a note to his concerned constituent from the Hillsdale District. He expressed appreciation for Howard Smith's recent communiqué and the additional information sent to his office. He shared all documents with members of his committee.

Marshall, whose district included Ann Arbor, opposed House Bill 75 for a number of reasons. But he was quick to point out that he was not alone; many other colleagues expressed similar concerns with the controversial legislation. He reassured Smith that all had "[given] this bill the 'working over' behind the scenes (sic) which it deserved." After considerable discussion, his fellow committee members decided to give it "unofficially the 'silent treatment'"—no further debate, no final decision. Lacking the Judiciary Subcommittee's stamp of approval, "there isn't one chance in a thousand that it will again see the 'light of day' [in] this session." He noted that Smith's mimeographs, including the surprisingly candid Brody letter, played a major role in effectively tabling the name change legislation.[49]

The disappointing news did not discourage the president of Michigan State College of Agriculture and Applied Science. After meeting with his legislative sponsor, John Hannah proposed a compromise. Maintain the current title but substitute "university" for "college." The Wolverine response was predictable. The latest proposal was merely smoke screen. Other than in official documents, most people generally referred to the school as Michigan State College.[50] Replacing one word in the current name would still give Hannah, at least in practice, what he really wanted—Michigan State University.[51] The revised bill went nowhere.

One month after first proposing a name change for the pioneer land-grant institution, members of both chambers of the Michigan legislature received a letter jointly signed by the chairman of the State

Board of Agriculture and the president of Michigan State College. It was official notice that the school's leadership would capitulate to the will of political forces in Lansing.

Based on protocol, the chairman of the State Board—Clark Brody—signed the letter. President John Hannah countersigned it. Regardless of documentary propriety, there was no doubt who had drafted that two-page statement. And reading between the lines, John Hannah was fuming. But the quintessential politician maintained his poise, at least in writing, while conceding defeat.

The president was surprised by the "violent objection" from the Board of Regents of the University of Michigan. He noted that many land-grant colleges had adopted the title of university. And there was "ample precedence" that schools with similar names could peacefully co-exist after a change. He cited examples involving Ohio, Pennsylvania, Florida, New York, and California. In each instance, the transition took place, for the most part, without incident. [52]

Hannah reiterated the two major reasons for the name change: to more adequately reflect the scope of degrees offered at the school and to acknowledge the position it held as a leading center for research. There was "no desire or intention to borrow the prestige or reputation of any institution."[53]

"It appears, however, that officials of the University of Michigan are apprehensive that confusion might result and that in some way the prestige of the [university] might be affected. While we do not think that there is any reason for their apprehension, it is our desire and purpose to avoid any action that might cause further controversy."[54]

Hannah concluded that it was in the best interest of all parties involved that sponsors of the bills before the legislature withdraw them for the time being. He emphasized that the State Board of Agriculture would review the matter and work towards a solution satisfactory for both institutions.

JOHN HANNAH never learned of the significant role Howard Remus Smith, let alone his old foe, Ralph Aigler, had played in this rare rejection he experienced at the State Capitol. In his opinion, the failure to advance House Bill 75 to the senate floor was due to counsel provided Harlan Hatcher by his law faculty.[55] Dean Blythe Stason's roundtable statement questioning the constitutionality of the proposed legislation was impressive, to say the least. Some of the brightest legal minds in the country, members of Hatcher's faculty, contributed. And it did not help matters that a majority of House and Senate members privy to that legal brief claimed either undergraduate or law school diplomas from the University of Michigan.[56] If Hannah was to succeed a second time around, he had to come up with a strategy to circumvent that Wolverine advantage.

Hail to the Victors, Ralph William Aigler included—at least for the moment.

CHAPTER 13

The Secretary of Offense

———

"I am and remain mindful of the conceivable pressure that
has been brought to bear upon you, as President of the
University of Michigan. Even so, does not every man who
becomes a leader in his field meet up with those challenges
to act as truth and courage demands.... Your opposition
to this change in name of Michigan State College can do
damage, both to you and the University. The request to
change this name will be granted, either now or later and
history will [one day] record the details of the endeavor."

A. FISK, THE STATE AGRICULTURAL COLLEGE '05; 7 APRIL 1955[1]

UNLIKE A FEW FELLOW GRADUATES that migrated to the greater Lansing
area, Claud Lamar Brattin ('12) never became a Michigan Mole. After
receiving his degree in mechanical engineering from the University
of Michigan, he worked in private industry near Cleveland. Michigan
Agricultural College eventually hired him as an instructor in drawing
and design in 1920.[2] A few years later, the land-grant institution, now
known as Michigan State College of Agriculture and Applied Science,
offered him tenure. And on July 1, 1955, after 35 years as professor
and ultimately department chair, he would retire from Michigan State
University of Agriculture and Applied Science.[3]

HE ALMOST threw it away. But there was something about the bulk mail glossy that caught his attention—didn't he just receive his quarterly *Letter to Michigan Alumni* a few weeks earlier?

He skimmed through the four-page newsletter; the special edition was entirely devoted to the current name change controversy.[4] Nothing unusual about that—just about everybody was talking about it around East Lansing. Apparently the Board of Regents back in Ann Arbor wanted to update alumni and friends of the university on its reasons for opposing the Spartans' initiative.

Recognizing that *Postscript: Letter to Michigan Alumni* might be of interest to Michigan State President John Hannah, he set it aside near his briefcase. The following morning Professor Claud Brattin personally delivered his copy to John Hannah's secretary in the administration building just east of Beaumont Tower. His good friend, preoccupied with responsibilities in Washington, could read it a few days later after returning to East Lansing for the weekend.

President Hannah was impressed with the quality of the throwaway brochure. Succinct and easily readable, the author thoroughly summarized Michigan's main reasons for opposing the name change. Clearly, this was a very professional job intended for one purpose: educate the Wolverine faithful.

But there was one particular comment on the first page that piqued his interest. "Perhaps the greatest opposition to the proposed change of name...has come not from the Regents or University alumni, but from Michigan State College alumni who are proud of a century of achievement as the College; and from farm people who fear the change would be a further step away from the main purpose for which the College was created."[5] Where in the world did the author, no doubt a university employee, come up with that assertion? Clark Brody had shared with him a letter from a somewhat disgruntled old Aggie, Howard Smith. The college had just honored the highly regarded alumnus one year earlier during spring commencement. Smith fervently objected to the name change. But that was it. Most Spartan alumni were in favor of the proposal.

A week later, shortly after conceding defeat to Harlan Hatcher, President Hannah shared copies of *Postscript: Letter to Michigan Alumni* with his board. He commented on the mistruth at the bottom of page one. His point was straightforward: as leaders of the college, they could take nothing for granted while dealing with the University of Michigan. During the brief discussion that followed, Board Chairman Brody remained surprisingly quiet.

John Hannah reminded the board that he had a job to finish in Washington. But once that task was completed in about four months, he would return to East Lansing and devote his undivided attention to this name change matter. The school's Centennial was less than a year away. With a little luck, he might be able to come up with a scheme to resurrect the debate. He desperately wanted "university" added to the school's official title before February of 1955—the inauguration of the yearlong celebration.

JOHN HANNAH tendered his resignation to Secretary of Defense Charles Wilson in late June of 1954. Four weeks later, he was back in charge as the full-time president of Michigan State College.

Planning for the Centennial had been in progress for some time. In fact, Hannah had been anticipating it since the day he assumed the president's office 13 years earlier. And now, finally free from obligations at the Pentagon, he could focus his attention on final preparations for the big event. After all, this was an unparalleled opportunity for the school to shine. Over 500,000 visitors, including numerous dignitaries, politicians, scientists, and members of the media, were expected to campus throughout the year.[6]

The U.S. Postal Service had already approved a 3-cent stamp to commemorate the first two academic institutions subsidized with state, and later federal, land-grant dollars—Michigan State College and Pennsylvania State University.[7] Hannah's connections in Washington, D.C. no doubt aided the cause.[8] But President Milton Eisenhower's relationship with older brother Dwight sealed the deal!

Scientific symposia, to be scheduled throughout the year, were in the works. Prominent agrarian researchers from around the world would be invited. A huge farming exposition celebrating the role of mechanization in agriculture was inked on the calendar for August. Over one hundred acres of campus south of the Red Cedar River would be cordoned off for the event.

Parades acknowledging landmarks in the college's storied history were planned throughout the spring and fall. A two-day Centennial Homecoming for returning alumni was scheduled for the Illinois game. Numerous parties, socials, and a parade down Grand River Avenue were anticipated for that weekend.

The 100-year anniversary of the founding of the Agricultural College of the State of Michigan would kick-off the historic 12 months of celebration. Coinciding with that birthday, Michigan State intended to bestow honorary doctor of law degrees on the presidents of five land-grant schools within the original Northwest Territory—all current members of the Big Ten. Penn State President Milton Eisenhower was included on the list for historical reasons. In a gesture of friendship, perhaps politically motivated, President Harlan Hatcher of the University of Michigan would also be offered a doctorate.

A few dignitaries and politicians, including Governor G. Mennen Williams, were invited as well.[9] It never hurt to acknowledge certain distinguished leaders, especially those influencing the flow of dollars from Lansing.

And as promised his State Board back in February, President Hannah would also begin planning for one final event to hopefully coincide with the Centennial year—a name change acknowledging the college's true status as a university. By late fall of 1954, after thoroughly reviewing Harlan Hatcher's defensive strategy, as clearly spelled out in *Postscript: Letter to Michigan Alumni,* he was ready for an offensive advance on the State Capitol. All he needed was some incident, perhaps even staged, to resurrect debate.

John Hannah was in luck—at least it sure seemed that way. In early January of 1955, the Lansing City Council passed a much-ballyhooed resolution requesting that the state legislature change the name of the college to Michigan State University of Agriculture and Applied Science. The student body, almost on cue, rallied behind the cause.[10]

President Hannah steadfastly denied any role in the resolution, let alone the students' response. The college had no intention of pursuing name change legislation during its centennial year—a potentially ugly political sideshow that might distract from the grand celebration. But with the council's request, and the groundswell of interest that followed, he had no choice but to "(make) an all-out effort to secure its approval." Despite his disclaimer, many people, members of the press included, still questioned the president's sincerity.[11]

A few weeks later, the State Board of Agriculture would meet in East Lansing for its monthly gathering. After President Hannah reviewed recent developments around town, his board unanimously approved a motion requesting "enactment by the Legislature authorizing the use of the name of Michigan State University of Agriculture and Applied Science."[12] The hurried resolution took place just days after a Centennial event in which President Harlan Hatcher received a friendly handshake and an honorary doctorate from Michigan State College of Agriculture and Applied Science![13]

AS EXPECTED, the latest news from East Lansing set off a seismograph back in Ann Arbor. But the university administration was well prepared for the aftershock.

During the last go around with President Hannah and his board, the Michigan regents privately raised the question whether elected officials had the constitutional privilege to change the name of the college. The framers of the current State Constitution of 1908 left that open for interpretation.[14] And in the opinion of university law school experts, the courts would probably side with the regents.[15] However, due to a successful ploy on the part of a few loyal Wolverines sitting on the House Judiciary Subcommittee, the court had no reason to address the issue at the time. But now that the college had resurrected the name change debate, and anticipating that John Hannah would be better prepared for the fight this time around, Harlan Hatcher and his board decided that this question of constitutionality must be confidently addressed. A thoroughly researched legal opinion supporting Michigan's stance would be hard to counter if the debate ultimately ended up in the State Supreme Court.

Hatcher contacted his law school dean. Professor Blythe Stason reminded the president that he had already reviewed this question a year earlier. That legal brief, drafted with the assistance of a few law school colleagues, was still pertinent. He also informed his boss that a member of the state Senate had requested a formal opinion from the attorney general's office shortly after House Bill 75 was tabled. The astute politician, anticipating Hannah's latest ploy, probably wanted to avoid another embarrassing public tit for tat that might cast further shame on both institutions. In a little noticed, long-since forgotten press release, Attorney General Frank Millard ruled that the legislature had no right to change the name of Michigan State if it led to "confusion or deception" with a "name previously adopted and in use by another entity operating in the [state's] educational field."[16] He concluded that only a constitutional amendment, approved by the citizenry, could legally change the name of the college. Despite possessing a Wolverine pedigree (BA '14, LLM '16), conflict of interest charges were never raised by the press. Millard's ruling conveniently endorsed Dean Stason's legal brief.[17] [18]

Unfortunately for Harlan Hatcher and the University of Michigan, Frank Millard was no longer attorney general for the State of Michigan. Democrat Thomas Kavanaugh, riding the coat tails of Governor G. Mennen Williams, had defeated the Wolverine in the recent November election. Millard's opinion was now irrelevant. But it didn't stop Stason from contacting the former attorney general for some political advice. And as luck would have it, Millard was able to help out. Two of his former associates, career state employees, remained on Kavanaugh's payroll. He agreed to cautiously ask them to render an unofficial opinion on this all-important constitutional question without their new boss's awareness. And as expected, Russell Searl ('26 LLM) and R. Glen Dunn ('19 BA, '20 LLM) were more than eager to aid their alma mater in this righteous cause. They completed their confidential assignment within a week. The Wolverine duo effectively upheld Frank Millard's previous ruling on the question.

Dean Stason shared the encouraging news with Hatcher. The bottom line: it appeared fairly certain that the name change, as proposed, was unconstitutional. But he reminded the president that this was not necessarily the view of the current attorney general. Nonetheless, should an opinion from Kavanaugh be requested in the near future, Searl and Dunn's presence in that office might come in handy. After all, as staff attorneys charged with researching constitutional questions for their boss, they did carry subtle clout in many decisions.

Professor Stason concluded his note by reminding President Hatcher that any leak to the press, especially regarding how this unofficial opinion came about, could prove extremely embarrassing for the University of Michigan.[19] The Searle-Dunn brief must kept under wraps.

Armed with Stason's affirming opinion, gained from two Wolverines embedded in the Office of the State Attorney General, President Harlan Hatcher felt quite confident that Michigan would eventually prevail in this latest challenge by the college.

BIGGIE MUNN'S recent success on the gridiron was in large part due to his 'multiple offense'—easily adaptable variations on the traditional T-formation intended to frustrate opposing coaches. "When teams figured out how to defend against a certain formation, Munn would simply devise a new one" to counter it.[20]

In preparing a plan to defeat the Wolverines a second time around, John Hannah would borrow from his head coach's philosophy on offensive schemes. Availing himself of Professor Claud Brattin's copy of *Postscript: Letter to Michigan Alumni*—a document that defined Michigan's somewhat limited defensive options—the president devised a grand strategy during the fall football season, well in advance of the Lansing City Council resolution of January.

The former assistant secretary of defense's first move was to gather together his troops and spell out his plan. The emphasis must be on educating all parties involved in this contentious issue—politicians, taxpayers, alumni, students, and members of the press—on the Spartan position. And to start the process, he had printed up a glossy document very similar to Arthur Brandon's bulk mailing to Wolverine alumni one year earlier. The throwaway spelled out in an easy-to-read format the case for change. *Michigan State: College or University? 10 Answers to That Question* was purportedly financed and published by students and alumni of the land-grant school. It was sent out to just about anyone of influence in the debate.[21]

The college's public relations department, in large part due to Hannah's insistence, worked overtime while preparing position statements on just about any question that might arise with a name change. Topics included: "The Matter of Infringement;"[22] "Confusion;"[23] "On the Matter of Constitutionality;"[24] and "The Matter of Precedent."[25] The school even went so far as to draft a statement "On the Matter of Costs Involved in the Change of Name."[26] (Based on its assistant comptroller's estimate, taxpayers would be out a grand total of $2,100. The two power plant smoke stacks carrying the letters "M.S.C." would remain unchanged. But should there be a groundswell of interest in modifying the chimneys, donations from alumni and friends could cover that add-on expense.)[27]

An extensive memorandum on the curricular growth of the school, dating back to its founding in 1855, was also drafted and shared with the media. Its point was straightforward: Michigan State had evolved over the past century.[28] A comprehensive list of recent name changes involving other institutions of higher learning—land-grant schools included—was also made available to reporters.[29]

Representatives of the school, board members included, were assigned an eight-page fact sheet on the name change issue to memorize. It was mandatory homework. Every conceivable question was considered—a brief answer followed. Hannah wanted simple, consistent replies from all Spartans at risk for an interview or a legislative subcommittee subpoena.

As coordinator for this offensive on Lansing, President Hannah would do what he did best—lobby state politicians. He penned personal letters to key legislative leaders while pleading the Spartans' cause. "Evidence has accumulated that the limitations imposed by being known throughout the world as a 'college' rather than as a 'university' have placed definite handicaps upon our students and upon the institution itself in its mission to serve all of the people who have so generously supported the College during its 100-year history."[30]

And to buttress his argument, he cited the following examples: graduates of the college were discriminated against in the job market when competing against students owning a university diploma; international students, a growing segment of the graduate school, experienced similar treatment—many foreign countries considered college as a mere extension of high school; faculty recruits, with interest in research, often turned down job offers because of the school's name—lack of affiliation with a 'university' might hinder their ability to gather grants; and graduate school candidates chose to pursue doctorates at other institutions—future employment in academia was tied to their association with those professors maintaining prominent research grants. [31]

The official title also hampered the college's ability to lure dollars from many foundations—bylaws quite often limited gifting to institutions with 'university' designation only. In addition, Hannah noted how the current name impacted the school's accreditation status. Apparently, in years past, the land-grant school's overall score had been reduced by its accrediting agency due to semantics—the distinction between university and college. By convention, certain mandated programs at Michigan State operated out of "departments within the college" rather than specific "schools within a university." The subtlety, in his opinion, unfairly penalized faculty and students of a bona fide university.[32]

Contrary to concerns emanating from Ann Arbor, as spelled out in *Postscripts: Letter to Michigan Alumni*, Hannah argued that changing only

David J. Young

one word in Michigan State's current title would lead to little confusion. He had a reassuring telegram from President Milton Eisenhower of Pennsylvania State University to support that claim.[33] And by maintaining the suffix of its current title, Michigan State would "preserve the (land-grant) traditions which have been developed by this institution through the years."[34]

Finally, the president addressed the constitutionality question—a major concern mentioned in *Postscripts*. It remained within the rights of the legislature, as borne out by constitutional tradition and historic precedence, to change the titles of state-supported institutions without need of a constitutional amendment. Hannah was confident that Attorney General Thomas Kavanaugh would concur. He closed by reminding the reader that "not only the students present and future, the alumni and faculty, but all the people of Michigan will be served by granting now our request" that the school's name "be changed to conform with the status it has long since achieved...."[35] And with public opinion polls overwhelming in favor of Hannah's cause, it was hard for any politician, including those with Wolverine blood, to ignore that appeal for support.

And so, by late February, well into the second week of the yearlong Centennial observance, John Hannah was well prepared to advance the State Board initiative to the legislature in Lansing. All he could do now was await a rebuttal from Ann Arbor.

THE MICHIGAN Board of Regents, in the guise of Harlan Hatcher, responded to the State Board of Agriculture's revised request for a name change within days of the announcement. A letter to Governor Williams and a few prominent state legislative leaders was mailed out; a position paper was included "because of the general confusion [among various constituencies] regarding the serious issues involved in [the] proposal."[36]

The president reminded the politicians that there would be no compromise on the current proposal. "It was and is the opinion of the Regents that any name that has the combination of words *Michigan* and *State* and *University* is an infringement upon the name of the *University*

192

of *Michigan*. Through 118 years in Ann Arbor the name University of Michigan has been built up to have meaning and prestige through its title and its accomplishments. It is not a name to be shared in any way, either by similarity or duplication." [37]

Hatcher then focused on the matter of confusion. Contrary to Michigan State's claim, there were considerable problems encountered by other states permitting like-named institutions to coexist. He cited examples in Ohio, Pennsylvania, Florida, and New York.

The university's position paper closed by reiterating its statement made one year earlier: "If the College wishes to take on a new name not in conflict with that of the University of Michigan, the Regents of the University of Michigan would have no objection."[38]

The position paper was reprinted just in time for the spring edition of *The Michigan Alumnus*;[39] no doubt, it got the dander up of a pack of Wolverine graduates. Surprisingly, the students in Ann Arbor failed to share their ire. It remained an ongoing frustration for the school's leadership.[40] [41]

The Michigan State student body, on the other hand, embraced the cause. In early March, class representatives delivered to the Capitol a petition with 15,000 signatures supporting the proposal. And alumni did their part to badger state government leaders.[42] Many Spartan graduates attended open hearings in legislative chambers. Thousands of others wrote letters to their representatives and senators.[43] [44]

By now, just about everyone in the state took a side in the name change controversy. In the interest of averting civil war, the Council of State College Presidents proposed that a joint committee of the Board of Regents and the State Board of Agriculture meet to arrive at some compromise on "a name or names for Michigan State College that will not be in conflict with the University's and will be acceptable to both institutions."[45] [46]

That meeting finally took place in mid-March at the Olds Hotel in downtown Lansing "in an atmosphere of cordiality and good will." [47] It accomplished nothing. Name confusion remained the major concern of the Wolverine contingency. The Spartan three "stated repeatedly the opinion of the [State] Board that this point has been magnified beyond all reasonable proportions and should not be permitted to becloud the real issue at stake."[48] The frustrated three delegates from Ann Arbor, in a gesture of goodwill (and perhaps an attempt at manipulating the media), offered their board's assistance in choosing an alternative, mutually acceptable name for Michigan State. The college emissaries acknowledged the offer; they would take it under advisement.

The respective representatives of the Regents and State Board "expressed their hope that a decision on this proposal will be reached in an atmosphere of reasonableness and fairness, and all deplore such elements of heated controversy and unseemly comments which have been permitted to intrude into the matter." [49] The six shook hands and departed the demilitarized zone.

The following day, the three Spartan board representatives met with their colleagues and President Hannah. After summarizing the course of events during the somewhat contentious meeting, it was their "unanimous opinion that the Board should reaffirm its stand with respect to the proposed revision in the name of Michigan State College." But in the interest of a lasting peace (and their own attempt at controlling the media), they recommended that their resolution from one month earlier be tweaked just a little. "Resolved that the State Board of Agriculture affirms and endorses its action of February 18, 1955, stating that it would welcome revision of the name of Michigan State College of Agriculture and Applied Science to Michigan State University of Agriculture and Applied Science." The revision further requested "expeditious enactment of House Bill 156 now before the Legislature be encouraged by all practical means." [50]

In other words, it was up to the University of Michigan to arrive at a name that would meet the Spartans' specifications. Lacking a suitable alternative, the college leadership would continue to lobby for passage of the current legislation.

The three Michigan regents reported back to their board as well. Mindful of Michigan State's intransigence—diplomatically spelled out in the latest proposal from the State Board—the regents passed their own resolution. In effect, they encouraged all loyal Wolverines to inundate the Lansing post office with letters to the governor and all state legislators expressing opposition to the name change bill.[51] Peace was not at hand!

Edward Kuich, the ardent—if not overzealous—Wolverine from Menominee, who had communicated with Governor Williams one year earlier, was quick to respond. His latest letter, like his previous one, spewed vitriol towards anything Green and White.

> The proponents of this bill feel the name of the College should be changed because...their degrees lack prestige, and they are unable to attract competent instructors. If my name was Hannah I would be utterly humiliated to admit these truths in the year of the school's 100th anniversary.[52]

And Eugene Mossner, the Wayne University law student who had typed a note to the governor one year earlier, likewise responded to the urgent request from Ann Arbor. But his letter was much more conciliatory (if not ingratiating).

> Let me say that my opposition to the name-change (sic) does not spring from animosity towards Michigan State College. It is one of the finest institutions of learning in the nation, in my opinion, and does deserve University status. But I am sure you will agree that other "University" names might be found than the one which (sic) is presently proposed in the bill....[53]

Twelve months ago, Mossner was hung up on semantics—the meaning of "college" and "university."[54] In the interim, he must have taken a required course in state government. The second year law student was now focused on the legislative process—how a bill ends up on the chief executive's desk. And in his opinion, despite acknowledging that the land-grant college was a valid university, the governor should still exercise his veto privilege. There must be no compromise on Michigan State borrowing from the university's time-honored name and reputation.[55]

BY LATE March, the legislators were pretty disgusted with antics on both sides of this divisive issue—mature adults behaving like children fighting in a sandbox.[56] [57] They were also sick and tired of getting all those letters from impassioned Spartans and Wolverines.[58]

Regardless of the statewide emotionalism tied to House Bill 156, Hannah's offensive scheme, based on his personal tally of House and Senate members' leanings, appeared to be working.[59] Following the meeting of board representatives from both schools at the Hotel Olds a few days earlier, the House Judiciary Subcommittee granted the presidents an opportunity to plead their case before a vote to send it to the floor. John Hannah was away in Alaska. Board member Frederick Mueller, a prominent Grand Rapids businessman, was asked to speak on his behalf. Harlan Hatcher would represent the University of Michigan.

Fritz Mueller was first up. The Aggie began his presentation by closely following John Hannah's script. But after a few minutes, he tossed aside his prepared statement and began speaking off the cuff. The wealthy Republican, owner of a very successful furniture manufacturing company he inherited from his father, assumed a populist's demeanor while alluding to the mission of land-grant schools. This debate wasn't about names, confusion, or constitutional infringement. This was all about conceit—shall we say arrogance? The University of Michigan, he charged, was an elitist institution. It trained the privileged few. Michigan State, on the other hand, was founded to serve the sons and daughters of common folk—farmers, laborers, teachers, factory engineers, bookkeepers, and small business owners. And it did so very well. Transitioning to the title "university" could only benefit those humble, hard-working kids looking for a break in life. Diplomas from a college didn't have quite the same value in the market place in the post war era.[60] [61]

President Hatcher was next up. He took no time in responding to a man born with a silver spoon in his mouth. While glaring over at Mueller, he raised his voice a few decibels and declared in no uncertain terms that the University of Michigan was also for the common man. "Do not let it get to your head that there is a differentiation in the clientele we serve. They are the people of this State, sir!"[62] His emphasis on "sir", a title traditionally reserved for aristocracy, was no doubt intentional. It appeared that Harlan Henthorne Hatcher could play that populist card too.

Neither side gained any points from the confrontation. It didn't matter. The members of the committee, both Republicans and Democrats, were well aware of current polls. They agreed to send the bill to the floor. The following day the House hastily approved the measure 88-14.[63]

According to legislative protocol, House Bill 156 would now be sent on to the Senate for a final review and vote. Fortunately for Harlan Hatcher and his regents, the Easter break gave the Wolverine contingency an opportunity to regroup and contemplate remaining options.

THE MESSAGE gained from that resounding House vote was loud and clear for the Michigan Board of Regents. In a last ditch effort at stemming the tide, President Hatcher decided to pursue a different tack. Rather than throwing sticks and stones at his adversary through interviews with the press, he would set aside those makeshift sandbox weapons and present his case like a rational, highly educated adult. He planned to pen a letter to the honorable members of the Senate.

Hatcher started out by taking the high road. He expressed great sorrow over "all the sound and fury generated by [the] sponsors [of this legislation], and the corresponding misunderstandings that have been propagated."[64] He avoided the temptation to point a finger at John Hannah.

I have always considered that Michigan State College under its historic name already had university status, and was surprised indeed to find that it was not proud of this great name, but sensitive to it. I felt honored to receive a degree at the Centennial Convention [six weeks ago] bearing [its] name in full, and I paid sincere tribute in friendship to the College on that notable occasion. I meant what I said.

Hatcher then cut to the chase. A few weeks earlier, he and his colleagues sitting on the Michigan Council of State College Presidents "urged the President of Michigan State College...to select a name that would not conflict with or infringe upon that of Michigan's already established and world-recognized state university." Unfortunately, "we were not able to dissuade the Michigan State College representatives from the regrettable course which has been followed."

Acknowledging that no one was going to reference the college "Michigan State University of Agriculture and Applied Science" other than in legal documents, Hatcher proposed that the legislature amend House Bill 156 to "require that any name adopted be actually used by the institution in its publications, letterheads, publicity and official statements." Regardless of John Hannah's very public reassurances, he was certain that in no time flat the school would be referred to as simply "Michigan State University." Hatcher latest ploy was a subtle attempt at handcuffing Hannah and his Spartan followers.

He closed his letter by reminding the senators that Michigan "would not be objecting to this particular name for our sister institution if it were nothing more than a happy birthday gesture in recognition of a centennial." But this proposed legislation was much more that that. "I pray that you, who love both institutions and have equal responsibility to both, will weigh earnestly the issues as set forth herein."

The attachment was nothing new—merely a restatement of the university's reasons for opposing the bill. But to demonstrate the regents' willingness to compromise, Hatcher did reference an offer they had made a few weeks earlier: a list of alternative names Wolverines could live with. Great Lakes University, Michigan Agricultural University, Michigan

State Central University, Michigan State Agricultural and Scientific University, Lansing State University, Michigan Lansing University, Michigan-Morrill State University, Michigan Northwest University, and Midwest State University were mentioned. The State Board was apparently unimpressed. The names were just as awkward as the current one.

Needless to say, Harlan Hatcher was well aware that this was a futile effort. It appeared too little too late for the University of Michigan—unless, of course, another miscue, similar to the Brody Fumble of '54, was discovered. Unfortunately for the Wolverine president, there were no Michigan Moles working in John Hannah's office back in December of 1951.

PERRY D. Chatterton grew up in Gladwin, Michigan. He later graduated from the County Normal School. The associate degree in teaching allowed him to work at a rural public grade school while continuing his undergraduate studies at Ferris Institute and later Central State Teachers College in Mount Pleasant. He would eventually earn master's in education from Michigan State College of Agriculture and Applied Science.

Chatterton moved to the greater Detroit area where he held various administrative positions within the Fitzgerald School System, ultimately serving as assistant superintendent. In recognition of his dedicated years of service to the district serving both Warren and VanDyke, Chatterton Middle School was named in his honor following his untimely death in August of 1963.[65]

In early December of 1951, President John Hannah received a letter postmarked Warren Township. High School Principal Perry Chatterton was impressed with Hannah's accomplishments in transitioning the college during the early post war years. Students were much better prepared for a changing world. He was quite excited about what the future held for Michigan State. Acknowledging Hannah's vision, he felt it critical that the school now embrace university status by including that designation within its official name.[66]

President Hannah replied a few days later. He thanked the Spartan graduate for sharing his thoughts and recommendations.

> Michigan State is, of course, a university, in the technical sense of the term, and has been for many, many years. It is recognized as such by other educational institutions and accrediting agencies, but the general public may have some misunderstanding of the point. On several occasions members of the Legislature have proposed the introduction of bills to change the name of the college to Michigan State University, but they have never been encouraged to do so [by me] for a couple of reasons: one is that it might lead to even more confusion to have two large state-supported institutions with similar names; the other is that the phrase "state college" has some traditional standing among the land-grant colleges. No doubt, in time, the word "university" will be added to the name of Michigan State, but I do not feel that it would be a good idea for the change to be promoted actively by officials of M.S.C.[67]

Hannah's surprising response to Chatterton could have set himself up as cannon fodder had Harlan Hatcher been aware of those comments four years later. At the very least, the Wolverine leader might have raised the credibility question. Were President Hannah's oft-repeated reassurances that the school would honor the proposed, somewhat awkward formal name sincere? Or would the suffix be ignored in favor of the truncated "Michigan State University"?

Fortunately for the State Board of Agriculture and Michigan State, the Chatterton communication, long since forgotten by John Hannah, was never discovered. The letters remained haphazardly buried with other unrelated documents in a closet adjacent to the president's office. Years later, following Hannah's retirement from the university, they would be discovered by college archivists and appropriately filed away in Box 61, folder 18 located in the basement of Conrad Hall.

AS PREDICTED by political pundits, the Michigan Senate overwhelmingly approved House Bill 156 shortly following Easter recess. The final tally was 23-2. It was only a matter of time before Governor G. Mennen Williams would sign the legislation into law. The regents' one remaining option was a lawsuit—challenge the legislature's right to change the name of Michigan State.

Anticipating this potential court action, members of the Senate Judiciary Committee had requested an official opinion from the Attorney General's office a few weeks earlier. Availing himself of what he thought was "an impartial, disinterested" legal staff,[68] Thomas Kavanaugh was able to complete the assignment just prior to the Easter break. And his conclusion, as Dean Stason had feared, was contrary to the confidential opinion the law professor had received from those embedded Wolverines now working for Kavanaugh. The state's chief legal officer found no "constitutional prohibition to the change in name proposal."[69] It was a reassuring opinion for Senate leaders on both sides of the aisle. After all, everyone at the Capitol wanted an end to this civil war, and the sooner, the better.

Regardless of a rumored lawsuit following the decisive Senate vote, Soapy Williams did the politically expedient thing and had his lieutenant governor, Philip Hart, sign the bill. (Williams was out of state on official business at the time.) In a prepared statement, the governor noted "the legislature certainly in its wisdom should have the discretion of changing the name from Michigan State College to Michigan State University."[70] In trying to bury this divisive issue once and for all, the popular state leader was undoubtedly sending a message to Ann Arbor.

The Michigan Regents, as expected, respectfully disagreed with both the attorney general and the governor. Harlan Hatcher was now instructed to explore legal recourse. The beleaguered president once again turned to his right-hand counselor—Dean Blythe Stason. Based on the legal scholar's recommendations, Michigan law school graduate and private attorney Thomas G. Long was retained by the university. He was instructed to begin drafting a Bill of Complaint should the Board of Regents decide to press forward with a suit in the near future.[71]

A few weeks later, after reflecting on "the subject of impending litigation," Stason appeared to have had a change of heart. The law professor now questioned the wisdom of suing a sister public institution—it might not be in the long-term best interests of the university. He shared his thoughts with President Hatcher.

> Speaking technically, I believe there is a better than fifty-fifty chance of convincing the court that the words "Michigan State University" would infringe unlawfully upon the name "University of Michigan." Perhaps there is a two-to-one chance of prevailing. However, we must be conscious of the fact that should the suit succeed, it would merely precipitate a request for a constitutional amendment to authorize the use of the name [in question]. Under the circumstances the Legislature would undoubtedly submit such a proposal to the electors, and it would [no doubt] receive a favorable majority at the polls.
>
> In short, we are confronted with the situation where we may win the battle but lose the war; and if the Regents should decide after weighing the pros and cons that the wiser course is to refrain from taking legal action, I would feel that they would be taking the proper action under the circumstances.[72]

Stason wasn't the only one advising the president on this delicate political dilemma. Vice President Marvin Niehuss, the man charged with coordinating the Wolverine Strategy since January, was in touch with several key legislative leaders in Lansing, many with Michigan pedigrees. The consensus was that it would not serve the university well by suing the college. "[Rather,] we should be good sports now that the matter has been settled."[73]

And with that wise recommendation in mind, gained from a legal scholar and a few savvy state politicians, Harlan Hatcher and his regents conceded defeat. The civil war was finally over.

SHORTLY AFTER the legislative victory, President John Hannah received a letter from his old buddy up in Minneapolis. Lew Morrill extended his congratulations for another victory over the Wolverines—this one unrelated to gridiron play. "Not only as an honorary alumnus, but for all the other reasons you so well understand, it gives me great happiness to send you this letter as the head of the 'Michigan State University.'"[74] Morrill failed to use the legally correct, suffixed name. It was not an oversight. Mindful of undue concern in Ann Arbor over name confusion, the old Buckeye took great delight in poking fun at Michigan and Harlan Hatcher in particular. After all, Morrill knew darn well that sooner or later everyone would be adopting his abbreviation.

Hannah replied to his colleague a few days later. While expressing appreciation for the recent letter, he noted, "there are many interesting facets to the story that I shall be glad to tell you about on some future date."[75] The two university leaders owned cottages in northern Michigan within a short drive of each other. No doubt Morrill was eagerly looking forward to that conversation on Hannah's porch, rum and Coke in hand, while overlooking a July sunset on Lake Michigan.

House Bill 156 would officially become law on July 1, 1955. Two months earlier, just a few weeks in advance of graduation ceremonies, the Michigan State senior class was given the opportunity to vote on how they might like their diplomas issued. The first option: receive a sheepskin at commencement with the current name "Michigan State College of Agriculture and Applied Science" printed at the top. The second option: defer receipt of a diploma for two weeks; the tardy document would be dated July 1 and issued with the school's new name, "Michigan State University of Agriculture and Applied Science," in bold classic Old English font.[76] A few weeks later, the tally was completed—the students almost unanimously favored the second option, "incorporating the name Michigan State University."[77] And in citing that decision in the official minutes for May 20, 1955, the State Board secretary inadvertently used the objectionable abbreviation. It appeared that Lew Morrill wasn't the only one ignoring the suffix. Fortunately for John Hannah, the Freedom of Information Act didn't become the law of the land until 1974.[78] In the meantime, the board minutes remained confidential, well out of reach of Wolverine skeptics, including Harlan Hatcher.

At the same convocation that the senior Class of 1955 would receive handshakes—and no diploma—from State Board Chairman Clark Brody and President John Hannah, Michigan State would also recognize for the second time in three years a distinguished alumnus. Howard Remus Smith, the proud 1895 graduate of The State Agricultural College, would now receive the Centennial Award.[79] Unlike the students, however, he chose to accept his certificate that very same day, imprinted with the current legal name, "Michigan State College of Agriculture and Applied Science." Following Hannah's ceremonial reading of the award, Brody, in his official capacity as chairman, congratulated the old Aggie while presenting him with the honorary document. But unlike one year earlier, there was no fumble during this hand-off!

IN SEPTEMBER of 1961, delegates about the state of Michigan convened in Lansing to begin rewriting the 1908 constitution. The document was adopted April 1, 1963. One noteworthy change involved the governance of all publically supported institutions. The voting public would now elect trustees for the major tax-supported schools. As a consequence, the State Board of Agriculture would no longer oversee the operations of Michigan State University of Agriculture and Applied Science. Acknowledging this change in governance, the constitutional convention decided there was no longer reason to maintain the suffix. On January 1, 1964 it became official state law. John Hannah's alma mater would once and for all be referenced as Michigan State University. Assistant Superintendent Perry D. Chatterton, the Spartan graduate school alumnus from Warren, Michigan and the Fitzgerald School District, would have been proud—unfortunately, he passed away five months prior to the announcement.[80]

Regardless of the latest (and hopefully final) name change, the fifth time in 110 years of existence, President Hannah was correct in his repeated assertions throughout the name change skirmish. Whether designated a "college" or "university," he was confident that the institution would always be referred to as simply Michigan State.[81] [82] Five decades later, signage adjacent to every campus entrance supports his assertion. "University" appears in smaller font below the bold vernacular.

SHORTLY AFTER having his lieutenant governor sign the peace treaty ending the intrastate civil war, Governor G. Mennen Williams issued a statement. As head of state, he wanted to promote the healing of some festering wounds sustained in various battles over the past year. "The state of Michigan is certainly big enough for two state-supported universities. We always have been proud of the... schools in Ann Arbor and East Lansing. We are sure that Michigan will receive continued service and increasing reputation from the good works of both institutions."[83] The governor proved prescient. Today, the people of Michigan remain proud owners of two pre-eminent universities, each with distinctly different missions in service to the state, the country, and the world.

Hail to the Victors—both Michigan and Michigan State!

Hannah v. Aigler: Case Law for a Rivalry

———

"The Hannah Committee...is in my opinion somewhat of a
joke. I suspect there are few institutions in the country that
carry on their athletic activities more callously than does
Michigan State, and President Hannah is the key to it all."

PROFESSOR RALPH W. AIGLER; 28 NOVEMBER 1951[1]

THE SUNDAY AFTERNOON FOOTBALL GAME in late November of 1921 involved makeshift teams from two neighboring towns in central Illinois.
It was not an unusual practice. Many communities about the Midwest
offered similar weekend entertainment—radio and television were dis-
tant dreams for a society in transition back in the early 1920s. But what
made this game different were the gridiron participants and the money,
a lot of it.

Taylorville had hosted Carlinville one year earlier. Small bets were
gathered that day—a common practice back then. The home team won,
10-7. Following the game, the disgruntled losers, financially poorer for
the experience, "loudly boasted" to anyone within earshot that next
year's outcome would be different. And to ensure that promise, a few
Carlinville residents quietly made "overtures" to certain members of a

prominent, very successful college football team located in northern Indiana. The ten athletes would each receive $200 (equivalent to $2,600 in 2014)[2] plus travel expenses to represent the community in the annual grudge match.[3]

Excited about their secret ploy to buy the outcome and, no doubt, make a few bucks on the side, "the persons who arranged the [plan] passed the word [on] to their friends to bet the limit [on the upcoming game being held in town]. These friends went to the bank, the family stocking, and the cupboard to bring forth, in some cases, the savings of years." Almost $50,000 was eventually wagered on the outcome by local town folk. Unfortunately for the original schemers, "each person who received the 'confidential' information apparently passed it on to another friend...." And before long, "the word spread through Macoupin and Montgomery counties," eventually ending up in their rivals' camp about 30 miles down the road.[4]

"Consternation, [as might be expected], spread through Taylorville at the idea of sending their team [of townies] against nationally known college players." A few community leaders decided to "fight fire with fire" and hired their own players from another collegiate powerhouse located about an hour away in Urbana. "Quietly the word was passed around [town] not to fear Carlinville—that a means of defeating their rivals' plans had been found." Needless to say, that community also went to the bank on that promise.[5]

Tickets were acquired and a few thousand people from both towns showed up to root on their favorite team. Final bets were collected before kickoff. Almost $100,000, equivalent to over $1.3 million today,[6] was wagered on the outcome.

The Taylorville-Carlinville story made national headlines. The late November scandal wasn't about scalpers selling tickets, venders pushing beer sales, or townies making wagers. Rather, it was all about the moonlighters—a handful of young men from two prominent football programs, Notre Dame and Illinois, competing in a semi-professional contest.[7] The practice was a violation of the recently revised amateur code of ethics—a promise all college athletes made to ensure fair competitive play between schools.

A few weeks later, a Milwaukee newspaper reported a similar escapade. A small group of Fighting Irish athletes were caught representing a local semi-professional club competing against a team from Racine, Wisconsin.[8]

The Big Ten responded swiftly to the threat—a professional creep into the intercollegiate game. Athletic directors promised to monitor student practices in the off-season.[9] Young men would now be obligated to sign a statement at the beginning of each season professing adherence to conference rules on pay-for-play, rules consistent with the 1916 code.[10] The penalty was harsh—ineligibility for the remainder of one's collegiate career.

After receiving word of the mortal sins committed by Notre Dame student's in violation of NCAA catechism, the Holy Cross priests conducted an investigation far removed from confessional boxes inside Sacred Heart Basilica. After meeting with the faculty oversight board, the sinners were given a harsh penance: irrevocable "suspension from future participation" in college athletics. Previously earned monograms were also "withdrawn."[11]

Professor George Shuster, secretary of the Notre Dame Faculty Board in Control, felt compelled to notify Michigan's faculty representative Ralph Aigler. The gesture, at the very least, acknowledged the expanded role the young law professor had already assumed within the Western Conference, and in only four years on the job. A few weeks later, Aigler responded on behalf of his Big Ten colleagues. He applauded the decisive action by the small Catholic school and encouraged ongoing administrative surveillance if this "grave menace" to the college game was to be defeated.[12]

And with that response, Ralph Aigler discovered his cause célèbre, far removed from the lecture hall, for the remainder of his career. The current transgressions by students, in the context of Michigan's recent Detroit Alumni Club booster scandal, [13] had convinced him that something must be done to address the allure of money in certain college sports. Within a few years, his office in the Law Quadrangle would become a bully pulpit for sermons on pure amateur play. His legal background, proficiency in debate, and long tenure as a representative no doubt aided that rise to power and influence in intercollegiate circles.[14]

While Professor Aigler was developing a national reputation in the aftermath of the Taylorville-Carlinville scandal, a former student of his was advancing in rank at a land-grant agricultural college located in East Lansing. By the early 1940s, John Hannah would assume a position of influence among institutions of higher learning as well—but as president of Michigan State College. In short order, he too would become a national figure in that debate regarding the definition of an amateur student athlete. And contrary to Aigler's fundamentalist reading of NCAA doctrine, Hannah would interpret those same words quite differently—all based on his concept of justice and fairness.

THE TRANSITION of the long-running Wolverine-Spartan series to rivalry had its origins with some decisions made by the State Board of Agriculture in November of 1926.[15] [16] Prompted by frustrated Aggie alumni tired with a losing football tradition, the administration adopted a few policies intended to mollify the grumbling graduates—and maybe bring a little money back to campus in the process. The Athletic Council was revamped; the faculty leadership was relegated to minority voting status; student and alumni representatives were added to the current mix.[17] And within a couple of years, a young, energetic head coach with a Rockne pedigree was hired to turn around the program in East Lansing. In short order, Jim Crowley proved to be a winner.

The intrastate series originated back in 1898 merely to appease some state politicians and their constituencies. There were very few reasons otherwise for the University of Michigan to contract with The State Agricultural College. And in later years, dismal gridiron performances by the Aggies failed to justify the dominant Wolverines' continuing the series. But by the early 1920s, with the advent of ticket sales, dollars could now be added to that short list of reasons for contracting with the hapless competitors from East Lansing. Michigan Agricultural College, after all, generated some pretty decent crowds at Ferry Field. The only stipulation imposed on the wannabes was that the annual contest be held in Ann Arbor and always the Saturday before the start of the Big Ten season, the Scrimmage Game weekend.

Faculty Representative Ralph Aigler's interest in the Aggies/ Spartans was marginal at best prior to 1929. The football program had a reputation for ruff play on the field—desperate tactics at trying to gain an occasional victory over the traditionally successful Wolverines.[18] But beyond that, he had little concern over contracts with the land-grant college.

That would all change after Coach Crowley's first year in East Lansing. The rumors were disturbing. Something was not right over at Michigan State. Aigler suspected lax leadership within the college administration. Early on, he would avail himself of a few loyal Wolverines living near the campus to stay updated on Crowley's shenanigans. But by the time John Hannah assumed the presidency of Michigan State, the law professor no longer needed espionage to monitor what was going on 60 miles away. The new president was quite open about his desire to use Jenison Awards to attract talented young football players to East Lansing—financial aid contrary to Big Ten and NCAA policies.

Ralph Aigler's obsession with righting an inherently unfair subsidy practice would play a major role in transitioning an irrelevant series, at least for most Michigan Wolverines, into a genuine rivalry—one that, unlike Ohio State's, would eventually include a trophy. But it was John Hannah's obsession with righting an inherently unfair scheduling arrangement that would ultimately cinch rivalry status for the long-running series. And the surest way to achieve that more equitable contractual understanding, at least in his opinion, was to make the Michigan game one of significance for both schools. Hannah would provide his coaching staff with additional Jenison dollars to acquire the skill set needed to field formidable teams. To further entice Fritz Crisler, however, he planned to expand Macklin Field to accommodate 52,000 paying customers. With a little additional political pressure from Lansing, there was no way the Michigan athletic director could turn down a Spartan offer to occasionally host a game in East Lansing and on a weekend later in the season.

Despite their differing stance on financial aid for student athletes, the gist of their strained if not contentious relationship over the years, Ralph Aigler and John Hannah were surprisingly of similar stock. Both men were raised in the Judeo-Christian tradition. Their fathers were affiliated with agriculture—they shared a common Protestant work ethic. The future academic leaders, both exceptional students, graduated from college but never pursued advanced degrees.[19] They were gifted and persuasive speakers; were committed to public service; and were devoted family men. They were also dyed-in-the-wool Republicans. Despite their conservative political leanings, the two men were ahead of time on questions of ethnic diversity and religious tolerance.[20] If they differed, it was in how each man would confront the simmering civil rights issue. Hannah, as his record demonstrated, favored expeditious action to right any inherent wrong for minorities on his campus.[21] Aigler, on the other hand, seemed to favor a slow, methodical approach, while utilizing the legislature and the courts, to advance civil rights.[22]

Adding to that list of similarities, neither man was an athlete in his youth, despite playing major roles in intercollegiate athletic policy years later. In fact, both had little interest in sports, even during their collegiate years. Yet following graduation, they became enthusiastic and loyal fans of their college teams. And in time, each man would profoundly influence the athletic tradition of his alma mater.

John Alfred Hannah's legacy to Michigan State University athletics lay in his quixotic obsession with gaining membership in the Big Ten. That affiliation not only improved Spartan competitive performance in football and other team sports, it also garnered the national spotlight he needed to transition the school into a major academic research institution, a far nobler endeavor.

Ralph William Aigler's legacy to University of Michigan athletics was equally significant. No doubt, his greatest achievement was leading the wandering Wolverines back into the Big Ten. Hiring Fritz Crisler to resurrect Michigan Football after the dark, scandalous years of the 1930s was almost as significant. And his promotion of the Ohio State rivalry requires no hyperbole.

In hindsight, and somewhat ironically, Aigler appeared to have also played a prominent role in the story of Spartan athletics. The competitive intercollegiate relationship between Michigan and Michigan State has been unique for many reasons. But now, historical intrigue can be added to that list. Aigler's covert ploy to purposely impede Hannah's quest for membership in the conference; his confidential role in offering advice and legal counsel to the commissioner during the Spartan Foundation investigation; his behind-the-scenes involvement in the Paul Bunyan Trophy escapade; and his bit (yet significant) part in the Brody Fumble miscue during the name change controversy demonstrate that point. Without Ralph William Aigler, the Spartan-Wolverine game would be just another annual intrastate contest. Like it or not, his role in transitioning this series to rivalry status must be added to his amazing legacy!

DURING ITS December 1953 meeting, the University Faculty Senate unanimously voted to reappoint Professor Ralph Aigler as its representative to the Intercollegiate Conference.[23] It was the 12th time that he had been selected to serve a three-year term, a tenure that began shortly after Michigan regained faculty control of its athletics and rejoined the Big Ten.

After so many years in office, it must have been difficult for Aigler to accept a term he knew would be truncated due to his mandatory retirement in June of 1955. The Faculty Senate eventually appointed another law professor, Marcus Plant, to serve out the remaining year of his three-year commitment.[24] [25]

Ralph Aigler, without a doubt, was the most powerful leader in the history of the Western Conference, at least when faculty input made a difference. Length of tenure alone might have earned him that distinction. But it was his skill in forensics—power of persuasion in debate—that positioned him well in influencing Big Ten policies and practices. His nine colleagues, other than those few with a legal background, were not quite up to task in challenging him on contentious issues. As a consequence, the faculty leadership eventually adopted Aigler's view of the world—strict constructionism, at least as it applied to the rules of conference play.

But it was his cause célèbre—defending and upholding the amateur code of ethics—that ultimately gained him his national reputation as perhaps the most dominant voice in all of intercollegiate athletics. That passionate conviction, for all intents and purposes, defined his life outside his legal circle. It would also set him up for disappointment, perhaps even despair, as he witnessed the conference and his alma mater gradually embrace the concept of "athletic" scholarships—subsidies he was convinced would one day destroy the amateur game.[26]

Wilfred Smith, the widely respected *Chicago Tribune* sports editor, penned a note to Aigler shortly following his retirement from the university. Mindful of the profound role he had played in the evolution of intercollegiate competition, Smith encouraged the professor to write his memoirs. The suggestion piqued the old Wolverine's curiosity.

Aigler wrote back to Smith expressing interest. Acknowledging that most sports enthusiasts would have little interest in what he might share, he still felt there was reason to put in writing what he had learned during his long tenure in "management and control" of intercollegiate athletics at the local, regional, and national levels. But what really intrigued the educator, even in retirement, was the role he might still play in "bringing about a re-examination of some fundamentals that are now so commonly being ignored."[27] Translated, he longed to jump back into the fray and influence debate on the evolving definition of the amateur athlete.

The book was never written. He probably felt it wouldn't sell many copies, even about Ann Arbor. But Aigler did gather his thoughts for a compendium of articles that appeared in the *Michigan Alumnus* the following year.[28] [29] [30] Although it may have generated little interest at the time, his comments on amateurism, athletics in the context of higher education, and the role of intercollegiate competition at Michigan, still have relevance today as college and conference leaders struggle to redefine the amateur game for the 21st century.

PROFESSOR RALPH Aigler became acquainted with first-year student John Hannah in the fall of 1921.[31] Hannah had transferred from Grand Rapids Community College after fulfilling basic college requirements. He planned to study law at the University of Michigan, a two-year program, with plans to one-day return to West Michigan. Nine months later, Hannah would drop out of school. He was somewhat troubled by the focus of a legal education—an overemphasis on the letter rather than the spirit of the law, especially in the context of "securing" justice for the individual.[32] Limited finances and uncertain job prospects back home may have also contributed to that decision.[33] Regardless, he would transfer to Michigan Agricultural College and study poultry science—a passion since childhood. His professors, Ralph Aigler included, wished the exceptionally bright student well.

Fifteen years later, in November of 1936, the student would unexpectedly cross paths with his professor. John Hannah was now Secretary of Michigan State College, President Robert Shaw's right hand man. The State Board of Agriculture was interested in applying for membership in the Big Ten. An ad hoc committee of three, including Hannah, was charged with exploring that strategic initiative.[34] [35] A few months later, it concluded there was little likelihood for success. The committee was convinced that the University of Michigan, in the guise of one influential law professor named Aigler, was spreading rumors about the college and its athletic operations.[36] There was no other plausible reason for the school's eventual rejection four weeks later. If there was anything gained from that exercise in futility, at least for Secretary Hannah, it was his appreciation of the persuasive power his one-time professor wielded in

Big Ten decisions. Any future applications by the college would need to take into account the prominent role Ralph Aigler played in conference politics.[37]

A few years later, they would finally reacquaint—but only in writing. Professor Aigler was now dean of the Western Conference faculty representatives. He was also a recognized leader in the national Purity Movement that opposed any form of financial aid for non-scholar athletes. John Hannah, on the other hand, had recently been appointed president of Michigan State College. He was only 39 years of age at the time.

Hannah was about to propose to the State Board of Agriculture his plan to subsidize student athletes. Just prior to announcing that proposal to his board, however, he urgently requested a meeting with the influential faculty representative in Ann Arbor.[38] His reason was vague.[39] But to ensure the encounter took place, Hannah reminded the professor that at one time he had been a student of his at the University of Michigan. Aigler was pleasantly surprised. They agreed to meet a few days later.[40][41]

The agenda was brief. Hannah wanted to personally inform Aigler of his subsidy plan to avoid any misunderstanding. He was well aware that the proposal conflicted with the conference leader's strict interpretation of the NCAA amateur code. Debating him would serve no purpose. The visit was merely a courtesy call. The good will engendered, however, might benefit Hannah sometime down the road, especially if the college ever planned another conference application drive.

The meeting never took place. Professor Aigler became seriously ill with a respiratory ailment that required a prolonged hospitalization in Ann Arbor and ultimate recuperation in the Arizona desert.[42] As a consequence, he formed an opinion of the Jenison Awards from other sources, most likely Michigan Moles.

Ralph Aigler and John Hannah would finally shake hands in February of 1946. The meeting was at the college president's prodding. Aigler offered counsel on how to properly tender an application for membership in the Big Nine. He was even willing to provide support for Hannah's cause—but it was conditional. The college had to demonstrate full compliance with the Intercollegiate Conference's handbook.[43] In other words, Hannah must rescind his Jenison Awards.

The two extended greetings again in the spring of 1947. At the time, President Hannah had requested time to meet with Big Nine faculty representatives during their May meeting in Highland Park, Illinois. He wanted to advance an application for membership in the Intercollegiate Conference. Professor Aigler was impressed with his former student's presentation. He handled all questions well, including those involving the controversial Jenison subsidy[44]—a program Hannah was now willing to terminate if it assured him membership. But it wasn't the right time for the faculty leadership to debate a replacement for the University of Chicago; there were more pressing issues to discuss at the moment, most notably a collective response to the forthcoming NCAA Sanity Code.

Ralph Aigler and John Hannah would meet one final time before the professor's retirement in summer of 1955. That encounter was not nearly as cordial as the previous two.

In the fall of 1951, shortly following the demise of the Sanity Code, the influential and highly regarded American Council on Education (ACE), a consortium of academic leaders and think tank representatives, decided to tackle the divisive financial aid question once and for all.[45] [46] It appointed a subcommittee of ten college and university presidents to draft a position paper. And somewhat unexpectedly, at least for Ralph Aigler, one of the leading proponents of grants for non-scholar athletes—John Hannah—was designated its chairman.[47] A few months later, the committee made its recommendations—they came as no surprise to the leader of the old Purity Movement.

The Hannah Committee effectively "open(ed) the door to athletic scholarships" by including vague language allowing financial aid for students that "demonstrated academic ability." In the chairman's respected opinion, that meant a boy was "teachable." There was no need to demonstrate scholarly aptitude. Needless to say, Ralph Aigler blew a fuse.[48]

Recognizing the importance of the Hannah Committee's statement, Aigler requested that the Big Ten leadership meet to discuss the controversial ACE report. He wanted his conference to be on record opposing its recommendation—the affirmation of the athletic scholarship. The Faculty Representatives Committee and the Council of Ten, including President Hannah, met in Chicago in early April of 1952 to address that concern.

Prior to sitting down across from each other, Ralph Aigler and John Hannah shook hands. Protocol demanded as much. They made little eye contact throughout the remainder of the meeting.

Professor Aigler took the offensive and "stated as emphatically as I could our concern and regret that the ACE Executive Committee had approved the Hannah Committee's recommendations..." In effect, it "put a stamp of approval on athletic scholarships."[49]

Hannah was invited to respond. With forensic skills gained from his one year in law school three decades earlier, the student effectively dodged his professor's attempt at debate. Instead, he discussed the politics behind the decision. If his committee was to arrive at any substantive statement, there had to be compromise. Acknowledging the reality of financial aid for non-scholar students, especially as it existed in the Deep South where athletic scholarships were already widely accepted, all the Hannah Committee could do was place restrictions on that practice—an attempt at avoiding an embarrassing marketplace atmosphere in which athletes' services were acquired by the highest bidder.[50] [51] [52] [53]

Regardless of the conference leaderships' decision concerning the ACE recommendations, Ralph Aigler knew the national debate was already past tense. Most schools and conferences about the country would soon embrace the practice, scholarship dollars for non-scholar student athletes. The Big Ten would remain one of the few holdouts—at least as long as he held a seat of influence in the conference. All he really had hoped to achieve from the gathering in Chicago was an opportunity to put the college president, his old adversary, on the spot, to challenge his integrity in front of his many influential friends on the Council of Ten. And that he had accomplished. Hannah's admission substantiated Aigler's long held belief—the Spartan leader had "personally wanted an approval of athletic scholarships" dating back at least a decade.[54]

One year following Professor Aigler's retirement from the University of Michigan, President Hannah asked Spartan Faculty Representative Leslie Scott to propose a more realistic handbook rule that would permit tuition, room and board, and books for the student athlete—a practice firmly in place in just about every major conference by now. He felt the proposal would "eliminate the hypocrisies in the present work programs" which were not only unrealistic but also completely unenforceable.[55] [56] In short order, the Intercollegiate Conference of Faculty Representatives would officially recognize the athletic scholarship. It had no choice if the membership was to remain competitive in contests with non-conference foes.[57]

RALPH AND Eileen Aigler moved to Arizona shortly after he received his last paycheck from the university. Retirement out in the desert was a relative term for the old professor. He still loved teaching and counseling young students; Hastings College of Law and the University of Arizona continued to request his services as a guest lecturer. He also maintained contact with hundreds of former Wolverine students—his wisdom and practical advice was still valued.

But within a few years, Aigler decided to call it quits. The years of service to law students, the University of Michigan, the Board in Control of Intercollegiate Athletics, the Intercollegiate Conference, the Association of American Law Schools, the American Bar Association, and the NCAA had taken a toll. His health was in decline. A little over five decades after graduating from the University of Michigan, he retired from public life while remaining near Tucson.

In May of 1964, Ralph William Aigler passed away following a brief illness. He was 79 years of age.

Five years later, President John Hannah would resign from Michigan State University after almost three decades in office. The challenge of leading a major public institution during the turbulent Viet Nam era had taxed his patience. He was 69 years at the time and had tired of debating radical students and mollifying liberal-leaning professors.[58]

But Hannah, like his one-time law professor, was not quite ready to officially retire. He accepted a position as director of the United States Agency for International Development (USAID). The experience rejuvenated him. After a four-year stint, he assumed leadership of the World Food Council, a new organization affiliated with the United Nations.[59] And as expected, he served with distinction. But the years of service to Michigan poultry farmers, the national Poultry Hatchery Code, the State Board of Agriculture and its college, the Department of Defense, the Civil Rights Commission, the federal government, and the United Nations had taken a toll. Almost six decades after graduating from Michigan Agricultural College, he retired from public life and returned to his small farm near Dansville, Michigan.

In February of 1991, John Alfred Hannah passed away following a protracted illness. He was 88 years of age.

Epilogue:
Employment Contracts

———

> On the surface the conclusion seems inescapable that, if
> the athlete has been the beneficiary of some economic
> advantage based in whole or in part upon his athletic
> ability or service, he no longer comes within the currently
> accepted definition of an amateur, and unless the term is
> redefined, it is intellectually dishonest for the institution
> to treat him as if he were still in that category.
>
> PROFESSOR EMERITUS RALPH W. AIGLER; 25 MAY 1957[1]

ED O'BANNON WAS AN ATHLETE "masquerading" as a student. He attended UCLA for four years but never graduated. "I was there strictly to play
basketball. I did basically the minimum to make sure I kept my eligibility academically so I could continue to play."[2] In 1995, UCLA won the
NCAA men's basketball national championship. O'Bannon was named
MVP. He played almost 10 years at the professional level (NBA, ABA,
and Europe) on a bum knee before retiring from competitive play. He
now works as a marketing director in Las Vegas; he sells used cars.[3]

In July of 2009, Ed O'Bannon, a one-time student-athlete who had
received a full athletic scholarship from one of the country's premier
institutions of higher learning, filed a lawsuit against the NCAA. He

argued that use of his likeness in a video game, sanctioned by that hugely profitable (and thereby powerful) organization, without his permission had deprived him of his right of publicity. In other words, O'Bannon wanted a share in the profits—dollars his alma mater gained from use of his image for commercial purposes.

A few years later, in April of 2014, Northwestern University football players cast votes on whether to unionize. They argued that their athletic scholarships were equivalent to salaries. As full-time employees of the institution, for all intents and purposes, they were due additional benefits including health insurance and disability coverage.

The NCAA, forced to respond to the O'Bannon charge, borrowed from an old definition of amateurism while pleading its case before a federal district judge in California. Its lawyers argued that abandoning that time honored concept "in which players participate for the love of the game [rather than for a share in the profits] would drive spectators away from college sports and would [also] upset the competitive balance among schools and conferences."[4] It proved to be a weak, somewhat hypocritical defense. Intercollegiate competition was originally intended for the students—the well being of the sponsor schools and community spectators was never the founders' intent. But with the advent of ticket sales to accommodate a growing number of alumni and townies eager to watch makeshift weekend entertainment, dollars unexpectedly entered into the mix. Quite suddenly, administrators realized that there was money to be made by supporting a college football program. And with the introduction of NBC's televised "game of the week" four decades later, those sponsoring schools and their contracting agent—the NCAA—would soon be mining gold! The initial contract signed in 1952 was worth $1.144 million in revenue for the organization. Two years later, due to the resounding success of the collaborative venture, the network increased its payout to almost $1.75 million.[5] Today, the NCAA reports annual revenue that exceeds $795 million, most of it derived from television and marketing rights fees.[6]

In early August of 2014, to no one's surprise, Judge Claudia Wilkin ruled in favor of O'Bannon and 19 former athletes who had also filed grievances. She based her decision on antitrust concerns, not an anachronistic definition of amateurism dating back to 1916. "The injunction...allows players at big schools to have money generated by television contracts put into a trust fund to pay [student athletes] when they leave" school after completing their years of competitive eligibility.[7] But in a "partial victory for the NCAA," the federal district judge ruled that it could "set a cap on money paid to athletes, as long as it allows at least $5,000 per athlete per year of competition."[8] And of perhaps greater significance, the court "rejected both the NCAA's definition of amateurism and its justification for not paying players." In effect, Wilken acknowledged the hypocrisy that exists in college athletics—a matter John Hannah, Ralph Aigler, and many other intercollegiate leaders had debated six decades earlier.

In response to the O'Bannon decision, the NCAA agreed to "allow the five wealthiest conferences in the country to set their own rules, paving the way for those 65 schools to potentially offer richer scholarships and health benefits to players."[9] That plan was officially approved by the NCAA membership in January of 2015. Unlike the traditional academic scholarship, the redefined athletic scholarship would now include a salary to cover "transportation and miscellaneous expenses."[10] In addition, the contract with the student would be irrevocable; no longer could a school or coach renege on a promise to educate an athlete due to a career ending injury or a failure to measure up to expectations.[11]

The NCAA decision also appeared to address the Northwestern unionization threat; the membership agreed to permit athletes to borrow against future earnings in order to purchase so-called loss-of-value insurance—products designed to compensate policyholders for injuries incurred during collegiate years that might impact future professional income. And somewhat surprisingly, perhaps in deference to that erstwhile (and honorable) Big Ten tradition of respecting free time for study, the representatives agreed to "rules changes that would eventually regulate time demands on athletes 'to ensure an appropriate balance between athletics participation and academic obligations and opportunities presented to students generally.'"[12]

EVERY STORY requires a protagonist. And in this epic tale about a relationship between two academic giants, both men of highest repute and integrity, John Hannah was cast in the good guy role. He earned it due to his convictions on justice and fairness in the context of financial aid for the needy or deserving college athlete. Unlike Ralph Aigler, who was obsessed with rules, regulations, and an idealistic definition of amateurism, Hannah was concerned about reality—the well being of the student. Participation in a college football program back then demanded at least 30 hours per week of a student athlete's free time, especially during the season. [13] Even with honed time management skills, that student had precious few hours for book study, let alone a part-time job to cover college costs. Hannah's Jenison Awards seemed honorable, especially for a young man contributing to his school's bottom line during Saturday afternoons in the fall.

Ralph Aigler was all about justice and fairness too. And like John Hannah, he was also a realist. But in this long-standing debate on financial aid for athletes, he differed from his one-time law student on three accounts.

The Michigan faculty representative was a staunch adherent of the revised amateur code of 1916. A student athlete enrolled in a college or university for one purpose: to gain an education. Competitive intercollegiate sports were an extracurricular activity intended "only for the pleasure and physical, mental, moral and social benefits directly derived" from student participation.[14] The code emphasized the critical role academic institutions, charged with a higher purpose, played in sponsoring these activities.[15] However, by the late 1920s, the pressure to win, as imposed on administrators by rabid alumni and fans, forced certain academic leaders to turn a blind eye to illegal recruiting and subsidizing practices at many colleges and universities. Michigan State was no exception. The practice was indefensible in the professor's opinion; it compromised institutional integrity; it also tilted the field of play in one direction. And for the impressionable student athlete, a potential leader in industry, government, or society years later, the message was loud and clear—cheating was acceptable.[16]

Putting aside the law professor's issues with institutional integrity and competitive fairness, Aigler was also concerned about the well being of the student—just like John Hannah. After all, that was the founders' reason for having faculty representatives, academicians protected by tenure, oversee the Intercollegiate Conference. But he also understood human nature very well, especially in the context of competitive amateur sport—football in particular at the time. Skilled young athletes, not necessarily prepared to meet the rigors of a college curriculum, were at-risk for being taken advantage of by opportunists, well-paid coaches willing to compromise personal integrity in the pursuit of gridiron victories. Once eligibility was expended, the ill-equipped student often left college with little to show for his commitment other than a few news clippings and a monogram sweater.

And in response to proponents of closely monitored institutional financial aid programs designed to hold in check opportunists, Professor Aigler was quick to point out "the same people who will cheat when [no financial-aid is] permissible will cheat when we allow it to [exist under strict guidelines]."[17] Even if there was a way to effectively control abuse, he was confident that the amateur game he greatly loved would eventually lose out—athletic scholarships, after all, were nothing more than employment contracts. Pay-for-play.

Sixty years later, Professor Aigler proved to be right. The athletic scholarship would ultimately lead to the demise of the amateur game as originally defined by the fledgling Intercollegiate Association of Amateur Athletes of America (later renamed the NCAA). The O'Bannon court decision and the NCAA's response, say as much. College athletes, at least those under contract for non-scholarly attributes, are effectively full-time employees of athletic departments—the entertainment divisions of our great colleges and universities. They are paid to perform—semi-professional athletes for all intents and purposes. Schoolwork is something they do in their limited free time.

It is unfortunate that all stories must also have an antagonist. Ralph William Aigler deserved a fairer shake.

BIBLIOGRAPHY

Behee, John R. *Fielding Yost's Legacy to the University of Michigan.* Ann Arbor: Uhlrich's Books, Incorporated, 1971.

Falla, Jack. *NCAA: The Voice of College Sports–A Diamond Anniversary History 1906- 1981.* Mission, Kansas: National Collegiate Athletic Association, 1981.

Hannah, John A. *A Memoir.* East Lansing: Michigan State University Press, 1980.

Kryk, John. *Natural Enemies: Major College Football's Oldest, Fiercest Rivalry– Michigan vs. Notre Dame.* Lanham, Maryland: Taylor Trade Publishing, 2007.

Kuhn, Madison. *Michigan State: The First One Hundred Years 1855-1955.* East Lansing: Michigan State University Press, 1955.

Lester, Robin. *Stagg's University: The Rise, Decline & Fall of Big-Time Football at Chicago.* Urbana and Chicago: University of Illinois Press, 1999.

Noer, Thomas J. *Soapy: A Biography of G. Mennen Williams.* Ann Arbor: University of Michigan Press, 2005.

Pollard, James E. *Ohio State Athletics: 1879-1959.* Columbus: The Athletic Department of Ohio State University, 1959.

Thomas, David A. *Michigan State College: John Hannah and the Creation of a World University, 1926-1969.* East Lansing: Michigan State University Press, 2008.

Watterson, John Sayle. *College Football: History, Spectacle, Controversy.* Baltimore and London: The Johns Hopkins University Press, 2000.

Widder, Keith R. *Michigan Agricultural College: The Evolution of a Land-Grant Philosophy, 1855-1925.* East Lansing: Michigan State University Press, 2005.

Young, David J. *Arrogance and Scheming in the Big Ten: Michigan State's Quest for Membership and Michigan's Powerful Opposition.* On-line: DJY Publishing, 2011.

E N D N O T E S

Archival documents will be referenced by name, date, institution, title of collection and its code, box number/folder and description while utilizing the following abbreviations:

-ACR1: (Michigan State) Athletic Council Records, UA4.4

-ACR2: (Michigan State) Athletic Council Records, UA4977

-ADUM: Athletic Department (University of Michigan) Records, 943 Bimu 2

-AEDR: Agricultural Economics Department Records, UA16.5

-AGRP: Alexander Grant Ruthven Papers, 86550 AC Aa 2

-BCIA: Board in Control of Intercollegiate Athletics (University of Michigan) Records, 8729
 Bimu F81 2

-BHL: Bentley Historical Library, University of Michigan

-BOT: Michigan State University Board of Trustees, UA1.0

-DICAP: Department of Intercollegiate Athletics Papers (Minnesota)

-GMWP: G. Mennen Williams Papers

-FRC: Faculty Representatives Committee

-HAF: Hannah Administrative Files, UA2.1.12

-HAP: Hannah Archives Project, UA2.1.12.2

-HHHP: Harlan Henthorne Hatcher Papers, 851647 Aa 2

-HOCP: Herbert Orin Crisler Papers, 85823 AC UAm Aa 2

-HP: Hannah Papers, UA2.1.12

-HPP: Hannah Presidential Papers Record, UA2.1.12

-HRSP: Howard Remus Smith Papers 00046

-ICA: (Michigan State) Intercollegiate Athletics, UA4.3

-ICFR: Intercollegiate Conference of Faculty Representatives

-JAHP: John A. Hannah Papers, UA2.1.12

-JAHPR: John A. Hannah Presidential Records, UA2.1.12

-MLNP: Marvin L. Niehuss Papers, Aa 2

-MAQR: Michigan Alumnus Quarterly Review

-MSUA: Michigan State University Archives and Special Collections

-RSP: Robert Shaw Papers, UA2.1.11

-RWAP: Ralph W. Aigler Papers, 87406 Aa 2

-RYP: Ralph Young Papers, UA17.114

-SBA: Minutes of the State Board of Agriculture

-TOSUA: The Ohio State University Archives

-UFAB: The University Faculty Athletic Board (Wisconsin)

-UIA: University of Illinois Archives

-UIA-ICI: University of Iowa Archives-Iowa City, Iowa

-UMA: University of Minnesota Archives

-UNDA: University of Notre Dame Archives

-UPA: University of Pittsburgh Archives

-UWA-M: University of Wisconsin Archives-Madison

-WC: Western Conference

-WIC: Western Intercollegiate Conference

PROLOGUE: THE MYTH

1. *The seven founders of the conference never named the association. Governance was delegated to their respective faculty representatives at the follow-up meeting in February of 1896. Original minutes referenced the "Intercollegiate Conference of Faculty Representatives." By default, this became the official title. Unofficial names included the Conference on Athletics, the Intercollegiate Conference, Big Seven, Big Nine, Big Ten, and Western Conference. In 1987, the presidents dropped the 1896 title in favor of The Big Ten Conference. Various names, consistent with the times, will be used throughout this historical exploration.*

2. Young. pp. 197-201.

3. Bachman, Charles. "The Athletic Side of JAH." Circa 1970. MSUA. HAP; Box 34, folder: 2 Bachman

4. *When Louis Elbel hailed the "champions of the West" in his rousing fight song, The Victors (1898), he was referencing the Western Conference, the popular name for the Big Seven at the time.*

CHAPTER 1: STILL IN CONTROL

1. Small Handbook. 10 Sept. 1908. UMA. DICAP; Box 13, folder: small handbooks 1895-1908, 1930,41

2. Min. of the ICFR. 6 Dec. 1912. UW-M. Pres. Van Hise Papers, Series 4/10/1; Box 36, folder: 549 Ehler, George

3. "Mem. of the Adm. Group." 19 Dec. 1941. MSUA. HPP; Box 63, folder 7: Schol.-Jenison 1942-45

4. "Statement of Floyd W. Reeves." 11 June 1970. MSUA. HAP; Box 34, folder 37, p. 18

5. SBA. 17 Mar. 1932. www.onthebanks.msu.edu

6. *The Intercollegiate Athletic Association of the United States (IAAUS) changed its name to the NCAA six years after it was founded in 1906.*

7. Falla. p. 25

8. Ibid.

9. Hannah, J. "Speech...NCAA." 9 Jan. 1946. BHL HOCP; Box 1, folder: top corr. MSU, clippings/misc.

10. "A Bulletin of Michigan State College," Volume 38, number 13: Mar. 1944. MSUA. JAHPR: Box 63, folder: 6 schol. 1941-55

11. Hannah, J. "Speech...NCAA." 9 Jan. 1946. BHL HOCP; Box 1, folder: top corr. MSU, clippings/misc.

12. Bachman, Charles. "The Athletic Side of JAH." Circa 1970. MSUA. HAP; Box 34, folder: 2 Bachman

13. Aigler to Richart. 21 Dec. 1948. UIA. Series 4/2/12; Box 3, folder: WIC 1948-49

14. Hannah. pp. 15, 124

15. Hannah to Hovde. 17 Sept. 1952. MSUA. JAHP; Box 90, folder: 22 misc. corr. "H"

16. SBA. 17 May 1945. www.onthebanks.msu.edu

17. Aigler to Long. 7 Oct. 1935. BHL. RWAP; Box 12, folder: athletics corr. 1933-36 "L" misc.

18. Rules, Regulations and Opinions of the ICFR-Rev. 1930. UMA. DICAP; Box 13, folder: 1930

19. Aigler to Young. 11 Feb. 1935. BHL. RWAP; Box 7, folder: corr. 1934-39 "X-Y-Z" misc. *Aigler reminded Young of his obligation to comply with the rules of the conference or face possible termination of a Big Ten contract with Michigan.*

20. Min. of the ICFR. 22 May 1937. BHL. ADUM; Box 84, folder: FR min.

21. Huston to Aigler. 4 Dec. 1936. BHL. RWAP; Box 7, folder: corr. 1934-39 NCAA

22. Young to Crisler. 28 Dec. 1942. BHL, HOCP, AC; Box 1, folder: top corr. MSU 1943-46

23. Crisler to Ruthven. 13 Jan. 1943. BHL, HOCP; Box 1, folder: top corr. MSU 1943-46

24. Crisler to Ruthven. 23 Jan. 1943. BHL. AGRP; Box 34, folder: 27

25. Hannah to Ruthven. 18 Mar. 1946. BHL, HOCP; Box 6, folder: BICA 1941-49, undated

26. Ruthven to Aigler. 21 Apr. 1932. BHL. RWAP; Box 4, folder: corr. 1929-33 Ruthven

27. Williams, Brian. "WWII and UM." E-mail to David Young. 22 Sept. 2013. *UM was involved with training 3700 young men in uniform by the end of 1943. JAG, Navy V-12, ASTP, and Army Japanese Language programs were also offered in Ann Arbor to aid the military cause.*

28. Kuhn, Madison. "John A. Hannah." Circa 1971. MSUA. HAP; Box: 34, folder: 27

29. Denison, James H. Untitled. 24 Jun. 1970. MSUA. HAP; Box: 34, folder: 8

30. Kelly to Cavanaugh. 25 Sept. 1946. UNDA, [UPCC 17/4]

31. Ruthven to Hannah. 23 Mar. 1946. BHL, HOCP; Box 1, folder: MSU top corr. 1943-46

32. Aigler to Richart. 14 Dec. 1948. UIA, Series 4/2/12; Box 3, folder: WIC 1948-49

33. Aigler to Richart. 16 May 1946. BHL. RWAP; Box 9, folder: corr. 1946-52 "H" misc.

34. Min. of the Mtg. of the Fac. Comm. on Athl. Policies. 23 May 1946. UPA, collection 9/2, FF1; Box 1

35. Thomas. p. 289

36. SBA. 16 Jan. 1947. www.onthebanks.msu.edu

37. First Session 10:30 Thursday," (Frank Richart personal notes). 29 May 1947. UIA. Series 4/2/12; Box 3, folder: conf. min. 1946-47

38. Joint Meeting. 29-30 May 1947. BHL. ADUM; Box 84, folder: FR min. 1941-1957

39. Hannah to Morrill. 2 June 1948. UMA, Pres. Office; Box 238, folder: PE and Athl. 1948-49

40. Falla. p. 22

41. Ibid. p. 131

42. Aigler to Wilson. 11 June 1946. BHL. RWAP; Box 10, folder: corr. 1946-52 Wilson, K.L.

43. Wilson to Aigler. 9 July 1946. BHL. RWAP; Box 10, folder: corr. 1946-52 Wilson, K.L.

44. Crisler to the President.... Jan. 1947. BHL. BICIA; Box 32, folder: BIC Rec.

45. Commissioner's Report to the Joint Conference. 6 Dec. 1951. BHL ADUM; Box 84; folder: FR Min. 1941-1957. *Prof. Karl Leib of Iowa coined the epithet "Sanity Code" to distinguish it from the earlier Purity Code.*

46. Wilson to FR and AD. Memo. 22 Jan. 1948. BHL. RWAP; Box 10, folder: corr. 1946-52 Wilson, K.L.

47. Aigler to Breneman. 7 July 1947. UIA. Series 4/2/17; Box 3, folder: WIC 1946-47

48. Richart to Breneman. 14 July 1947. UIA. Series 4/2/17; Box 3, folder: WIC 1946-47

49. Min. of the ICFR. 29-31 May 1947. BHL. RWAP; Box 14, folder: athletics 1947 meeting min.

50. Morrill to Rottschaefer.... 17 May 1946. UMA, Pres. Office; Box 238, folder: PE and athl. 1945-47

51. Morrill to Rottschaefer. 9 July 1947. UMA, Pres. Office; Box 238, folder: PE and athl. 1948-49

52. Hannah to Morrill. 17 Nov. 1947. UMA, Pres. Office; Box 238, folder: PE and athl. 1948-49

53. Morrill to Rottschaefer. 9 July 1947. UMA, Pres. Office; Box 238, folder: PE and athl. 1948-49

54. Denison, James H. 5 Nov. 1969. "Intercollegiate Conference." MSUA. HP; Box 80, folder: 12

55. Morrill to Rottschaefer. 9 July 1947. UMA, Pres. Office; Box 238, folder: PE and athl. 1948-49

56. Morrill to Rottschaefer. 16 Sept. 1948. UMA, Pres. Office; Box 238, folder: PE and ʌ 1948-49

57. Min. of the IC Mtg. of ADs. 16 May 1948. UWA-M. UFAB, Series 5/21/6; Box 1, folder: WC min. 1947-54

58. Morrill to Rottschaefer. 16 Sept. 1948. UMA, Pres. Office; Box 238, folder: PE and athl. 1948-49

59. Rottschaefer to Richart. 20 May 1948. UIA. Series 4/2/12; Box 3, folder: WIC 1947-48

60. Min. of the ICFR. 16 May 1948. UFAB, Series 5/21/6; Box 1, folder: WC min. 1947-54

61. Min. of the IC Joint Mtg. of the FRs and the ADs. 29 May 1948. BHL. ADUM; Box 84, folder: Big Ten dir. mtg. 3/41-7/52

62. Morrill to Rottschaefer. 16 Sept. 1948. UMA, Pres. Office; Box 238, folder: PE and athl. 1948-49

63. Min. of the ICFR. 27-29 May 1948. UWA-M. UFAB; Series 5/21/6; Box 1, folder: WC min. 1947-51

64. Aigler to Wilson. 19 Apr. 1948. BIIL. RWAP; Box 10, folder: corr. 1946-52 personal

65. Hannah. p. 119

66. Hannah to Morrill. 2 June 1948. UMA, Pres. Office; Box 238, folder: PE and athl. 1948-49

67. Morrill to Hannah. 24 Apr. 1947. UMA, Morrill, J.L.; Box 1, folder: corr, A-L, Ha-He

68. Morrill to Rottschaefer. 16 Sept. 1948. UMA, Pres. Office; Box 238, folder: PE and athl. 1948-49

69. Denison, James H. 5 Nov. 1969. "Intercollegiate Conference." MSUA. HP; Box 80, folder: 12

70. Rottschaefer to Morrill. 26 Feb. 1948. UMA, Pres. Office; Box 238, folder: PE and athl. 1948-49

71. Aigler to Richart. 14 Dec. 1948. UIA. Series 4/2/12; Box 3, folder: WIC 1948-49

71. Ibid.

72. Morrill to Rottschaefer. 16 Sept. 1948. UMA, Pres. Office; Box 238, folder: PE and athl. 1948-49

73. Hannah to Morrill. 15 Dec. 1948. UMA, Pres. Office; Box 238, folder: PE and athl. 1948-49

74. Aigler to Mem. of the Board. 16 Dec. 1948. BHL. RWAP; Box 10, folder: corr. 1946-52 personal

75. Richart to Emmons. 21 Dec. 1948. UIA. Series 4/2/12; Box 3, folder: WIC 1948-49

76. Aigler to Mem. of the Board. 16 Dec. 1948. BHL. RWAP; Box 10, folder: corr. 1946-52 personal

CHAPTER 2: ONLY A MATTER OF TIME

1.   Richart to Aigler. 17 Dec. 1948. UIA. Series 4/2/12; Box 3, folder: WIC 1948-49

2.   NCAA: Bulletin No. 2. 12 July 1948. UWA-M. UFAB, Series 5/21/6; Box 1, folder: WC min. 1947-51

3.   SBA 15 Jan. 1948. www.onthebanks.msu.edu. *Consistent with the recently passed Sanity Code, the Board revised all rules regarding subsidies. A Faculty Committee on Scholarships would dispense all grants. A student had to fulfill a scholastic aptitude benchmark for eligibility. The award would be renamed Michigan State College Scholarships.*

4.   Hannah to Richart. 23 Jan. 1948. UIA, Series 4/2/112; Box 3, folder: WIC 1947-48

5.   Hannah to Aigler. 23 Jan. 1948. BHL. RWAP; Box 9, folder: corr. 1946-52 "H" misc.

6.   Aigler to Hannah. 26 Jan. 1948. BHL. RWAP; Box 9, folder: corr. 1946-52 "H" misc.

7.   Crisler to Little, ... 30 Mar. 1949. BHL. RWAP; Box 9, folder: corr. 1946-52 "E" misc.

8.   Min. of the IC Mtg. of the ADs and Head Football Coaches. 13 Dec. 1949. BHL. ADUM; Box 84, folder: Big 10 records 1941-52

9.   Little to Blommers,..... 23 Apr. 1949. UWA-M. UFAB, Series 5/21/7; Box 1, folder: WC files

10. Richart to Aigler. 17 Dec. 1948. UIA. Series 4/2/12; Box 3, folder: WIC 1948-49

11. Min. of the ICFR. 19-20 May 1949. BHL. ADUM; Box 84, folder: FR min. 1941-57

12. Little to Hannah. 27 May 1949. UWA-M. UFAB, Series 5/21/7; Box 1, folder: WC files

13. Rules... of the ICFR-Rev. 1930. UMA. Intercollegiate Athletic Papers; Box 13, folder: IC min.

14. Aigler to Spoelstra. 27 Apr. 1949. BHL. RWAP; Box 10, folder: corr. 1946-52 "B" misc.

15. Spoelstra to Aigler. 14 Apr. 1948. BHL. RWAP; Box 10, folder: corr. 1946-52 "B" misc.

16. Spoelstra to Aigler. 2 June 1949. BHL. RWAP; Box 10, folder: corr. 1946-52 "B" misc.

17. Aigler to Richart. 21 Dec. 1948. UIA. Series 4/212; Box 3, folder: WIC 1948-49

18. Thomas. p. 11

19. Denison, James. 24 June 1970. Untitled. MSUA. HAP; Box 34, folder: 8

20. Hurst to Hannah. 4 Dec. 1961 (received Nov. 9, 1961). MSUA. JAHR; Box 57, folder: 44

21. Hannah to Hurst. 10 Nov. 1961. MSUP. JAHR; Box 57, folder: 44

22. Hannah to Fitzgerald. 13 Nov. 1961. MSUA. JAHR; Box 57, folder: 44

23. Aigler to Griffith. 14 Dec. 1929. BHL. RWAP; Box 3, folder: corr. Griffith 1930

24. Griffith to Works. 3 Mar. 1936. BHL. RWAP; Box 6, folder: corr. 1934-39

25. Aigler to Ruthven. 10 Dec. 1937. BHL. RWAP; Box 7, folder: corr. 1934-39 Ruthven

26. Aigler to Spoelstra. 27 May 1949. BHL. RWAP; Box 10, folder: corr. 1946-52 "E" misc.

27. Aigler to Salsinger. 12 Feb. 1943. BHL. RWAP; Box 8, folder: corr. 1940-45 "S" misc.

28. Lynah to Aigler. 1 Oct. 1951. BHL. RWAP; Box 10, folder: corr. 1946-52 "L" misc.

29. Falla. p. 134

30. Watterson. pp. 214-218

31. Lynah to Aigler. 1 Oct. 1951. BHL. RWAP; Box 10, folder: corr. 1946-52 "L" misc.

32. Griffith to St. John. 11 Sept. 1941. TOSUA, DA (RG 9/e-1/9), "IC: Comm.: Corr. (Griffith): 1941-42 (Folder 2/2)."

33. Griffith to St. John. 17 Feb. 1943. TOSUA, DA (RG 9/e-1/9), "IC: Comm.: Corr. (Griffith): 1942-43 (Folder 2/2)."

34. Griffith to St. John. 7 December 1943. TOSUA, DA (RG 9/e-1/9), "IC: Comm.: Corr. (Griffith and St. John): 1940-46."

35. Richart to Pollard. 11 Mar. 1949. UIA. Series 4/2/12; Box 3, folder: WIC 1948-49.

36. Hannah, J. "Speech...NCAA." 9 Jan. 1946. BHL. HOCP; Box 1, folder: top corr. MSU clippings/misc..

37. Aigler to Spoelstra. 27 May 1949. BHL. RWAP; Box 10, folder: corr. 1946-52 "E" misc.

38. Spoelstra to Aigler. 2 June 1949. BHL. RWAP; Box 10, folder: corr. 1946-52 "B" misc.

39. Wilson to Little. 19 Apr. 1949. UWA-M. UFAB, Series 5/21/7; Box 1, folder: WC Gen. files

40. Aigler to Wilson, ... 25 Mar. 1949. UWA-M. UFAB, Series 5/21/7; Box 1, folder: WC Gen. files

41. Aigler to Richart. 21 Dec. 1948. UIA. Series 4/2/12; Box 3, folder: WIC 1948-49

42. Aigler to Richart. 14 Dec. 1948. UIA. Series 4/2/12; Box 3, folder: WIC 1948-49

43. Aigler to Wilson, ... 25 Mar. 1949. UWA-M. UFAB, Series 5/21/7; Box 1, folder: WC Gen. files

44. Aigler to Richart. 21 Dec. 1948. UIA 4/2/12; Box 3, folder: WIC 1948-49

45. Aigler to Richart. 14 Dec. 1948. UIA. Series 4/2/12; Box 3, folder: WIC 1948-49

46. Aigler to Wilson, ... 28 Jan. 1949. UWA-M. UFAB, Series 5/21/7; Box 1, folder: WC Gen. files

47. Aigler to Wilson. 31 Jan. 1949. BHL. RWAP Box 10, folder: corr. 1946-52 Wilson, K.L. 2/2

48. Aigler to Richart. 21 Dec. 1948. UIA. Series 4/2/12; Box 3, folder: WIC 1948-49

49. Aigler to Reed. 5 May 1952. BHL. RWAP; Box 10, folder: corr. 1946-52 Reed, William

50. Aigler to Richart. 21 Dec. 1948. UIA. Series 4/2/12; Box 3, folder: WIC 1948-49

51. Aigler to Wilson, ... 28 Jan. 1949. UWA-M. UFAB, Series 5/21/7; Box 1, folder: WC Gen. files

52. Aigler to Reed. 19 May 1952. BHL. RWAP; Box 10, folder: corr. 1946-52 Reed, William

CHAPTER 3: KING OF THE HILL

1. "From Titles to Tackles." Cook, Granger. *Res Gestae*, Vol. IV, No. 2; BHL. RWAP; Box 17, folder: clippings

2. "William Aigler b. 24 Nov. 1845 probably Juniata County, Pennsylvania." Jones Genealogy. <http://www.jonesgenealogy.net/getperson.php?personID=12193

3. Etter, Les. "Biographical Sketch of Prof. Ralph W. Aigler." *Sport News: University of Michigan.* Circa 1965. BHL. RWAP; Box 17, folder: Biographical

4. "Have Finished Their Course—Twelve Graduates Received Diplomas Wednesday Evening." *Bellevue Gazette*, 14 June 1901.

5. Loewenberg, Freddi. "Sports Enthusiast: Civil Law Expert to Retire in June." *Michigan Daily.* Circa July 1955. BHL. RWAP; Box: 17, folder: Aigler Nite, 1955 2/2

6. Aigler to Scroggs. 20 Apr. 1922. BHL. RWAP Box 1, folder: 1921 corr. "P-Z" misc.

7. "Early This Morning." *Bellevue Gazette*, 3 Dec. 1969.

8. Oddo, William. "Re: follow-up." E-mail to David J. Young. 20 Mar. 2013. *Oddo is regarded as the community historian for Bellevue, Ohio ("Stories of Old Bellevue"). He shared this tidbit of Ohio history with me from his research.*

9. Williams, Brian A. "Re: history of law school, stadium capacities." E-Mail to David J. Young. 15 Nov. 2010. *Prior to 1928, college students could enroll in an undergraduate law program at UM. The university also offered a master's degree (LL.M) and a doctorate of laws (LL.D).*

10. "Memorial Service." Circa 1964. BHL. RWAP; Box 17, folder: Biographical

11. Griffith to Healy. 27 Mar. 1934. BHL. RWAP; Box 6, folder: corr. 1934-39

12. Etter, Les. "Biographical Sketch of Prof. Ralph W. Aigler." *Sport News: University of Michigan.* Circa 1965. BHL. RWAP; Box 17, folder: Biographical

13. Sunderland to Aigler. 10 Sept. 1907. BHL. RWAP; Box 8, folder: corr. 1940-45 R. Aigler

14. Etter, Les. "Biographical Sketch of Prof. Ralph W. Aigler." *Sport News: University of Michigan.* Circa 1965. BHL. RWAP; Box 17, folder: Biographical

15. "U.M. Professor Roasts Regents and Board in Control, Advocating Return to Western Conference Without Concessions." *The News Tribune*, 6 Dec. 1912. BHL. RWAP; Bio-news

16. Aigler, Ralph W. "Control of IC Athletics at Michigan." *The MAQR*, 10 Aug. 1957.

17. Ibid.

18. Behee. pp. 59-84.

19. http://www.razorrobotics.com/knowledge/?title=Ralph_W._Aigler

20. Sunderland to Aigler. 10 Sept. 1907. BHL. RWAP; Box 8, folder: corr. 1940-45 R. Aigler

21. Undated. BHL. RWAP; Box 17, folder: Biographical

22. Smith, Allan F. "Ralph W. Aigler." 63 Mich. L. Rev. 2 1964-1965.

23. Mathews to Martin. 27 Mar. 1926. BHL. RWAP; Box 12, folder: corr. 1933-36 "M"

24. Undated. BHL. RWAP; Box 17, folder: Biographical

25. Linotyper's Copy Sheet, undated. BHL. RWAP; Box 17, folder: Biographical

26. Arbuckle to Aigler. BHL. RWAP; Box 9, folder: corr. 1946-52 "A" misc.

27. Aigler to McShane. 9 July 1951. BHL. RWAP Box 10, folder: corr. 1946-52 "Mc" misc.

28. Ibid.

29. Smith, Allan F. "Ralph W. Aigler." 63 Mich. L. Rev. 2 1964-1965.

30. Mathews to Martin. 27 Mar. 1926. BHL. RWAP; Box 12, folder: corr. 1933-36 "M"

31. Aigler to Rapp. 26 Feb. 1936. BHL. RWAP Box 12, folder: athl. corr. 1933-36 "R" misc.

32. Aigler to Evans. 22 Nov. 1929. BHL. RWAP; Box 8, folder: corr. 1940-45 "E-F" misc.

33. Phillips to Aigler. 13 Sept. 1939. BHL. RWAP; Box 8, folder: corr. 1940-45 "P" misc.

34. Evans to Aigler. 24 Nov. 1939. BHL. RWAP; Box 8, folder: corr. 1940-45 "E-F" misc.

35. Aigler to McCormick, 10 June 1936. BHL. RWAP; Box 12, folder: corr. 1933-36 "M" misc.

36. McCormick to Aigler, 22 Aug. 1936. BHL. RWAP; Box 12, folder: corr. 1933-36 "M" misc.

37. Smith, Allan F. "Ralph W. Aigler." 63 Mich. L. Rev. 2 1964-1965.

38. Aigler, Ralph W. "Control of IC Athletics at Michigan." *The MAQR*, 10 Aug. 1957.

39. Ibid.

40. Ibid. p. 316. *Aigler served 42 years on the BIC dating back to 1913 when he was appointed to complete a 2-year term by a dean. Following readmission into the WC, depending on bylaws, he was either reappointed by the president (16 years), the faculty senate (11 years), or the BIC (13 years). BIC members would select him on 12 separate occasions to represent UM at Big Ten meetings.*

41. St. John to Griffith. 11 Sept. 1941. TOSUA DA (RG 9/e-1/9), "IC: Comm.: Corr. (Griffith): 1941-42 (Folder 1 of 2)."

42. Griffith to St. John. 17 Feb. 1943. TOSUA DA (RG 9/e-1/9), "IC: Comm.: Corr. (Griffith): 1942-43 (Folder 2 of 2)."

43. Griffith to St. John. 7 Dec. 1943. TOSUA, DA (RG 9/e-1/9), "IC: Comm.: Corr. (Griffith and St. John): 1940-46."

44. Richart to Pollard. 11 Mar. 1949. UIA. Series 4/2/12; Box 3, folder: WIC 1948-49

45. Richart to Little. 12 Mar. 1948. UIA. Series 4/2/12; Box 3, folder: Dec. '47 meeting

46. Aigler, Ralph W. "Amateurism and IC Athletics." *The MAQR*, 25 May 1957.

47. Aigler to Pollard. 19 June 1945. BHL. RWAP; Box 8, folder: corr. 1940-45 "P" misc.

48. Aigler, Ralph W. "Amateurism and IC Athletics." *The MAQR*, 25 May 1957.

49. Aigler, Ralph W. "Control of IC Athletics at Michigan." *The MAQR*, 10 Aug. 1957.

50. Aigler to Murfin. 10 Nov. 1936. BHL. RWAP; Box 12, folder: corr. 1935-36.

51. Mackey to Aigler. 27 Jan. 1947. BHL. RWAP; Box 10, folder: corr. 1946-52

52. Aigler to Mackey. 11 Feb. 1947. BHL. RWAP; Box 10, folder: corr. 1946-52

53. Mackey to Aigler. 17 Feb. 1947. BHL. RWAP; Box 10, folder: corr. 1946-52

54. Linotyper's Copy Sheet, undated. BHL. RWAP; Box 17, folder: Biographical

55. Aigler to Griffith, 10 Sept. 1935. BHL. RWAP; Box 6, folder: corr. 1934-39 Griffith 4/34-1/36

56. Aigler to Griffith, 13 Aug. 1941. BHL. RWAP; Box 8, folder: Wilson, K.L.

57. Aigler to Griffith, 17 May 1939. BHL. RWAP; Box 6, folder: corr. 1934-39 Griffith 9/37-2/39

58. Aigler to Griffith, 5 May 1939. BHL. RWAP; Box 6, folder: corr. 1934-39 Griffith 1/37-7/39

59. Griffith to Aigler, 24 Apr. 1939. BHL. RWAP; Box 6, folder: corr. 1934-39 Griffith 1/37-7/39

60. Aigler to Griffith, 25 Apr. 1939. BHL. RWAP; Box 6, folder: corr. 1934-39 Griffith 1/37-7/39

61. Aigler to Salsinger. 5 Feb. 1937. BHL. RWAP; Box 7, folder: corr. 1934-39 "S" misc.

62. Aigler to Wilson. 2 July 1948. BHL. RWAP; Box 10, folder: corr. 1946-52 Wilson, K.L.

63. Aigler to Shuster. 5 Jan. 1921. BHL. RWAP; Box 1, folder: 1921 corr. "P-Z" misc.

64. Aigler, Ralph W. "Commercialism in IC Athletics." Circa 1952. BHL. RWAP; Box 13, folder: athl., IC 1929, 52

65. Salsinger to Aigler. 9 Jan. 1945. BHL. RWAP; Box 7, folder: corr. 1934-39 Ruthven

66. Tapping to Aigler. 25 Apr. 1955. BHL. RWAP; Box 17, folder: Aigler Nite, 1955 1/2

67. Pollard. p. 79

68. Laylin to Aigler, 5 Oct. 1933. BHL. RWAP; Box 12, folder: athl. corr. 1933-36 "L" misc.

69. Aigler to Laylin, 7 Oct. 1933. BHL. RWAP; Box 12, folder: athl. corr. 1933-36 "L" misc.

70. Ibid.

71. Aigler to Ruthven, 30 Sept. 1941. BHL. RWAP; Box 8, folder: corr. 1940-45 "H" misc.

72. Widder. pp. 377-78, 387-88

73. Rockne to Young. 19 July 1929. UNDA, [UADR 22/25]

74. SBA. 17 Mar. 1926. www.onthebanks.msu.edu

75. "Report of the Committee on Methods of Supervision of Intercollegiate Athletics Michigan State College." 1 Mar. 1927. MSUA, ACR1. Box: file drawer, folder: 12. *The board was reorganized based on the recommendation of the Committee on Methods and Supervision. The goal was to "insure faculty control of athletics and…to provide for a larger alumni and student representation on such board." Despite that honorable "goal," the faculty retained only four seats on the athletic council.*

Alumni representatives held the other seven positions. "...The Committee feels that in every reasonable way alumni opinion with reference to the athletic situation at the college should be obtained and given careful consideration, and that the alumni should be kept as fully informed as possible on this subject."

76. Ibid.

77. SBA. 24 Nov. 1926. www.onthebanks.msu.edu

78. Min. of the Meeting of the Stockholders and Directors of the ICAA. 7 Dec. 1940. BHL. ADUM; Box 84, folder: ADs Office, Big Ten Comm. Min. 1932-40. *Following WWI, an Army report noted that one-third of all enlistees were physically unfit for service. It recommended that high schools and colleges assume a role in conditioning the nation's youth for any future military conflict. As a result, universities created Physical Education degrees to meet the growing demand for qualified instructors.*

79. Lester. pp. 137-38

80. "Report of the Committee...." 1 Mar. 1927. MSUA. ACR1; Box: file drawer, folder: 12

81. Byers to Richart. 12 Apr. 1948. UIA, Series No. 4/2/12; Box 3, folder: commissioner 1947-48

82. Young to Rockne. 15 July 1929. UNDA, [UADR 22/25]

83. Rockne to Young, 19 July 1929. UNDA, [UADR 22/25]

84. Kryk. pp. 81-113

85. Young to Rockne. 15 July 1929. UNDA, [UADR 22/25]

86. Rockne to Young, 19 July 1929. UNDA, [UADR 22/25]

87. Rockne to Young, 17 June 1929. UNDA, [UADR 22/25]

88. SBA. 17 July 1929. www.onthebanks.msu.edu

89. Young to Rockne. 15 July 1929. UNDA, [UADR 22/25]

90. Widder. p. 390.

91. Falla. p. 24-26.

92. Ibid. p. 22.

93. Waterson. pp. 164-170.

94. Griffith to Conference ADs.... 5 Sept. 1944. TOSUA, DA (RG 9/e-1/10), "IC: Comm.: Corr. (Griffith): 1944-45."

95. Waterson,. p. 183.

96. Falla. pp. 22-24.

97. Rockne to Young. 17 June 1929.UNDA, [UADR 22/25]

98. SBA. 18 Dec. 1929. www.onthebanks.msu.edu

99. Devine, Tommy. "The Michigan State Construction Job." *Sport* Dec. 1953. MSUA. RYP; Box 903, folder: 72

100. Aigler to Griffith. 1 Oct. 1935. BHL. RWAP; Box 6, folder: corr. 1934-39, Griffith 4/34-1/36.

101. Falla, p. 22.

102. *Outlaw—"outside the law"—lacking conference oversight to ensure compliance with rules on recruiting, eligibility, and subsidizing of athletes.*

103. Rules...of ICFR-rev. 1930. UMA, DICAP; Box 13, folder: small handbooks 1895-1908, 1930, 41.

104. Aigler to Young. 11 Feb. 1935. BHL. RWAP; Box 7, folder: corr. 1934-39 "X-Y-Z" misc.

105. Aigler to Long. 7 Oct. 1935. BHL. RWAP; Box 12, folder: athl. corr. 1933-36 "L" misc.

106. Aigler to Griffith. 14 Mar, 1938. BHL. RWAP; Box 6, folder: Griffith 1934-39 9/37-7/39

107. Griffith to Aigler 23 Feb. 1931. BHL. RWAP; Box 3, folder: Griffith 1931

108. Aigler to Griffith. 26 May 1938. BHL. RWAP; Box 6, folder: corr. 1934-39

109. Aigler to Griffith. 14 Mar. 1938. BHL. RWAP; Box 6, folder: Griffith 1934-39 9/37-7/39

110. Bogienski, Stephen, "'Jim Crowley Signs as Coach at Fordham." *Michigan State News*, 5 Jan. 1933.

111. Stradley, B.S. "Michigan State College of Agriculture and Applied Science-1933." 26 Apr. 1933. MSUA. RSP; Box 840, folder: 71

112. "This and That." Sports Editor, *Michigan State News*, 5 Jan. 1933.

113. "The Conference and the NCA." Circa Feb. 1931. BHL. RWAP; Box 3, folder: corr. 1929-32 Griffith

114. Stradley, B.S. "Michigan State College of Agriculture and Applied Science-1933." 26 Apr. 1933. MSUA. RSP; Box 840, folder: 71

115. Ibid. *MSC records indicated that Crowley graduated with an LL.B in 1921 based on Stradley's report.*

116. Lysy, Peter. "Re. James Harold Crowley." E-Mail to David J. Young. 8 Jan. 2013. *Crowley briefly studied undergraduate law at Notre Dame. He failed to obtain a degree or graduate.*

117. Flory, Julie A. "Re: James H. Crowley." E-Mail to David Young, 11 Jan. 2013. *The Office of the Registrar verified that Crowley attended classes at Notre Dame during his senior year but did not graduate.*

118. Fountain, John W. (with Wong, Edward). "Notre Dame Coach Resigns After 5 Days and a Few Lies." *New York Times*, 15 Dec. 2001. *Almost 70 years later, newly hired ND Coach George O'Leary would have welcomed some of Crowley's Irish luck regarding resume inconsistencies. A few days after he accepted the job, reporters inadvertently discovered some inaccuracies in his curriculum vitae. He resigned shortly thereafter.*

119. Works to Shaw. 26 Apr. 1933. MSUA. RSP, Box 840, folder: 71.

120. SBA. 1 June 1932. www.onthebanks.msu.edu

121. Byers to Richart. 12 Apr. 1948. UIA, Series No. 4/2/12; Box 3, folder: commissioner 1947-48

122. Aigler to Griffith. 1 October 1935. BHL. RWAP; Box 6, folder: corr. 1934-39, Griffith 4/34-1/36.

123. SBA. 29 June 1922. www.onthebanks.msu.edu

124. Emmons to FRs. Circa 22 Feb. 1953. UWA-M. UFAB, Series 5/21/7; Box 2, folder: WC Gen. files

CHAPTER 4: A CALL TO DUTY

1. Falla. p. 52

2. Richart to Hannah. 14 Dec. 1948. UIA, Series 4/2/12; Box 3, folder: WIC 1947-48

3. Crisler to the President, ... Jan. 1947. BHL. BICIA; Box 32, folder: Oct. 1949-Feb. 1955, annual reports

4. Wilson to FRs and ADs: Memo. 22 Jan. 1948. BHL. RWAP; Box 10, folder: corr. 1946-52 Wilson, K.L.

5. Aigler to Smith. 20 Jan. 1950. BHL. RWAP; Box 10, folder: corr. 1946-52 "S" misc.

6. Crisler to the President, ... Jan. 1947. BHL. BICIA; Box 32, folder: Oct. 1949-Feb. 1955, annual reports

7. Wilson to FRs and ADs: Memo. 22 Jan. 1948. BHL. RWAP; Box 10, folder: corr. 1946-52 Wilson, K.L.

8. Aigler to Smith. 20 Jan. 1950. BHL. RWAP; Box 10, folder: corr. 1946-52 "S" misc.

9. SBA. 15 Jan. 1948. www.onthebanks.msu.edu.

10. NCAA: Bulletin No. 2. 12 July 1948. UWA-M, UFAB, Series 5/21/6; Box 1, folder: WC min. 1947-51

11. Aigler to Breneman. 7 July 1948. UIA, Athl. Comm. Chairman and FR file 1907-49. Series 4/2/12; Box 3, folder: WIC 1946-47

12. Richart to Breneman. 14 July 1947. UIA, Athl. Comm. Chairman and FR file 1907-49. Series 4/2/12; Box 3, folder: WIC 1946-47

13. Aigler to Wilson, ... 28 Jan. 1949. UWA-M UFAB, Series 5/21/7; Box 1, folder: WC Gen. files

14. Aigler to Mem. Of Board. 16 Dec. 1948. BHL. RWAP; Box 10, folder: corr.1946-52 Wilson, K.L. 2/2

15. "Claud Erickson Distinguished Alumni Award." 5 Dec. 2009. College of Eng., MSU. <http://www.egr.msu.edu/alumni/awards/erickson>.

16. SBA. 29 June 1922. www.onthebanks.msu.edu.

17. "Claud Erickson Distinguished Alumni Award." 5 Dec. 2009. College of Eng., MSU. <http://www.egr.msu.edu/alumni/awards/erickson>.

18. Vescio, Portia. MSU Archives, Claud R. Erickson Papers; processed by Portia Vescio, Apr. 2007.

19. "Claud Erickson Distinguished Alumni Award." 5 Dec. 2009. College of Eng., MSU. <http://www.egr.msu.edu/alumni/awards/erickson>.

20. SBA. 22-23 July 1927. www.onthebanks.msu.edu.

21. SBA. 18 May 1933. www.onthebanks.msu.edu.

22. SBA. 19 Apr. 1934. www.onthebanks.msu.edu.

23. "Claud Erickson Distinguished Alumni Award." 5 Dec. 2009. College of Eng., MSU. <http://www.egr.msu.edu/alumni/awards/erickson>.

24. Hannah to Shaw. 23 Nov. 1938. MSUA. BOT; Box 1884, folder: 8 sup. mat. 11/23/38.

25. Ibid.

26. Ibid.

27. Hannah to Dirks. 3 June 1940. MSUA. BOT; Box 1885, folder: 15 sup. mat. 7/5/40.

28. Erickson to Hannah. 1 June 1940. MSUA. BOT; Box 1885, folder: 15 supp. material 7/5/40

29. Hannah to Dirks. 3 June 1940. MSUA. BOT; Box 1885, folder: 15 sup. mat. 7/5/40.

30. SBA. 17 Jan. 1946. www.onthebanks.msu.edu.

31. "Born of Controversy: The GI Bill of Rights." *US Dept. of Veterans Affairs.* 2/9/12. http://www.gibill.va.gov/benefits/history_timeline/

32. Ibid. pp. 7, 11

33. Denison, James H. "Untitled." 24 June 1970. MSUA. HAP; Box 34, folder: 8 Denison

34. Thomas. p. 11

35. Hannah. pp. 76-77.

36. Denison, James H. "Untitled." 24 June 1970. MSUA. HAP; Box 34, folder: 8 Denison

37. Ibid.

38. Michigan State College: Urgent Building Needs for Rehabilitation and Improvement of Instructional Plant: Veterans' Aid Program. 4 Feb. 1946. MSUA. HAP; Box 34, folder: 8 Denison

39. SBA. 21 Feb. 1946. www.onthebanks.msu.edu.

40. Denison, James H. "Untitled." 24 June 1970. MSUA. HAP; Box 34, folder: 8 Denison

41. SBA. 21 Feb. 1946. www.onthebanks.msu.edu.

42. Hannah. pp. 58-59.

43. Hannah to Ruthven. 18 Mar. 1946. BHL. HOCP; Box 1, folder: MSU corr. 1943-46 topical. *Hannah noted that MSC had gained $15 million dollars over two years for a building program (financed by the VBP), equivalent to $144 million in 2013 (MeasuringWorth.com).*

44. Memo: Postwar Victory Building Program. Circa Jan. 1946. MSUA. AEDR; Box 2309, folder: 24

45. SBA. 21 Feb. 1946. www.onthebanks.msu.edu.

46. SBA. 17 May 1945. www.onthebanks.msu.edu.

47. Michigan State College: Urgent Building Needs for Rehabilitation and Improvement of Instructional Plant: Veterans' Aid Program. 4 Feb. 1946. MSUA. HAP; Box 34, folder: 8 Denison

48. SBA. 17 Jan. 1946. www.onthebanks.msu.edu.

49. McDonel to Hannah. 4 Jan. 1946. MSUA. BOT; Box 1891, folder: 12 sup. mat. 1/17/46.

50. McDonel to Erickson. 21 June 1946. MSUA. BOT; Box 1892, folder: 4 sup. mat. 6/20/46.

51. MeasuringWorth.com.

52. McDonel to Hannah. 31 Jan. 1949. MSUA. BOT; Box 1895, folder: 17 sup. mat. 2/10/49.

53. *Erickson's decision to end his confidential gifting to the college predated State Board member Frederick Mueller's planned review of his lucrative contract in June of 1950. As will be seen, the consultant appeared to contribute to his Spartan Foundation instead of gifting to the board.*

54. *Aigler's original estimate of 100 beneficiaries included senior class members no longer attending school in East Lansing.*

55. Aigler to Wilson, ... 28 Jan. 1949. UWA-M. UFAB, Series 5/21/7; Box 1, folder: WC Gen. files

56. Hannah to Little. 1 June 1949. UWA-M. UFAB, Series 5/21/7; Box 1, folder: WC Gen. files

57. Wilson to Harden. Circa May 1954. MSUA. JAHP; Box 69, folder 38 Athl. Council

58. Scott to Hannah. 22 Aug. 1955. MSUA. JAHP; Box 69, folder 38 Athl. Council

59. Hannah to Athl. Coun. 4 Aug. 1954. MSUA. JAHP; Box 69, folder 38 Athl. Council

60. Scott to Hannah. 22 Aug. 1955. MSUA. JAHP Box 69, folder 38 Athl. Council

CHAPTER 5: PRELUDE TO PROBATION

1. Wallace, Francis. "Test Case at Pitt: The Facts about College Football Play for Pay." *The Saturday Evening Post*, 28 Oct. 1930. UPA, 9/10-A: Box 1, folder: FF772.

2. Falla. pp. 130-31

3. Waterson. p. 208

4. Ibid. p. 202

5. St. John to Crisler. 27 Dec. 1944. BHL. BICIA; Box 30, folder: papers 1944 Jan.

6. Aigler, Ralph W. "Control of IC Athletics at Michigan." *The MAQR,* 10 Aug. 1957,

7. "Vet Fritz Crisler Retiring." *Big Spring Daily Herald,* 30 June 1968.

8. Aigler, Ralph W. "Control of IC Athletics at Michigan." *The MAQR,* 10 Aug. 1957

9. Mackey to Aigler. 27 Jan. 1947. BHL. RWAP; Box 10, folder: corr. 1946-52

10. Aigler to Mackey. 11 Feb. 1947. BHL. RWAP; Box 10, folder: corr. 1946-52

11. Aigler to Mullendore. 24 Jan. 1951.; BHL. RWAP; Box 10, folder: corr. 1946-52 "M" misc.
    (ME-MY). *Aigler greatly respected Crisler's leadership and administrative skills. "…I think if in earlier
    years he had started along certain paths, he would have been a first-class businessman, doctor or lawyer,
    or even a university president." He noted that a number of professional football teams sought his coach-
    ing services. One club also wanted him to run its front office. A large manufacturing company in Detroit
    tried to entice him to direct its operations. Both the University of California—Berkley and the University
    of Southern California offered him coaching opportunities. As Aigler suggested years later, Crisler was
    driven by a higher purpose—dollar enticement, in Crisler's opinion, was an insult to his integrity. He
    opted to stay in Ann Arbor.*

12. Aigler, Ralph W. "Control of IC Athletics at Michigan." *The MAQR,* 10 Aug. 1957

13. Aigler to Lorenz. 19 Feb. 1945. BHL. RWAP; Box 10, folder: Wilson, Tug

14. Aigler to Lorenz. 28 Feb. 1945 BHL. RWAP; Box 10, folder: corr. 1946-52 personal

15. Lorenz to Aigler. 23 Feb. 1945. BHL. RWAP; Box 10, folder: Wilson, Tug

16. St. John to Crisler. 27 Dec. 1944. BHL. BICIA; Box 30, folder: papers 1944 Jan.

17. Lorenz to Aigler. 2 Jan. 1945. BHL. RWAP; Box 12, folder: corr. A-Z misc.

18. Aigler to Rottschaefer. 3 Mar. 1948. BHL. RWAP; Box 10, folder: 1946-52 Rottschaefer,
    Henry

19. Reed to Aigler. 3 Dec. 1953. BHL. RWAP; Box 10, folder: corr. 1946-52 Reed, William

20. Min. of the ICFR. 9-10 March 1945. UIA, Series 4/2/12; Box 2, folder: conf. min. 1944-45

21. *SUI faculty representative Karl Leib was the popular choice among the academicians. He later assumed
    the presidency of the NCAA. Leib played a pivotal role in ensuring passage of the controversial Sanity
    Code.*

22. Lorenz to Aigler. 2 Jan. 1945. BHL. RWAP; Box 12, folder: athl. 1941-45 corr. A-Z misc.

23. Lorenz to Aigler. 23 Feb. 1945. BHL. RWAP; Box 10, folder: Wilson, Tug

24. Aigler to Lorenz. 28 Feb. 1945. BHL. RWAP; Box 10, folder: corr. 1946-52 personal

25. Aigler to Lorenz. 19 Feb. 1945. BHL. RWAP; Box 10, folder: Wilson, Tug

26. Min. of the ICFR. 9-10 Mar. 1945. UIA. Series 4/2/12; Box 2, folder: conf. min. 1944-45. *With military rule of conferences soon to be past tense, the planned agenda focused on eligibility and subsidy issues for returning vets. At the end of the second day of meetings, however, the chairman announced the appointment of Professor Aigler to serve on the ad hoc committee charged with revising the duties of the commissioner in addition to the eligibility issue. It is inferred that Aigler addressed his other concerns during those meetings that prompted that final announcement.*

27. Wallace, Francis. "Test Case at Pitt: The Facts about College Football Play for Pay." *The Saturday Evening Post*, 28 Oct. 1930. UPA, 9/10-A: Box 1, folder: FF772.

28. Wallace, Francis. "The Football Laboratory Explodes-The Climax in the Test Case at Pitt." *The Saturday Evening Post*, 4 Nov. 1930. UPA, 9/10-A: Box 1, folder: FF772.

29. Wilson to Aigler. 9 July 1946. BHL. RWAP; Box 10, folder: corr. 1946-52 Wilson, K.L.

30. Waterson. pp. 205-6

31. Falla. p. 132

32. Ibid.

33. Aigler to Griffith. 17 Jan. 1939. BHL. RWAP; Box 6, folder: 1934-39 Griffith 9/37-7/39

34. Aigler to Owens. 23 Jan. 1939. BHL. RWAP; Box 6, folder: 1934-39 Griffith 9/37-7/39

35. Lester, Robin. p. 132

36. Waterson. pp. 152-54

37. "Commercialism in IC Athletics." Aigler, Ralph W. Circa 1952. BHL. RWAP; Box 13, folder: athl. IC. 1929, 52

38. *The American Professional Football Association was organized in 1920. It was renamed the National Football League a few years later. The American Football League survived for two years in the early 1940s. The regional Pacific Coast Professional Football League was active from 1945-48. The All-America Football Conference existed from 1946-49. Of interest to Wolverine fans, the Los Angeles Dons, one of the AAFC clubs, actively recruited Michigan's Crisler to serve as its general manager in February of 1947. He declined the $25,000/year offer (twice his current salary) to remain in Ann Arbor.* [Aigler to Hattendorf. 17 Feb. 1947. BHL. RWAP; Box 9, folder: corr. 1946-52 "H" misc. (HA-HN)]. *Later that year UM would win a national championship. The AAFC folded shortly thereafter.*

39. Aigler to Wilson. 29 Apr. 1946. BHL. RWAP; Box 10, folder: Wilson, Tug

40. Min. of the ICFR. 9-10 Mar. 1945. UIA, Series 4/2/12; Box 2, folder: conf. min. 1944-45

41. Aigler to Richart. 9 Nov. 1944. BHL. RWAP; Box 8, folder: corr. 1940-45 Richart

42. Richart to Aigler. 29 Dec. 1944. BHL. RWAP; Box 8, folder: corr. 1940-45 Richart

43. Min. of the ICFR. 9-10 Mar. 1945. UIA. Series 4/2/12; Box 2, folder: conf. min. 1944-45

44. Aigler to Salsinger. 16 Mar. 1945. BHL. RWAP; Box 8, folder: corr. 1940-45 "S" misc.

45. Aigler to Paige. 26 Dec. 1930. BHL. RWAP; Box 4, folder: corr. 1929-33 Paige

46. Aigler to Owens. 10 Jan. 1945. BHL. RWAP; Box 8, folder: corr. 1940-45 "N-O" misc.

47. *The Council's name varied depending on the size of the conference.*

48. Rottschaefer to Morrill. 26 Feb. 1948. UMA, Pres. Office; Box 238, folder: PE and athl. 1948-49

49. Morrill to Presidents ... 10 Dec. 1947. UIA-ICI. V. Hancher Papers, RG 05.01.11; Box 209, folder: 171

50. Aigler to Rottschaefer. 3 Mar. 1948. BHL. RWAP; Box 10, folder: corr. 1946-52 Rottschaefer

51. Aigler to Wilson. 18 Apr. 1947. BHL. RWAP; Box 3, folder: 1947 Illinois scandal

52. Crisler to the President ... Jan. 1948. BHL. RWAP; Box 13, folder: athl. 1940-48 BIC

53. Aigler to Breneman. 7 July 1947. UIA. Athl. Comm. Chairman and FRs File 1907-49, Series 4/2/12; Box 3, folder: WIC 1946-47

54. Richart to Breneman. 14 July 1947. UIA. Athl. Comm. Chairman and FRs File 1907-49, Series 4/2/12; Box 3, folder: WIC 1946-47

55. Min. of the ICFR. 29-31 May 1947. UMA, Pres. Office; Box 238, folder: PE and athl. 1945-47

56. Rottschaefer to Morrill. 3 Sept. 1947. UMA, Pres. Office; Box 238, folder: PE and athl. 1945-47

57. Min. of the ICFR 5-6 June 1948. UWA-M. UFAB, Series 5/21/6; Box 1, folder: WC min. 1947-51.

58. Morrill to McCormick ... 27 Aug. 1947. UMA, Pres. Office; Box 238, folder: PE and athl. 1945-47

59. Roan to Nunn. 29 July 1947. UMA, DICAP; Box 6, folder: J.L. Morrill President

60. Morrill to Rottschaefer. 16 Sept. 1947. UMA, Pres. Office; Box 238, folder: PE and athl. 1945-47

61. Morrill to McCormick. 4 Mar. 1947. UMA, DICAP; Box 6, folder: Michigan "M" policy

62. Hannah to Kimpton. 27 Feb. 1946. MSUA. Floyd Reeves Papers, UA 21.12.1; Box 115, folder: 21

63. Aigler to Richart. 21 Dec. 1948. UIA. Series 4/2/12; Box 3, folder: WIC 1948-49

64. Morrill to McCormick. 4 Mar. 1947. UMA, DICAP; Box 6, folder: Michigan "M" policy

65. Morrill to Rottschaefer. 27 Aug. 1947. UMA, Pres. Office; Box 238, folder: PE and athl. 1945-47

66. Rottschaefer to Morrill. 3 Sept. 1947. UMA, Pres. Office; Box 238, folder: PE and athl. 1945-47

67. Morrill to Rottschaefer. 16 Sept. 1947. UMA, Pres. Office; Box 238, folder: PE and athl. 1945-47

68. Rottschaefer to Morrill. 3 Sept, 1947. UMA, Pres. Office; Box 238, folder: PE and athl. 1945-47

69. Morrill to Rottschaefer. 16 Sept. 1947. UMA, Pres. Office; Box 238, folder: PE and athl. 1945-47

70. Morrill to McCormick, ... 27 Aug. 1947. UMA, Pres. Office; Box 238, folder: PE and athl. 1945-47

71. Morrill to Nunn. 27 Aug. 1947. UMA, Pres. Office; Box 238, folder: PE and athl. 1945-47

72. Morrill to Rottschaefer. 16 Sept. 1947. UMA, Pres. Office; Box 238, folder: PE and athl. 1945-47. *Morrill's intentions were spelled out in a draft letter to George E. Corrothers dated Sept. 18, 1947 and included at the bottom of the Sept. 16th letter to Rottschaefer.*

73. Morrill to Presidents. 10 Dec. 1947. UMA, Pres. Office; Box 238, folder: PE and athl. 1945-47

74. 390Min. of ICFR. 12-13 Dec. 1947. UIA. Series 4/2/12; Box 3, folder: Dec. '47 meeting

75. Joint Luncheon Mtg. 28 Feb. 1948. UMA, Pres. Office. Box 238, folder: PE and athl. 1948-49

76. Aigler to Rottschaefer. 3 Mar. 1948. BHL. RWAP; Box 10, folder: corr. 1946-52 Rottschaefer

77. Morrill to Wells. "Proposal By The 'Council of Ten' For Consideration By The ICFR." 21 Apr. 1952. BHL. RWAP; Box 10, folder: corr. 1946-52 NCAA. *By the spring of 1952 it was apparent that Wilson was not meeting the expectations of the Council. Morrill proposed greater involvement by the presidents in oversight of the conference and its commissioner.*

78. Aigler to The FRs. 23 Apr. 1952. BHL. RWAP; Box 10, folder: corr. 1946-52 NCAA. *This memo summarizes Morrill's memo to Indiana President Herman B. Wells dated 4/21/1952.*

79. Min. of the Joint Group of the IC. 5-6 Dec. 1952. UWA-M. UFAB, Series 5/21/6; Box 1, folder: WC min. 1947-51. *The Council of Ten, on the recommendation of the FRC, now hired the commissioner. He was required to meet with the council twice a year to discuss job performance.*

80. Min. of the IC Mtg. of the ADs. 16 May 1948. UWA-M. UFAB, Series 5/21/6; Box 1, folder: WC min. 1947-54

81. Min. of the ICFR. 5-6 June 1948. UWA-M. UFAB, Series 5/21/6; Box 1, folder: WC min. 1947-51

82. Min. of the IC: Joint Mtg. of FRs and ADs. 29 May 1948. UIA. Series 4/2/13; Box 3, folder: WIC 1947-48

83. Hovde to Lundquist. 12 Aug. 1948. BHL. RWAP; Box 10, folder: corr. 1946-52 "L" misc.

84. Min. of the IC: Joint. Mtg. of FRs and ADs. 29 May 1948. UIA. Series 4/2/13; Box 3, folder: WIC 1947-48

85. Hovde to Lundquist. 12 Aug. 1948. BHL. RWAP; Box 10, folder: corr. 1946-52 "L" misc.

86. Aigler to Lundquist. 12 Aug. 1948. BHL. RWAP; Box 10, folder: corr. 1946-52 "L" misc

87. Min. of IC: Joint Mtg. of FRs and ADs. 29 May 1948. UIA. Series 4/2/13; Box 3, folder: WIC 1947-48

88. Richart to Pollard. 11 Mar. 1949. UIA. Series 4/2/12; Box 3, folder: WIC 1948-49

89. Ibid. *Richart questioned the wisdom of adopting Aigler's strict scholarship rules that exceeded the Sanity Code benchmark. He felt the Wolverine and a few other passionate leaders were unduly influencing votes among conference colleagues.*

90. Aigler to Wilson. 17 Apr. 1947. BHL. RWAP; Box 3, folder: corr. 1929-33 J.L. Griffith

91. Aigler to Breneman. 7 July 1947. UIA. Series 4/2/17; Box 3, folder: WIC 1946-47

92. Richart to Breneman. 14 July 1947. UIA. Series 4/2/17; Box 3, folder: WIC 1946-47

93. Crisler to Wilson. 4 May 1948. BHL. ADUM; Box 31, folder: papers 1948 May

94. Hovde to Lundquist. 23 July 1948. BHL. RWAP; Box 10, folder: corr. 1946-52 "L" misc.

95. Hovde to Morrill. 29 Sept. 1948. UMA, Pres. Office; Box 238, folder: PE and athl. 1948-49

96. Little to Lundquist. 17 Aug. 1948. UWA-M. UFAB, Series 5/21/7; Box 1, folder: WC gen. files

97. Richart to Lundquist. 15 Aug. 1948. UIA. Series 42/12; Box 1, folder: WIC min. 1947-48

98. Aigler to Lundquist. 12 Aug. 1948. BHL. RWAP; Box 10, folder: corr. 1946-52 "L" misc.

99. Lundquist to Richart. 11 Aug. 1948. UIA. Series 4/2/12; Box 3, folder: WIC 1947-48

100. Richart to Lundquist. 13 Aug. 1948. UIA. Series 4/2/12; Box 3, folder: WIC 1947-48

101. Lundquist to Richart. 1 Sept. 1948. UIA. Series 4/2/12; Box 3, folder: WIC 1947-48

102. *The traditional way to punish a program was by quietly imposing a scheduling boycott. It was left to the athletic director to figure out why he was unable to sign biennial contracts with a conference foe, a practice I term 'vigilante justice.'*

103. Min. of IC—Mtg. of the ADs. 30 Nov. 1948. UWA-M. UFAB, Series 5/21/6; Box 1, folder: WC min. 1947-51

104. Wilson to Crisler. 28 Oct. 1948. BHL. BICIA; Box 31, folder: Papers 1948 Nov.

105. Lundquist to Richart. 1 Sept. 1948. UIA. Series 4/2/12; Box 3, folder: WIC 1947-48

106. *Ohio State and Illinois planned to boycott Purdue. Michigan's Crisler was impressed with the corrective action plan and decided not to discipline the school.*

107. Hovde to Morrill. 29 Sept. 1948. UMA, Pres. Office; Box 238, folder: PE and athl. 1948-49

108. Wilson to Aigler. 24 Oct. 1949. BHL. RWAP; Box 10, folder: corr. 1946-52 personal. *Wilson expresses appreciation for Aigler's willingness to help him during his early, challenging years in office.*

CHAPTER 6: A COMMISSIONER UNDER SIEGE

1. Aigler to Yost. 21 Jan. 1921. BHL. BICIA; Box 4, folder: Jan

2. "Report of the Field Sec. R.H. Clancy, ..." 16 June 1920. BHL. BICIA; Box 3, folder: June

3. Aigler to Wilson. 10 Apr. 1952. BHL. RWAP; Box 10, folder: corr. 1946-52 Wilson, K. L. 1952

4. Wilson to Larkins. 9 May 1949., DA (RG 9/e-1/10), "IC: Comm.: Corr. (Wilson): 1947-51."

5. *As will be seen, similar practices were taking place in East Lansing. The Spartan Foundation and its subsidiary Century Club had a loose relationship with assistant field secretary Jack Breslin, a college employee. The only difference—the commissioner forewarned OSU of a potential handbook violation. Michigan State was not afforded the same courtesy.*

6. Larkins to Wilson. 13 May 1949. TOSUA, DA (RG 9/e-1/10), "IC: Comm.: Corr. (Wilson): 1947-51."

7. Wilson to Larkins. 27 May 1949. TOSUA, DA (RG 9/e-1/10), "IC: Comm.: Corr. (Wilson): 1947-51."

8. Bevis to Larkins. 19 May 1949. TOSUA, DA (RG 9/e-1/10), "IC: Comm.: Corr. (Wilson): 1947-51."

9. Wilson to Larkins. 27 May 1949. TOSUA, DA (RG 9/e-1/10), "IC: Comm.: Corr. (Wilson): 1947-51."

10. Aigler to Wilson. 10 April 1952. BHL. RWAP; Box 10, folder: corr. 1946-52 Wilson, K. L. 1952

11. Min. of the IC-Mtg. of the ADs. 24-26 May 1951. UWA-M. UFAB, Series 5/21/6; Box 1, folder: WC min. 1947-51

12. Commissioner's Report.... 6 Dec. 1951. UWA-M. UFAB, Series 5/21/7; Box 2, folder: WC gen. files

13. Min. of the IC: Mtg. of ADs. 8-11 Dec. 1949. BHL. ADUM; Box 84, folder: Big Ten records 1941-52

14. Min. of the IC: Mtg. of ADs. 20 Nov. 1949. BHL. ADUM; Box 84, folder: Big Ten records 1941-52

15. Wilson to Conf. Pres..... 25 June 1952. BHL. RWAP; Box 10, folder: corr. 1946-52 Reed, William

16. Min. of the IC: Mtg. of ADs. 20 Nov. 1949. BHL. ADUM; Box 84, folder: Big Ten records 1941-52

17. Aigler to Blommers. 8 Dec. 1952. BHL. RWAP; Box 9, folder: corr. 1946-52 "B" misc.

18. Blommers to Aigler. 17 Dec. 1952. BHL. RWAP; Box 9, folder: corr. 1946-52 "B" misc.

19. Blommers to Aigler. 15 Apr. 1952. BHL. RWAP; Box 9, folder: corr. 1946-52 "B" misc.

20. "File Wilson." 7 Dec. 1952. BHL. RWAP; Box 10, folder: corr. 1946-52 Wilson, K. L. 1952

21. Wilson to Brechler. 23 Nov. 1952. BHL. RWAP; Box 10, folder: corr. 1946-52 Reed, William 1952

22. Blommers to Aigler. 17 Dec. 1952. BHL. RWAP; Box 9, folder: corr 1946-52 "B" misc.

23. Aigler to Reed. 12 Dec. 1952. BHL. RWAP; Box 10, folder: corr. 1946-52 Reed, William

24. "File Wilson." 7 Dec. 1952. BHL. RWAP; Box 10, folder: corr. 1946-52 Wilson, K. L. 1952

25. Aigler to Reed. 12 Dec. 1952. BHL. RWAP; Box 10, folder: corr. 1946-52 Reed, William

26. Aigler to Blommers. 8 Dec. 1952. BHL. RWAP; Box 9, folder: corr. 1946-52 "B" misc.

27. Aigler to Reed. 9 Dec. 1952. BHL. RWAP; Box 10, folder: corr. 1946-52 Reed, William

28. Aigler to Reed. 9 Dec. 1952. BHL. RWAP; Box 10, folder: corr. 1946-52 Reed, William

29. Blommers to Aigler. 15 Apr. 1952. BHL. RWAP; Box 9, folder: corr. 1946-52 "B" misc.

30. Blommers to Aigler. 17 Dec. 1952. BHL. RWAP; Box 9, folder: corr 1946-52 "B" misc.

31. Aigler to Richart. 14 Dec. 1948. UIA. Series 4/2/12; Box 3, folder: WIC 1948-49

32. Blommers to Aigler. 15 Apr. 1952. BHL. RWAP; Box 9, folder: corr. 1946-52 "B" misc.

33. Blommers to Aigler. 17 Dec. 1952. BHL. RWAP; Box 9, folder: corr. 1946-52 "B" misc.

CHAPTER 7: HELP WANTED

1. Spezia, Mark. "Flint Man Enters MSU Hall of Fame." *Flint Journal*, 22 Sept. 2007

2. Interview with George Guerre. 10 Oct. 2013. East Lansing, Michigan.

3. Scholarship Meeting. 18 June 1947. MSUA. RYP; Box 907, folder: 6 corr. scholarships 1947. *The meeting addressed how to dispense Jenison Awards to those receiving dollars through the GI Bill. Any shortage was covered by Jenison's endowment.*

4. Summer Scholarships. 19 June 1947. MSUA. RYP; Box 907, folder: 6 corr. Schol. 1947

5. SBA. 17 May 1945. www.onthebanks.msu.edu

6. Hannah to Young. 19 May 1945. MSUA. HPP; Box 63, folder: 7 Schol.-Jenison 1942-45

7. Little to Blommers, ... 23 Apr. 1949. UWA-M; UFAB, Series 5/21/7; Box 1, folder: WC files

8. Min. of the IC—Mtg. of the ADs. 8-11 Dec. 1949. UWA-M; Series 5/21/6; Box 1, folder: WC files

9. Interview with George Guerre, 7 Dec. 2012. East Lansing, Michigan.

10. Gen. Reg. XIV, Recruiting (Effective date, June 6, 1949). UWA-M. Univ. Fac. Athl. Series 5/21/6; Box 1, folder: WC files

11. Interview with George Guerre, 7 Dec. 2012. East Lansing, Michigan. *See Ch. 6 notes.*

12. SBA. 18 May 1950. www.onthebanks.msu.edu

13. Badgley, Megan. "Forest H. Akers: Not Just A Clever Name for a Golf Course." Exhibit/MSU Archives. June 2010. www.onthebanks.msu.edu

14. Hannah. p. 70

15. *The gift would be worth approximately $435,000 in 2013 (MeasuringWorth.com)*

16. SBA. 15 February 1948. www.onthebanks.msu.edu

17. Interview with George Guerre. 10 Oct. 2013. East Lansing, Michigan. *Akers found employment for many Spartans athletes with Dodge Motors.*

18. "MSU's Jack Breslin, 68, Died Today." *MSU News.* 2 Aug. 1988. MSUA; MSU Information File-Breslin, Jack

19. DiBiaggio, John. Eulogy: Jack Breslin. 4 Aug. 1988. MSUA; MSU Information File-Breslin, Jack

20. Telephone interview with Brian Breslin. 10 Oct. 2009. *Brian shared memories of his father while growing up in East Lansing.*

21. "Bio. Information-Jacweir (Jack) Breslin." Undated. MSUA. MSU Information File-Breslin, Jack

22. *This is based on a review of "The Wolverine," the college yearbook. The archives and Varsity S Club lack any additional information regarding his collegiate years.*

23. *The Wolverine*-1943, p. 233. *Based on the Alpha Tau Omega (ATO) write-up in the yearbook, Breslin may not have attended college during 1940-41; he appeared to have returned briefly to campus in the fall of 1941. He ultimately pledged ATO in the fall of 1942, equivalent to his sophomore year.*

24. "Mem. of the Adm. Group." 19 Dec. 1941. MSUA. HPP; Box 63, folder: 7: Schol.-Jenison 1942-45

25. Telephone interviews with Brian Breslin. 10 Oct. 2009, 19 Oct. 2013. *Brian shared a few stories of his father's upbringing.*

26. Annual report of the BICIA. Jan. 1944. BHL. AGRP; Box 36, folder: 22 1944

27. "Decision Made By President: Drain of Student Body Due To Military Demands Causes Action." *Lansing State Journal,* 10 Aug. 1943.

28. "Answer Still Remains 'No'- Army Says It's a Closed Question; Congress Petition Ignored." *Lansing State Journal,* 6 Aug. 1943.

29. "Bachman Will Continue Work." *Lansing State Journal,* 12 Aug. 1943.

30. Alderton, George S. "Scranton Plays State Saturday." *Lansing State Journal,* 24 Sept. 1944.

31. Alderton, George S. "Bachman Has 60 Candidates On 1944 Squad." *Lansing State Journal,* 9 Sept. 1944.

32. Alderton, George S. "Scranton Plays State Saturday—Spartans Return to Intercollegiate Football Wars This Week After Two-Year Absence." *Lansing State Journal,* 24 Sept. 1944.

33. Vescio, Portia. "A few questions." E-Mail to David J. Young. 28 Oct. 2013. *The archivist confirmed that Breslin had been awarded a "Jenison Scholarship" for the academic years of 1944-45* (RYP; Box 907, folder: 10-16).

34. Alderton, George S. "Coaches Will Train Squads – Varsity Mentors to Prepare Athletes for Games in All Sports." *Lansing State Journal,* 19 Aug. 1943.

35. *The Wolverine* -1945, p. 199

36. *The Wolverine* -1946

37. DiBiaggio, John. Eulogy: Jack Breslin. 4 Aug. 1988. MSUA. MSU Information File-Breslin, Jack

38. Interview with George Guerre. 10 Oct. 2013. East Lansing, Michigan. *Guerre, a close friend of Jack Breslin's, shared this story with me.*

39. SBA. 18 May 1950. www.onthebanks.msu.edu

40. SBA. 15 Jan. 1948 www.onthebanks.msu.edu

41. *Due to graduation of 30 seniors in the interim, the list was down to 70 by Jan. of 1949.*

42. Alderton, George S. "Jealous Rivals Seen in Big 10 Slap at M.S.C.-Probation Is Decreed by Wilson." *Lansing State Journal,* 23 Feb. 1953.

43. Erickson to Harden. 23 July 1953. MSUA. ACR2; Box 2, folder: 27

44. Alderton, George S. "Jealous Rivals Seen in Big 10 Slap at M.S.C.-Probation Is Decreed by Wilson." *Lansing State Journal,* 23 Feb. 1953.

45. Emmons to Wilson. 16 Feb. 1953.UWA-M. UFAB, Series 5/21/7; Box 2, folder: WC gen. files. *In script at the bottom left of the letter, Wisconsin faculty representative Kurt Wendt noted that Erickson was founder and president.*

46. Erickson to Harden. 23 July 1953. MSUA. ACR2; Box 2, folder: 27

47. MeasuringWorth.com

48. Alderton, George S. "Jealous Rivals Seen in Big 10 Slap at M.S.C.-Probation Is Decreed by Wilson." *Lansing State Journal,* 23 Feb. 1953.

49. Emmons to FRs. Circa 22 Feb. 1953. UWA-M. UFAB, Series 5/21/7; Box 2, folder: WC gen. files

50. Alderton, George S. "Jealous Rivals Seen in Big 10 Slap at M.S.C.-Probation Is Decreed by Wilson." *Lansing State Journal,* 23 Feb. 1953.

51. Interview with Guerre, George. 5 Feb. 2010. East Lansing, Michigan.

52. "Report to the WC." Harden, Edgar L. 6 Aug. 1953. MSUA. ACR2; Box 2, folder: 27

53. Ibid.

CHAPTER 8: MICHIGAN MOLES

1. Aigler to Rottschaefer. 3 Mar. 1948. BHL. RWAP; Box 10, folder: corr. 1946-52 Rottschaefer, Henry. (Italics added.)

2. Crisler to Wilson. 20 Sept. 1951. BHL. BICIA; Box 32, folder: papers 1951, Sept. *Crisler references a private conversation with Wilson during conference meetings to address the commissioner's revised duties. That encounter took place during late Feb. at the Chicago LaSalle Hotel* (Min. of the IC—Meetings of the ADs 22-25 Feb. 1951. UWA-M, UFAB, Series 5/21/6; Box 1, folder: WC min. 1947-51.)

3. Aigler to Long. 7 Oct. 1935. BHL. RWAP; Box 12, folder: corr. 1933-36 "L" misc. *Aigler references a confidential accrediting agency (NCA) investigation of MSC that took place shortly after Crowley departed East Lansing for Fordham. His source informed him that MSC had passed muster, much to Aigler's surprise. In point of fact, the school was at risk of probation had Crowley remained at MSC.*

4. Wilson to Aigler. 9 June 1947. BHL. RWAP; Box 10, folder: corr. 1946-52 Wilson, K.L. 1/2. *Wilson comments on reports that Michigan alumni were attending the outing. The fact that Aigler was able to compose a letter to Hannah, outlining the details of Munn's comments, implied that he heard about it through one of the Wolverines in the audience.*

5. Aigler to Wilson, ... 28 Jan. 1949. UWA-M. UFAB, Series 5/21/7; Box 1, folder: WC gen. files

6. Aigler to Little, ... 25 Mar. 1949. UWA-M. UFAB, Series 5/21/7; Box 1, folder: WC gen. files

7. Crisler to Wilson. 20 Sept. 1951. BHL. BICIA; Box 32, folder: papers 1951 Sept.

8. Appendix A: Commissioner's Report to the Joint Conference. 6 Dec. 1951. UMA, Pres. Office; Box 239, folder: PE and athl., IC 1949-52

9. Interview with Joanne Snider. 7 Dec. 2012. *Joanne was Ed Vandervoort's youngest daughter. She shared with me documents highlighting her father's athletic and business careers; membership cards from both the Downtown Coaches Club and the Century Club were included.*

10. Alderton, George S. "Jealous Rivals Seen in Big 10 Slap at M.S.C.-Foundation Ex-Head Denies Wilson Charge: Erickson Says Big Ten Chief Saw Books Back in Dec., 1951." *Lansing State Journal*, 23 Feb. 1953.

11. Jenkins to Harden. 30 July 1953. MSUA. ACR2; Box 2, folder: 27

12. Emmons to FRs Circa 22 Feb. 1953. UWA-M. UFAB, Series 5/21/7; Box 2, folder: WC gen. files

13. Erickson to Harden. 23 July 1953. MSUA. ACR2; Box 2, folder: 27

14. Alderton, George S. "Jealous Rivals Seen in Big 10 Slap at M.S.C.-Foundation Ex-Head Denies Wilson Charge: Erickson Says Big Ten Chief Saw Books Back in Dec., 1951." *Lansing State Journal*, 23 Feb. 1953.

15. Alderton, George S. "MSC Plans No Appeal in Big Ten Case: Loan List Disclosed By Emmons." *Lansing State Journal*, 24 Feb. 1953. *The booster organizations were respectively: Five-A Club (An Athlete to Ann Arbor Annually), Frontliners Club, Mendota Club, and I-Club.*

16. Alderton, George S. "MSC Plans No Appeal in Big Ten Case: Loan List Disclosed By Emmons." *Lansing State Journal*, 24 Feb. 1953.

17. Crisler to Wilson. 24. Sept. 1951.BHL. BICIA; Box 32, folder: papers 1951 Sept.

18. Yost to Aigler. 31 Dec. 1920. BHL. BICIA; Box 3, folder: Dec.

19. Behee. p. 88

20. Thomas. p. 20-21

21. Devine, Tommy. "Michigan State Challenges the Big Ten to Clean House." *Sports Illustrated* (sic), 18 June 1949. MSUA, JHP; Box 80, folder: 13

22. Turnbull, George. "Vandervoort's Leaves Sporting Goods Legacy." BNET. 1; 4/04. <http://findarticles.com/p/articles/mi_qa5316/is_>

23. Young to Rockne. 15 July 1929.UNDA, [UADR 22/25]

24. Rockne to Young. 19 July 1929. UNDA, [UADR 22/25]

25. Interview with Joanne Snider. 7 Dec. 2012. East Lansing, Michigan.

26. Min. of the IC—Mtg. of the ADs 22-25 Feb. 1951. UWA-M, UFAB, Series 5/21/6; Box 1, folder: WC min. 1947-51

27. Wilson to Crisler. 19 Sept. 1951. BHL. BICIA; Box 32, folder: papers 1951, Sept.

28. Crisler to Wilson. 27 Sept. 1951. BHL. BICIA; Box 32, folder: papers 1951, Sept.

29. Emmons to FRs. Circa 22 Feb. 1953. UWA-M. UFAB, Series 5/21/7; Box 2, folder: WC gen. files

30. Interview with Joanne Snider. 7 Dec. 2012. East Lansing, Michigan.

31. Crisler to Little, ... 30 Mar. 1949. BHL. HOCP; Box 1, folder: top corr. MSU 1947-49

32. Wilson to Aigler. 11 Mar. 1953. BHL. RWAP; Box 10, folder: corr.1946-52 Wilson, K.L. 1952

33. Wilson to Crisler. 19 Sept. 1951. BHL. BICIA; Box 32, folder: papers 1951, Sept.

34. Memo. to Conf. FRs and ADs. 7 March 1952. UWA-M, Series 5/21/7; Box 2, folder: WC gen. files

35. *Vandervoort assumed the presidency on July 1, 1952. He unexpectedly passed away a few days later.*

36. Morrill to McCormick. 4 Mar. 1947. UMA, Dept. Athl. Papers; Box 6, folder: Michigan "M" policy

37. Crisler to Wilson. 27 Sept. 1951. BHL. BICIA; Box 32, folder: papers 1951, Sept.

38. Emmons to FRs. Circa 22 Feb. 1953. UWA-M. UFAB, Series 5/21/7; Box 2, folder: WC gen. files

39. Erickson to Harden. 23 July 1953. MSUA. ACR2; Box 2, folder: 27

40. Emmons to Wilson. 16 Feb. 1953.UWA-M. UFAB, Series 5/21/7; Box 2, folder: WC gen. files. *Kurt Wendt noted that Erickson was founder/ president.*

41. Wilson to Hannah. 14 Feb. 1953. BHL. HOCP; Box 1, folder: top corr. MSU 1953

42. Harden to Wilson. 10 Sept. 1953. MSUA. ACR2; Box 2, folder: 27

43. Wilson to Hannah. 14 Feb. 1953. BHL. HOCP; Box 1, folder: top corr. MSU 1953

44. Crisler to Wilson. 27 Sept. 1951. BHL. BICIA; Box 32, folder: papers 1951, Sept.

45. Harden to Wilson. 10 Sept. 1953. MSUA. ACR2; Box 2, folder: 27

46. Aigler to Rottschaefer. 3 Mar. 1948. BHL. RWAP; Box 10, folder: corr. 1946-52 Rottschaefer,

47. Emmons to FRs. Circa 22 Feb. 1953. UWA-M. UFAB, Series 5/21/7; Box 2, folder: WC gen. files. *Emmons quotes a 5/17/1952 letter from Wilson to Hannah that summarized the commissioner's recent visit with him. Despite promising that the matter would remain confidential and limited to his immediate staff, Ralph Aigler was aware of all that transpired. This appeared to substantiate his plan to direct the investigation from Ann Arbor rather than to have Wilson do so from Chicago. Various communications with Wilson and Reed over the interim support this point.*

48. Falla. p. 219

49. Reed to Crisler. 2 Feb. 1946. BHL. BICIA; Box 31, folder: papers 1946 Feb

50. Min. of the IC-Mtgs. of the ADs. 24-26 May 1951. UWA-M. UFAB, Series 5/21/6; Box 1, folder: WC min. 1947-51

51. Commissioner's Report.... 6 Dec. 1951. UWA-M. UFAB, Series 5/21/7; Box 2, folder: WC gen. files

52. Reed to Aigler. 20 May 1952. BHL. RWAP; Box 10, folder: corr. 1946-52 Reed, William

53. Min. of the IC-Mtgs. of the ADs. 24-26 May 1951. UWA-M. UFAB, Series 5/21/6; Box 1, folder: WC min. 1947-51

54. Emmons to FRs. Circa 22 Feb. 1953. UWA-M. UFAB, Series 5/21/7; Box 2, folder: WC gen. files

55. Handbook of the ICFR-Rev. 1941. UMA, DICAP; Box 13, folder: small handbook 1941. *In the revision, under "Organization and Procedure," it is stated "a member institution becomes ineligible for*

membership if its governing body fails to respect its delegation of control over intercollegiate athletics to its faculty." The FRC, by tradition, was granted that oversight responsibility.

56. Commissioner's Report .... 6 Dec. 1951. BHL. ADUM; Box 84, folder: ADs 3/41-7/52

57. Alderton, George S. "Jealous Rivals Seen in Big 10 Slap at M.S.C.-Foundation Ex-Head Denies Wilson Charge: Erickson Says Big Ten Chief Saw Books Back in December, 1951." *Lansing State Journal*, 23 Feb. 1953.

58. Harden to Wilson. 10 Sept. 1953. MSUA. ACR2; Box 2, folder: 27

59. Erickson to Harden. 23 July 1953. MSUA. ACR2; Box 2, folder: 27

60. Alderton, George S. "Jealous Rivals Seen in Big 10 Slap at M.S.C.-Foundation Ex-Head Denies Wilson Charge: Erickson Says Big Ten Chief Saw Books Back in Dec., 1951." *Lansing State Journal*, 23 Feb. 1953.

61. Erickson to Harden. 23 July 1953. MSUA. ACR2; Box 2, folder: 27

62. Emmons to FRs. Circa 22 Feb. 1953. UWA-M. UFAB, Series 5/21/7; Box 2, folder: WC gen. files

63. Alderton, George S. "Jealous Rivals Seen in Big 10 Slap at M.S.C.-Hannah's Statement." *Lansing State Journal*, 23 Feb. 1953.

64. Hannah to Wilson. 10 Feb. 1953. BHL. RWAP; Box 10, folder: corr. 1946-52 "M" misc. (ME-MY)

65. Emmons to FRs. Circa 22 Feb. 1953. UWA-M. UFAB, Series 5/21/7; Box 2, folder: WC gen. files

66. Ibid.

67. SBA. 17 May 1945. www.onthebanks.msu.edu

68. SBA. 17 Jan. 1946. www.onthebanks.msu.edu

69. SBA. 18 Apr. 1946. www.onthebanks.msu.edu

70. SBA. 15 June 1950. www.onthebanks.msu.edu

71. SBA. 13 July 1950. www.onthebanks.msu.edu

72. *Based on a review of board minutes, Erickson's last gift to the college was in Feb. of 1949, around the time the Spartan Foundation was organized.*

73. Alderton, George S. "Jealous Rivals Seen in Big 10 Slap at M.S.C.-Foundation Ex-Head Denies Wilson Charge: Erickson Says Big Ten Chief Saw Books Back in Dec., 1951." *Lansing State Journal*, 23 Feb. 1953.

74. SBA. 17 Apr. 1952. www.onthebanks.msu.edu

75. Erickson to Hannah. 2 Apr. 1952. MSUA. BOT; Box 1899, folder: 11 sup. mat. 4/17/52

76. Alderton, George S. "Jealous Rivals Seen in Big 10 Slap at M.S.C.-Hannah's Statement." *Lansing State Journal*, 23 February 1953.

77. Emmons to FRs. Circa 22 February 1953. UWA-M. UFAB, Series 5/21/7; Box 2, folder: WC gen. files

78. Alderton, George S. "Jealous Rivals Seen in Big 10 Slap at M.S.C.-Probation Is Decreed By Wilson." *Lansing State Journal*, 23 Feb. 1953.

79. Reed to Aigler. 20 May 1952. BHL. RWAP; Box 10, folder: corr. 1946-52 Reed, William

80. Aigler to Reed. 5 May 1952. BHL. RWAP; Box 10, folder: corr. 1946-52 Reed, William

81. Reed to Aigler. 20 May 1952. BHL. RWAP; Box 10, folder: corr. 1946-52 Reed, William

82. Aigler to Reed. 19 March 1952. BHL. RWAP; Box 10, folder: corr. 1946-52 Reed, William

83. Reed to Aigler. 20 May 1952. BHL. RWAP; Box 10, folder: corr. 1946-52 Reed, William

84. Ibid.

85. Emmons to FRs. Circa 22 Feb. 1953. UWA-M. UFAB, Series 5/21/7; Box 2, folder: WC gen. files

86. Hannah to Wilson. 10 Feb. 1953. BHL. RWAP; Box 10, folder: corr. 1946-52 "M" misc. (ME-MY)

87. Ibid.

88. Ibid.

89. Ibid.

90. *Legal representation is common practice in the high stakes game of intercollegiate athletics today. Hannah's use of Kim Sigler, former governor of Michigan, as the college's counsel set precedence.*

91. Emmons to FRs. Circa 22 Feb. 1953. UWA-M. UFAB, Series 5/21/7; Box 2, folder: WC gen. files

92. Ibid.

93. Alderton, George S. "Jealous Rivals Seen in Big 10 Slap at M.S.C.-Hannah's Statement." *Lansing State Journal*, 23 Feb. 1953.

94. Hannah to Wilson. 10 Feb. 1953. UWA-M. UFAB, Series 5/21/7; Box 2, folder: WC gen. files

95. Aigler to Wilson, Blommers, Little. 28 Jan. 1949. UWA-M. UFAB, Series 5/21/7; Box 1, folder: WC Gen. files. *In Jan. of 1949, MSC announced that it was ready for the Committee of Three investigation. Aigler was stunned by how quickly the college addressed the faculty representatives' remaining concerns about the college's compliance. He proposed that the committee delay its investigation to allow more time to uncover any additional wrongdoings overlooked in East Lansing.*

96. "Spartans Accept Trophy For National Grid Title." *Lansing State Journal*, 2 Feb. 1953.

97. SBA. 5 June 1952. www.onthebanks.msu.edu

98. Ibid.

99. SBA. 18 Dec. 1952. www.onthebanks.msu.edu

100. SBA. 9 Aug. 1951. www.onthebanks.msu.edu

101. SBA. 31 Dec. 1952. www.onthebanks.msu.edu

102. Hannah. pp. 48-49

103. Combs, William H. Untitled. 11 Jan. 1971. MSUA. HAP; Box 34, folder: 7 written corr. Combs

104. Min. of the IC—Joint Dinner Mtg. of the FRs and ADs. 19 May 1949. BHL. ADUM; Box 84, folder: Big Ten Directors Committee Min. 3/41-7/52. *The "Crisler Asterisk" Motion was a proposal advanced by the director immediately following MSC's tentative selection for membership in 12/1948. He wanted to appease coaches angered over having to compete against "hired" talent. His motion became conference policy in 5/1949 following the FRC approval of the Committee of Three report certifying the college's compliance with the Intercollegiate Handbook.*

105. Min. ICFR. 19-20 May 1949. BHL. ADUM; Box 84, folder: FRs Min. 1941-1957

CHAPTER 9: AN ACT OF CONTRITION

1.   Aigler to Griffith. 17 Feb. 1932. BHL. RWAP; Box 3, folder: Griffith, John 1932

2.   SBA. 31 Dec. 1952. www.onthebanks.msu.edu

3.   Thomas. pp. 149-53

4.   Hannah to Wilson. 23 Dec. 1952. UWA-M. UFAB, Series 5/21/7; Box 2, folder: WC gen. files

5.   Aigler to Reed. 2 Feb. 1953. BHL. RWAP; Box 10, folder: corr. 1946-52 Reed, William

6.   Hannah to Wilson. 10 Feb. 1953. UWA-M. UFAB, Series 5/21/7; Box 2, folder: WC gen. files

7.   *In 2012, University of Michigan English Professor Anne Curzan was appointed the school's faculty representative to the Big Ten.* (http://www.mgoblue.com/genrel/022112aaa.html). *She is the grand daughter of Ralph Aigler's old nemesis—John Hannah! Areas of research interest for Curzan include linguistics and lexicography.* (http://www-personal.umich.edu/~acurzan).

8.   Hannah to Wilson. 10 Feb. 1953. UWA-M. UFAB, Series 5/21/7; Box 2, folder: WC gen. files xyz

9.   Ibid.

10. Ibid.

11. Ibid.

12. Wilson to Hannah. 14 Feb. 1953. UMA. Pres. Office; Box 239, folder: PE and athl., IC 1953

13. Ibid.

14. Ibid.

15. Ibid.

16. Wilson to The Council.... 14 Feb. 1953. UMA. Pres. Office; Box 239, folder: PE and athl., IC 1953

17. Aigler to Nichols. 27 Feb. 1953. BHL. RWAP; Box 10, folder: corr. 1946-52

18. McDonel to FRs. In Re. Complaint of K.L. Wilson vs. MSC. UWA-M. UFAB, Series 5/21/7; Box 2, folder: WC gen. files

19. Emmons to Wilson. 16 Feb. 1953. UWA-M. UFAB, Series 5/21/7; Box 2, folder: WC gen. files

20. Emmons to FRs. Circa 22 Feb. 1953. UWA-M. UFAB, Series 5/21/7; Box 2, folder: WC gen. files

21. Aigler to Reed. 17 Feb. 1953. BHL. RWAP; Box 10, folder: corr. 1946-52 Reed, William

22. Aigler to Rottschaefer. 16 Feb. 1953. BHL. RWAP; Box 10, folder: corr. 1946-52 Rottschaefer, Henry

23. Aigler to Reed. 17 Feb. 1953. BHL. RWAP; Box 10, folder: corr. 1946-52 Reed, William

24. Aigler to Reed. 19 Feb. 1953. BHL. RWAP; Box 10, folder: corr. 1946-52 Reed, William

25. Aigler to Nichols. 27 Feb. 1953. BHL. RWAP; Box 10, folder: corr. 1946-52

26. Untitled Appellate Board Decision. Circa 22 Feb. 1953. BHL. RWAP; Box 10, folder: corr. 1946-52 Reed, William

27. Aigler to Nichols. 27 Feb. 1953. BHL. RWAP; Box 10, folder: corr. 1946-52

28. Minutes of the ICFR. 22 Feb. 1953. BHL. ADUM; Box 84, folder: FR min. 1941-57

29. Aigler to FRs. 24 Feb. 1953. UWA-M. UFAB, Series 5/21/7; Box 2, folder: WC gen. files

30. Aigler to Nichols. 27 Feb. 1953. BHL. RWAP; Box 10, folder: corr. 1946-52

31. Wilson to Conf. FRs-Memo. 15 Sept. 1953. BHL. RWAP; Box 10, folder: corr. 1946-52 personal

32. Aigler to Reed. 5 Mar. 1953. BHL. RWAP; Box 10, folder: corr. 1946-52 Reed, William

33. Crisler to Wilson. 15 Apr. 1953. BHL. HOCP; Box 1, top. corr. MSU 1953

34. Min. ICFR. 10-12 Dec. 1953. UMA. Pres. Office; Box 239, folder: PE and athl., IC 1953

35. Crisler to Wilson. 15 Apr. 1953. BHL. HOCP; Box 1, top. corr. MSU 1953

36. "Min. of the IC of ADs." 29-31 May 1952. BHL. ADUM; Box 84, folder: Big Ten Dir. Comm. 1941-52

37. Young. pp. 278-284. *Tier-two schools were quite frustrated with scheduling antics of the elite conference programs. Alternative ways of contracting to ensure fairness (in dates and venues) had been debated as far back as the spring of '48.*

38. "Min. of the IC-ADs." 4-6 December 1952. BHL. ADUM; Box 84, folder: Big Ten Dir. Comm. 1941-52, 1941-57.

39. Aigler to FRs. 24 Feb. 1953. UWA-M. UFAB, Series 5/21/7; Box 2, folder: WC gen. files

40. Wilson to Aigler. 11 Mar. 1953. BHL. RWAP; Box 10, folder: corr. 1946-52 Wilson, K.L. 1952

41. College Football Data Warehouse: cfbdatawarehouse.com. *A review of scheduling patterns, in the context of historical events, tends to support this conjecture.*

42. Aigler to Wilson. 19 May 1953. BHL. RWAP; Box 10, folder: corr. 1946-52 Wilson, K.L. 1952

43. Ibid.

44. Harden to Wilson. 10 Sept. 1953. MSUA. ACR2; Box 2, folder: 27

45. Mtgs of the Joint Group … 28-29 May 1953. UMA. Pres. Office; Box 239, folder: PE and athl., IC 1953

46. Mtgs. of the Joint Group … 28-29 May 1953. UMA. Pres. Office; Box 239, folder: PE and athl., IC 1953

47. Ackley to Hatcher. 2 July 1954. BHL. HOCP; Box 6, folder: UM BICIA papers 1953-54

48. "Council Appointments." 1 Aug. 1953. *Spartan Alumni Magazine—The Record.* MSUA. ACR2; Box 2, folder: 27

49. Harden to Wilson. 10 Sept. 1953. MSUA. ACR2; Box 2, folder: 27

50. "Spartans' Edgar Harden Busy Getting Acquainted with New Athletic Directors." *Lansing State Journal,* 26 July 1953. MSUA. ACR2; Box 2, folder: 27

51. Wilson to Harden. 30 June 1953. MSUA. ACR2; Box 2, folder: 27

52. "Spartans' Edgar Harden Busy Getting Acquainted with New Athletic Directors." *Lansing State Journal.* 26 July 1953. MSUA. ACR2; Box 2, folder: 27

53. "Harden Gets Acquainted with Post." *Michigan State News.* 29 July 1953. MSUA. ACR2; Box 2, folder: 27

54. Harden to Wilson. 6 Aug. 1953. MSUA. ACR2; Box 2, folder: 27

55. Hannah to Emmons. 6 Jan. 1953. MSUA. JAHP Box 69, folder 38 Athl. Council, gen. 1954-58

56. Aigler to FRs. 24 Feb. 1953. UWA-M. UFAB, Series 5/21/7; Box 2, folder: WC, gen. files

57. Harden to Wilson. 6 Aug. 1953. MSUA. ACR2; Box 2, folder: 27

58. Ibid.

59. Harden, Edgar L. "Report to the Western Conference." 6 Aug. 1953. MSUA. ACR2; Box 2, folder: 27

60. *In point of fact, Breslin was actually promoted—and with a salary increase! Mindful of his role in recruiting him back to East Lansing, John Hannah apparently felt an obligation to protect his mentee.*

Over the next 16 years, he would advance in rank to become Secretary of the University, Secretary of the Board of Trustees, and eventually executive VP of MSU.

61. Harden, Edgar L. "Report to the Western Conference." 6 Aug. 1953. MSUA. ACR2; Box 2, folder: 27

62. Ibid.

63. Haley to Harden. 3 Aug. 1953. MSUA. ACR2; Box 2, folder: 27

64. Jenkins to Harden. 30 July 1953. MSUA. ACR2; Box 2, folder: 27

65. Harden, Edgar L. "Report to the West. Conf." 6 Aug. 1953. MSUA. ACR2; Box 2, folder: 27

66. Harden to Wilson. 6 Aug. 1953. MSUA. ACR2; Box 2, folder: 27

67. Wilson to Harden. 30 June 1953. MSUA. ACR2; Box 2, folder: 27

68. Wilson to The Conf. FRs. 15 Sept. 1953. BHL. RWAP; Box 10, folder: corr. 1946-52 personal

69. Harden to Wilson. 10 Sept. 1953. MSUA. ACR2; Box 2, folder: 27

70. Emmons to FRs. Circa 22 Feb. 1953. UWA-M. UFAB, Series 5/21/7; Box 2, folder: WC gen. files

71. Alderton, George S. "Jealous Rivals Seen in Big 10 Slap at M.S.C.—Hannah's Statement." *Lansing State Journal*, 23 Feb. 1953.

72. "Summary and Conclusion (Report of Dean Edgar L. Harden to Commissioner Wilson)." 12 Sept. 1953. BHL. RWAP; Box 10, folder: corr. 1946-52 personal

73. Ibid.

74. Harden to Wilson. 10 Sept. 1953. MSUA. ACR2; Box 2, folder: 27

75. Ibid. *Underlined emphasis was included in Harden's official transcript.*

76. Wilson to The Conf. FRs. 15 Sept. 1953. BHL. RWAP; Box 10, folder: corr. 1946-52 personal.

77. Aigler to Reed. 5 Mar. 1953. BHL. RWAP; Box 10, folder: corr. 1946-52 Reed, William

78. "FOR RELEASE TO AM'S OF FRIDAY, SEPT. 18," Western Conference Service Bureau. 18 Sept. 1953. UMA. Pres. Office; Box 239, folder: PE and IC 1953

79. Aigler to Reed. 19 May 1952. BHL. RWAP; Box 10, folder: corr. 1946-52 Reed, William

80. Aigler to Wilson. 11 June 1948. BHL. RWAP; Box 10, folder: corr. 1946-52 Wilson, K.L.

81. Aigler to Reed. 19 May 1952. BHL. RWAP; Box 10, folder: corr. 1946-52 Reed, William

82. Aigler to Reed. 5 March 1953. BHL. RWAP; Box 10, folder: corr 1946-52 Reed, William

CHAPTER 10: MR. CLEAN

1. Smith to Crisler. 20 Jan. 1955. BHL. HOCP; Box 1, folder: top. corr. MSU 1954-60, 1965-66.

2. Crisler to Smith. 1 Feb. 1955. BHL. HOCP; Box 1, top. corr. MSU 1954-60, 1965-66

3. Min. of the IC Mtg. of the ADs and Football Coaches. 13 Dec. 1948. BHL. ADUM; Box 84, folder: Big 10 records 1941-52. *Crisler proposed that Spartan football competition not count until all Jenison Awardees had used up their eligibility—intended to appease angry coaches and directors unwilling to compete against "hired" talent.*

4. Young. pp. 323-325.

5. Thomas. p. 286

6. Hannah, J. "Speech ... NCAA." 9 Jan. 1946. BHL. HOCP; Box 1, folder: top. corr. MSU, clippings and misc.

7. Hannah to Hovde. 17 Sept. 1952. MSUA. JAHP; Box 90, folder: 22

8. Young. pp. 197-203

9. Lester. p. 137

10. Bachman, Charles. "The Athletic Side of JAH." Circa 1970. MSUA. HAP; Box 34, folder: 2 Bachman

11. "Michigan State Football Date." Feb. 1949. BHL. HOCP; Box 1, folder: top. corr. MSU 1947-49

12. Young. pp. 54-55

13. Ibid. pp. 54-58

14. Aigler to Ruthven. 30 Sept. 1941. BHL. RWAP; Box 8; folder: corr. "H" misc.

15. Min. of the Mtg. of the BICIA. 27 Jan. 1949. BHL. BICIA; Box 40, folder: min. 2/38-6/50

16. Crisler to Young. 29 Jan. 1949. BHL. HOCP; Box 1, folder: top. corr. MSU 1950-52

17. Young to Crisler. 23 Feb. 1949. BHL. HOCP; Box 1, folder: top. corr. MSU 1950-52

18. Min. of the Mtg. of the BICIA. 27 Jan. 1949. BHL. BICIA; Box 40, folder: min. 2/38-6/50

19. Aigler to Ruthven. 30 Sept. 1941. BHL. RWAP; Box 8; folder: corr. "H" misc.

20. Crisler to Young. 29 Jan. 1949. BHL. HOCP; Box 1, folder: top. corr. MSU 1950-52

21. *The Spartans had a non-conference game against Marquette University the following weekend.*

22. Jenkins, Guy H. "State of GOP Eyes Strong Ticket for '56." *Grand Rapids Press*, 21 May 1956.

23. Min: BICIA. 16 Oct. 1953. BHL. HOCP; Box 6, folder: BIC Papers: 1953-1954. *(Unless cited otherwise, all quotes for this section derive from this document.)*

24. Williams to Hatt. 24 Nov. 1953. BHL. GMWP; Box 103, boards and commissions, 1953, folder: colleges, state, UM

25. Harden to Crisler. 17 Nov. 1953. BHL. HOCP; Box 1, folder: top. corr. MSU 1953.

26. Noer. p. 144

27. Ibid. p. 142

28. Harden to Crisler. 17 Nov. 1953. BHL. HOCP; Box 1, folder: top. corr. MSU 1953.

29. Williams to Crisler. 14 Oct. 1953. BHL. GMWP; Box 103, boards and commissions, 1953, folder: colleges, state, UM

30. Crisler to Williams. 15 Oct. 1953. BHL. GMWP; Box 103, boards and commissions, 1953, folder: colleges, state, UM

31. Wilson to Hannah. 14 Feb. 1953. UWA-M. UFAB, Series 5/21/7; Box 2, folder: WC, gen. files

32. Crisler to Smith. 1 Feb. 1955. BHL. HOCP; Box 1, folder: top. corr. MSU 1953.

33. Neisch to Crisler. 14 Oct. 1953. BHL. HOCP; Box 1, folder: top. corr. MSU 1953.

34. Bigby to Crisler. 15 Oct. 1953. BHL. HOCP; Box 1, folder: top. corr. MSU 1953.

35. Williams to Rogers. 19 Nov. 1953. BHL. GMWP; Box 103, boards and commissions, 1953, folder: colleges, state, UM

36. Min: BICIA. 16 October 1953. BHL. HOCP; Box 6, folder: BIC Papers: 1953-1954

37. Ibid.

38. Hibbard to Crisler. 21 December 1951. BHL. HOCP; Box 1, folder: top. corr. MSU 1950-52

39. Min: BICIA. 16 October 1953. BHL. HOCP; Box 6, folder: BIC Papers: 1953-1954

40. Ibid.

41. Ibid.

42. Ibid.

43. Ibid.

44. King to Williams. 4 Nov. 1953. BHL. GMWP; Box 103, boards and commissions, 1953, folder: colleges, state, UM

45. Ibid.

46. *Three schools may have quietly boycotted the Spartans. The 1955-56 schedules were supposed to be drafted during the December '52 meetings. For various reasons, no doubt one involving rumors of a Spartan investigation, the ADs tabled plans. Four weeks later, still lacking word on the commissioner's investigation, they again deferred drafting schedules. Finally, on 3/4/1953 the directors announced plans. Ohio State, Northwestern, and Iowa were not included on the Spartan's schedule* (Football Schedule Mtg. of the Conf. ADs and Football Coaches. 4-5 Mar. 1953. BHL. ADUM; Box 84, folder: Big Ten Dir. Comm. 1941-52, 1941-57). *In May of 1954, the directors met to arrange contracts for 1957-58. The three schools again failed to sign-up with MSC* (Meeting of the Conf. ADs and Football Coaches. 25-27 May 1954. BHL. ADUM; Box 84, folder: Big Ten Directors Committee 1941-52, 1941-57). *The boycott appeared to end in Jan. 1957* (Min. of Schedule Meeting of IC-ADs and Football Coaches." 7 Jan. 1957. BHL. ADUM; Box 84, folder: Big Ten Dir. Comm. 1941-52, 1941-57).

47. King to Williams. 4 Nov. 1953. BHL. GMWP; Box 103, boards and commissions, 1953, folder: colleges, state, UM

48. Smith to Crisler. 20 Jan. 1955. BHL. HOCP; Box 1, folder: top. corr. MSU 1953.

49. Crisler to Smith. 1 Feb. 1955. BHL. HOCP; Box 1, folder: top. corr. MSU 1953.

50. King to Williams. 4 Nov. 1953. BHL. GMWP; Box 103, boards and commissions, 1953, folder: colleges, state, UM

51. United Press Release-untitled. 19 Nov. 1953. BHL. GMWP; Box 103, boards and commissions, 1953, folder: colleges, state, UM

52. Hatt to Williams. 13 Nov. 1953. BHL. GMWP; Box 103, boards and commissions, 1953, folder: colleges, state, UM

53. Williams to Hatt. 13 Nov. 1953. BHL. GMWP; Box 103, boards and commissions, 1953, folder: colleges, state, UM

54. King to Williams. 4 Nov. 1953. BHL. GMWP; Box 103, boards and commissions, 1953, folder: colleges, state, UM

55. Williams to Hatt. 24 Nov. 1953. BHL. GMWP; Box 103, boards and commissions, 1953, folder: colleges, state, UM

56. Williams to Hannah. 5 Nov. 1953. BHL. GMWP; Box 103: boards and commissions, 1953; colleges, state, UM

57. Williams to Hatcher. 5 Nov. 1953. BHL. RWAP; Box 10, folder: corr: "U-V-W" misc.

58. Hatcher to Williams. 6 Nov. 1953. BHL. HOCP, Box 1, folder: top. corr. MSU 1953.

59. "Statement by Harlan Hatcher, ... " 6 Nov. 1953. BHL. HOCP; Box 1, folder: top. corr. MSU 1953.

60. Hatcher to Williams. 6 Nov. 1953. BHL. HOCP, Box 1, folder: top. corr. MSU 1953.

61. Ibid.

62. (Photo of Munn, Williams, players, and trophy). *Lansing State Journal,* 15 Nov. 1953.

63. Rogers to Williams. 19 Nov. 1953. BHL. GMWP; Box 103, boards and commissions, 1953, folder: colleges, state, UM

64. Williams to Rogers. 19 Nov. 1953. BHL. GMWP; Box 103, boards and commissions, 1953, folder: colleges, state, UM

65. Smith to Crisler. 20 Jan. 1955. BHL. HOCP; Box 1, top. corr: MSU 1953.

66. Crisler to Smith. 1 Feb. 1955. BHL. HOCP; Box 1, top. corr: MSU 1953.

67. Operation Rescue to Williams. 11 Jan. 1955. BHL. GMWP; Box 159, folder: boards and commissions, colleges, state, MSU rename 1955

68. Min: BICIA. 16 October 1953. BHL. HOCP; Box 6, folder: BIC Papers: 1953-1954

CHAPTER 11: DECISIONS

1. Hannah to Emmons, Young. 19 Feb. 1953. MSUA. JAHP; Box 69, folder: 38 Athletic Council, general 1954-58. *Hannah shared this quote with every new player, coach and administrator signing on at Michigan State. Its origin dates back to a conversation President Shaw had with sports writer George Alderton of the* Lansing State Journal.

2. Aigler to Wilson. 25 Feb. 1953. BHL. RWAP; Box 10, folder: corr. 1946-52 Wilson, K.L. 1952

3. Emmons to FRs. Circa Feb. 1953. UWA-M. UFAB, Series 5/21/7; Box 2, folder: WC gen. files

4. Hannah to Emmons. 6 Jan. 1953. MSUA. JAHP; Box 69 folder: 38 Athletic Council gen. 1954-58

5. Aigler to FRs. 24 Feb. 1953. BHL. RWAP; Box 10, folder: corr. 1946-52 Reed, William

6. Min. of the IC ADs. 29-31 May 1952. BHL. ADUM; Box 84, folder: Big 10 Rec. 1941-52

7. Min. of the IC ADs. 4-6 Dec. 1952. BHL, ADUM; Box 84, folder: Big 10 Rec. 1941-52

8. Football Schedule Mtg. of the Conf. ADs.... 4-5 Mar. 1953. BHL, ADUM; Box 84, folder: Big 10 Rec. 1941-52

9. Meetings of the Conf. ADs ... 25-27 May 1954. BHL, ADUM; Box 84, folder: Big 10 Rec. 1941-52

10. Aigler to Wilson. 25 Feb. 1953. BHL. RWAP; Box 10, folder: corr. 1946-52 Wilson, K.L. 1952

11. Harden to Wilson. 10 Sept. 1953. MSUA. ACR2; Box 2, folder: 27. *Hannah had previously granted Harden complete authority and responsibility regarding the internal investigation of the college during his sabbatical year in Washington. There was no need for the faculty representative to alert his boss of plans to interact with Aigler.*

12. Harden to Aigler. 15 Dec. 1953. BHL. RWAP; Box 9, folder: corr. 1946-52 "H" misc. (HA-HN)

13. Aigler to Reed. 5 Mar. 1953. BHL. RWAP; Box 10, folder: corr. 1946-52 Reed, William

14. King to Williams. 4 Nov. 1953. BHL. GMWP; Box 103, boards and commissions, 1953, folder: colleges, state, UM

15. Min,: BICIA. 16 October 1953. BHL. HOCP; Box 6, folder: BIC Papers: 1953-1954

16. Mtgs. of the Conf. ADs and Football Coaches. 25-27 May 1954. BHL, ADUM; Box 84, folder: Big 10 Rec. 1941-52. *As will be seen, following Wilson's Feb. '54 summary report on the Spartans' probationary year, the directors gathered a few months later to make schedules for 1957-58; they were unsuccessful for various reasons; contracts were finally arranged months later. Although never divulged, a review of scheduling patterns over the four years ('55-'58) would suggest there was a prolonged boycott*

but it involved three rather than four programs: OSU, Iowa, and NW. The three holdouts would resume/
start contracting with the Spartans as of 1959.

17. "Timetable for Unveiling, Presentation of 'Bunyan' Trophy Is Worked Out—University Displays Little Enthusiasm For Project." *Lansing State Journal*, 13 Nov. 1953

18. *That loss to Purdue also ended a 3-year 28-game winning streak.*

19. *The Crisler Asterisk Motion effectively declared that the Spartans were ineligible for conference titles in football until all Jenison Award athletes had completed eligibility. Competition with MSC was permissible; losses would not count against a member's record however. In addition to that sanction, based on scheduling patterns, it appeared that Illinois, Iowa, Wisconsin, and Northwestern athletic directors maintained a boycott against Michigan State's football program. Unlike its cohorts, Iowa's disciplinary action lasted only three years (1950-52).*

20. 789Slingerlend, L. "Spartans Rejoice, Wolverines Glum, but Unashamed." *Lansing State Journal*, 15 Nov. 1953

21. "Timetable for Unveiling, Presentation of 'Bunyan' Trophy Is Worked Out—University Displays Little Enthusiasm For Project." *Lansing State Journal*, 13 Nov. 1953

22. Alderton, George S. "Spartans Sure of Title Share..." *Lansing State Journal*, 15 Nov. 1953

23. Slingerlend, L. "Spartans Rejoice, Wolverines Glum, but Unashamed." *Lansing State Journal*, 15 Nov. 1953

24. (Photo of Munn, Williams, players, and trophy). *Lansing State Journal*, 15 Nov. 1953

25. Spoelstra, Watson. "How Did Crisler Vote? 'For MSC From the Start.'" *Detroit News*, 23 Nov. 1953.

26. Report of the BICIA. Jan. 1954. BHL. HOCP; Box 6, folder: 1953-54 BIC Annual Report. *Crisler summarizes the history of the WC's association with the Rose Bowl dating back to 1902.*

27. To the Presidents ... Jan. 1948. BHL. RWAP; Box 13, folder: athl., BIC, 1940-48

28. The Min. Joint Mtg. of the ICFR and ADs. 13 Dec. 1946. BHL. ADUM; Box 84, folder: Big Ten Dir. Comm. min. 1941-52

29. Crisler to Aigler. 22 Apr. 1940. BHL. RWAP; Box 10, folder: A-Z misc. athl. 1939-41

30. Ibid.

31. Ibid.

32. Aigler to Wilson. 29 Apr. 1946. BHL. RWAP; Box 10, folder: Wilson, Tug

33. Aigler to Salsinger. 15 Nov. 1948. BHL. RWAP; Box 12, folder: A-Z misc. athl.

34. Aigler to Wilson. 29 Apr. 1946. BHL. RWAP; Box 10, folder: Wilson, Tug

35. To the President.... Jan. 1948. BHL. RWAP; Box 13, folder: athl., BIC, 1940-48

36. Report of the BICIA. Jan. 1954. BHL. HOCP; Box 6, folder: 1953-54 BIC Annual Report

37. Ibid.

38. Min. of ICFRs. 28-29 May 1953. BHL. ADUM; Box 84, folder: Big 10 directors' min., file 3/41-7/52. *The influence of the presidents was noted in the tally. Hannah and Lew Morrill opposed all post-season bowls; their FRs' votes reflected that. Northwestern and Wisconsin also sided with the minority. Despite sharing the same concerns of his UM faculty senate, Aigler eventually voted with the majority in extending the contract.*

39. Spoelstra, Watson. "Second Poll Is Possible For Big Ten." *Detroit News,* 16 Nov. 1953. *The faculty chose the first five representatives to Pasadena based on a suggestion offered by Herbert Crisler back in 1940 (*Crisler to Aigler. 22 April 1940. BHL. RWAP; Box 10, folder: A-Z misc. athletics 1939-41). *Expediency may have contributed to the practice. The Inter-Conference Agreement was signed only five weeks before the 1947 Rose Bowl. There was little time to draft a Big Nine protocol for selecting a representative. By default, the faculty took on the responsibility. In 1951 the FRs appropriately delegated that task to the ADs. They would merely rubber-stamp the selection.*

40. Aigler to Harris. 9 Dec. 1953. BHL. RWAP; Box 9, folder: corr. 1946-52 "H" misc. (HA-HN)

41. Brannagan, Thomas. "Athletic Directors Say 'Football' Will Be Key for Rose Bowl Nomination." *Lansing State Journal,* 17 Nov. 1953.

42. Harman to Crisler. 17 Nov. 1953. BHL. HOCP; Box 1, folder: top. corr. MSU 1953

43. Nichols to Crisler. 20 Nov. 1953. BHL. HOCP; Box 1, folder: top. corr. MSU 1953

44. Aigler to Nichols. 27 Feb. 1953. BHL. RWAP; Box 10, folder: corr. 1946-52

45. Nichols to Crisler. 20 Nov. 1953. BHL. HOCP; Box 1, folder: top. corr. MSU 1953

46. Spoelstra, Watson. "How Did Crisler Vote? 'For MSC From the Start.'" *Detroit News,* 23 Nov. 1953.

47. Brannagan, Thomas. "Athletic Directors Say 'Football' Will Be Key for Rose Bowl Nomination." *Lansing State Journal,* 17 Nov. 1953

48. "Probation of Spartans No Bowl Factor—Big 10 Team To Be Picked On Merit." *Chicago Tribune,* 17 Nov. 1953.

49. Ibid.

50. Spoelstra, Watson. "How Did Crisler Vote? 'For MSC From the Start.'" *Detroit News,* 23 Nov. 1953.

51. Smallegan, Jim. "Rose Bowl Sparks Big MSC Rally." *Detroit News,* 23 Nov. 1953.

52. Goodsell to The Editor. 24 Nov. 1953. BHL. HOCP; Box: 1, folder: top. corr. MSU 1953

53. Smith, Wilfred. "Michigan State Picked For Rose Bowl." *Chicago Tribune,* 23 Nov. 1953.

54. Hannah to Foster. 5 Mar. 1960. MSUA. JAHP; Box 44, folder: 44 *Hannah made it a practice, as the Foster letter illustrates, to gift MSC-produced maple syrup (and also extension service-grown blueberries) to Council of Ten colleagues and other prominent university leaders such as ND's Rev. Ted Hesburgh. Prior to joining the Big Nine, however, he would gift only certain Council of Nine colleagues he considered very good friends—members he could count on for support if ever requested. Morrill, Hovde and Wells were included on that list.*

55. Spoelstra, Watson. "How Did Crisler Vote? 'For MSC From the Start.'" *Detroit News*, 23 Nov. 1953.

56. Young. pp. 277-292.

57. Spoelstra, Watson. "How Did Crisler Vote? 'For MSC From the Start.'" *Detroit News*, 23 Nov. 1953.

58. Ibid.

59. Ibid.

60. Brannagan, Thomas. "Athletic Directors Say 'Football' Will Be Key for Rose Bowl Nomination." *Lansing State Journal*, 17 Nov. 1953.

61. Spoelstra, Watson. "How Did Crisler Vote? 'For MSC From the Start.'" *Detroit News*, 23 Nov. 1953.

62. Young to Crisler. (Western Union) 23 Nov. 1953. BHL. HOCP; Box 1, folder: top. corr. MSU 1953

63. *Spartan fan David Burgess shared a note (Nov. 2013) written by Munn expressing this opinion. It was penciled in the margin of a copy of Spoelstra's Detroit News 11/23/54 article.*

64. (Handwritten note). Hannah, John A. 20 Nov. 1954. *The MSC president wrote a note to his athletic director (Munn) at the halftime of the '54 UM-OSU game (the score was tied). At the time, the Wolverines were 6-2 (one conference loss) and the Buckeyes 8-0. Anticipating a UM victory, and thus a conference tie with OSU, Hannah proposed the following press release: "In spite of the fact that we were deeply disappointed last year when the University of Michigan did not vote for M.S.C. to represent the Big Ten in the Rose Bowl—we feel that it is desirable for the State of Michigan to be represented and M.S.C. is voting for the University of Michigan." Munn penciled in the following: "Letter or note written by Pres. Hannah, 1954 Last game of season when Ohio and Mich. game was on (TV). This was at halftime." As it turned out, there was no need for a press release—OSU outplayed UM in the final quarter and ended the season undefeated. David Burgess shared the penciled notes with me. They remain in my possession.*

65. "Michigan State Students Hold Celebration." *Chicago Tribune*, 23 Nov. 1953.

66. Harden to Hannah. 4 Mar. 1954. MSUA. JAHP; Box 69, folder: 38

67. Wilson to Harden. Circa Mar. 1954. MSUA. JAHP; Box 69, folder: 38

68. Harden to Hannah. 4 Mar. 1954. MSUA. JAHP; Box 69, folder: 38

69. Aigler to Wilson. 23 Nov. 1953. BHL. RWAP; Box 10, folder: corr. 1946-52 personal

70. Smith, Wilfred. "Big Ten May Act On Spartan Ban." *Detroit News,* 10 Dec. 1953.

71. Spoelstra, Watson. "Second Poll Is Possible For Big Ten." *Detroit News,* 17 Nov. 1953.

72. Aigler to Wilson. 23 Nov. 1953. BHL. RWAP; Box 10, folder: corr. 1946-52 personal

73. Min. of ICFR. 10-12 Dec. 1953. UMA. Pres. Office; Box 239, folder: PE and athl., IC 1953

74. Wilson to Conf. FRs-Memo. 15 Sept. 1953. BHL. RWAP; Box 10, folder: corr. 1946-52 personal

75. Min. ICFR. 10-12 Dec. 1953. UMA. Pres. Office; Box 239, folder: PE and athl., IC 1953

76. Ibid. *By conference tradition, a simple majority ruled on all tallies. A favorable decision was noted in the minutes as "voted" or "unanimously voted." An unfavorable poll was declared, "Motion lost."*

77. "Whiter Than Lilies For Red Rose Bowl." *Detroit News,* 12 Dec. 1953. *Contrary to the commissioner's comments reported in the* News, *the confidential conference minutes noted that the motion to approve was "voted," implying no unanimity.*

78. "Dr. R.S. Shaw Dies Here at 81." *Lansing State Journal,* 8 Feb. 1953

79. Alderton, George S. "The Sport Grist—Back to Football." *Lansing State Journal,* 10 Feb. 1953

80. Hannah to Emmons. 19 Feb. 1953. MSUA. JAHP; Box 69, folder: 38

81. Harden to Hannah. 4 Mar.1954. MSUA. JAHP; Box 69, folder: 38

82. Wilson to Aigler. 11 Mar. 1953. BHL. RWAP; Box 10, folder: corr. 1946-52 Wilson, K.L. 1952

83. Hannah to Munn, Scott. 21 May 1956. MSUA. HAF; Box 41, folder: 5 IC athletics

84. *Aigler had attended at least four of the first seven games in Pasadena: '47 Illinois, '48 Michigan, '51 Michigan, and '53 Wisconsin. His presence at the other three contests could not be verified.*

85. Crisler to Aigler. 22 Apr. 1940. BHL. RWAP; Box 10, folder: A-Z misc. athl. 1939-41

86. Report of the BICIA. Jan. 1954. BHL. HOCP; Box 6, folder: 1953-54 BIC Annual Report

87. Aigler to Harris. 9 Dec. 1953. BHL. RWAP; Box 9, folder: corr. 1946-52 "H" misc. (HA-HN)

88. Royce to Hannah. 5 Jan. 1954. MSUA. JAHP; Box 62, folder: 71 Rose Bowl 1953-54

89. Mogge to Hannah. 6 Jan. 1954. MSUA. JAHP; Box 62, folder: 71 Rose Bowl 1953-54

90. Telford to Hannah. 8 Jan. 1954. MSUA. JAHP; Box 62, folder: 71 Rose Bowl 1953-54

91. Zimmerman to Harden. 21 Jan. 1954. MSUA. JAHP; Box 62, folder: 71 Rose Bowl 1953-54

92. SBA. 15 Jan. 1954. www.onthebanks.msu.edu

93. Hannah. p. 114

94. SBA. 18 Dec. 1953. www.onthebanks.msu.edu

95. McDonel to Young. 21 Dec. 1953. MSUA. BOT; Box 1901, folder: 23 sup. mat. 12/18/53. *Young was offered a one-year furlough beginning in July of 1954; retirement would take place 12 months later. The practice allowed Hannah the opportunity to replace his athletic director that much earlier.*

96. Harden to Hannah. 4 Mar. 1954. MSUA. JAHP; Box 69, folder: 38

97. Spoelstra, Watson. "Munn Promoted; Daugherty Coach." *Detroit News*, 15 Jan. 1954.

98. SBA. 15 Jan. 1954. www.onthebanks.msu.edu

99. "DiMaggio, Monroe Honeymoon." *Lansing State Journal*, 15 Jan. 1954.

100. "University Tag Sought by MSC." *Ann Arbor News,* 15 January 1954. *The Ann Arbor paper printed the story on page 3 adjacent to numerous other incidental news reports. The* Lansing State Journal *included the announcement in its "Bulletins" section. The* Detroit Free Press *buried the announcement inside its first section. There was no mention of the college's name-change plans in the* Detroit News *that day.*

101. SBA. 15 Jan. 1954. www.onthebanks.msu.edu

Chapter 12: The Brody Fumble

1. Aigler to Nienhuss. 25 Jan. 1954. BHL, RWAP; Box10, folder: corr. 1946-52

2. Brennan, Thomas E. "A Portrait of Augustus B. Woodward." 9 Oct. 2001. *Michigan State Supreme Court*

3. Stason to Hatcher, (Memo). 25 Feb. 1955. BHL. HHHP; Box 53, folder: MSU name and letters/Stason

4. Kuhn. pp. 302-303

5. Stason to Hatcher, (Memo). 25 Feb. 1955. BHL. HHHP; Box 53, folder: MSU name and letters/Stason

6. Morrill to Hatcher. 30 Aug. 1948. UMA. James L. Morrill Papers; Box 1, folder: Ohio corr. F-H

7. Morrill to Hannah. 24 May 1951. UMA. James L. Morrill Papers; Box 1, folder: corr. A-L, HA-HE Morrill to Hatcher.

8. 878Morrill to Pollard. 28 May 1951. UMA. James L. Morrill Papers; Box 2, folder: corr. PO-PZ

9. "Will M.S.C. Be M.S.U. Next Year?" *Lansing State Journal,* 16 Jan. 1954.

10. Hannah to Williams. 18 Jan. 1954. MSUA. BOT, sup. mat.; Box 1902, folder: 1, 1/15/54

11. Stason to Hatcher, (Memo). 25 Feb. 1955. BHL. HHHP; Box 53, folder: MSU name/letters to Blythe

12. Hatcher to Williams. 27 Jan. 1954. BHL. GMWP; Box 129, folder: Boards and Commissions, 1954: colleges, state, MSU

13. Hatcher to Williams. 28 Feb. 1955. BHL. GMWP; Box 159, folder: Boards and Commissions, 1955: colleges, state, MSU renaming. *Italics were originally underlined.*

14. Salsinger to Aigler. 31 Jan. 1943. BHL. RWAP; Box 8, folder: corr. 1940-45 "S" misc.

15. Min: BICIA. 16 October 1953. BHL. HOCP; Box 6, folder: BIC Papers: 1953-1954

16. "Contents." Circa Jan. 1954. BHL. MLNP; Box 4, folder: top. files, 1953-54 (E-P), MSC-name change

17. Stason to Hatcher. 22 Jan. 1954. BHL. HHHP; Box 53, folder: MSU name change, letters from Stason

18. Sellers, Ashley. "E. Blythe Stason—Engineer of Administrative Law." 59 *Michigan Law Review* (1960-61), p. 191

19. Stason to Hatcher. 22 Jan. 1954. BHL. HHHP; Box 53, folder: MSU name change, letters from Stason

20. "Attorney General Says Legislature Can Give MSC Title of University." *Ann Arbor News*. 1 Apr. 1955. BHL. MLNP; Box 4, folder: top. files, 1953-54 (E-P), MSC-name change

21. *Postscript: Letter to Michigan Alumni*, winter issue: Feb. 1954. MSUA. BOT; Box 1902, folder: 5 sup. mat. 2/19/54

22. Young. pp. 80-81

23. Kuich to Williams. 8 Feb. 1954. BHL. GMWP; Box 159, folder: Boards and Commissions, 1954: colleges, state, MSU.

24. Ibid.

25. Ibid.

26. Blackford to Kuich. 10 Feb. 1954. BHL. GMWP; Box 159, folder: Boards and Commissions, 1954: colleges, state, MSU.

27. Mossner to Williams. 28 Jan. 1954. BHL. GMWP; Box 159, folder: Boards and Commissions, 1954: colleges, state, MSU

28. Aigler to Wilson. 11 June 1948. BHL. RWAP; Box 10, folder: corr. 1946-52 Wilson, K.L.

29. SBA 18 Dec. 1953. www.onthebanks.msu.edu

30. Proposed New Legislation. Circa 18 Jan. 1954. MSUA. BOT; Box 1902, folder 1, sup. mat. 11/15/54

31. Hannah to Carr. 18 Jan. 1954. MSUA. BOT; Box 1902, folder 1, sup. mat. 11/15/54

32. Ibid.

33. "Definitions." Circa January 1954. MSUA. BOT; Box 1902, folder 1, sup. mat. 11/15/54

34. Ibid.

35. Biographical Note. Circa 2001. MSUA. HRSP

36. Filley, H. Clyde. "Howard R. Smith." Lincoln: Neb. Hall of Agric. Achievement, 1957. MSUA. HRSP

37. Biographical Note. Circa 2001. MSUA. HRSP

38. SBA 15 Jan. 1954. www.onthebanks.msu.edu

39. Smith to Aigler. 22 Jan. 1954. BHL. RWAP; Box 10, folder: corr. 1946-53

40. Ibid.

41. Aigler to Niehuss. 20 Jan. 1954. BHL. RWAP; Box 10, folder: corr. 1946-53

42. Brody to Smith. 21 Jan. 1954. BHL. RWAP; Box 10, folder: corr. 1946-53

43. Ibid.

44. Aigler to Niehuss. 20 Jan. 1954. BHL. RWAP; Box 10, folder: corr. 1946-53

45. Aigler to Niehuss. 25 Jan. 1954. BHL. RWAP; Box 10, folder: corr. 1946-53

46. Aigler to Hatcher. 5 Feb. 1954. B BHL. RWAP; ox 9, folder: corr. 1946-53 "H" (HA-HN)

47. Smith to Aigler. 22 Jan. 1954. BHL. RWAP; Box 10, folder: corr. 1946-53

48. Aigler to Hatcher. 5 Feb. 1954. BHL. RWAP; Box 9, folder: corr. 1946-53 "H" (HA-HN)

49. Marshall to Smith. 2 Feb. 1954. BHL. RWAP; Box 9, folder: corr. 1946-53 "H" (HA-HN)

50. "Fight on MSC Name Reopens: New Senate Proposal Brings Objections From U-M Officials." *Grand Rapids Press.* 10 Feb. 1954. BHL. MLNP; Box 4, folder: top. files, 1953-54 (E-P), MSC-name change

51. "Regents Explain Opposition." *Postscript: Letter to Michigan Alumni,* winter issue: Feb. 1954. MSUA. BOT; Box 1802, folder: 5 sup. mat. 2/19/54

52. Brody and Hannah to Mem. of the Mich. Leg. 15 Feb. 1954. BHL. HHHP; Box 53, folder: MSU name/letters to Stason.

53. Ibid.

54. Ibid.

55. Hatcher to Williams. 27 Jan. 1954. BHL. GMWP; Box 129, folder: Boards and Commissions, 1954: colleges, state, MSU

56. Thomas. p. 255

CHAPTER 13: THE SECRETARY OF OFFENSE

1. Fisk to Hatcher. 7 Apr. 1955. BHL. GMWP; Box 159, folder: Boards and commissions, 1955: colleges, state, MSU rename

2. *The Michigan Alumnus,* Vol. 36, no. 27. 3 May 1930

3. *"The Record." Spartan Alumni Magazine,* Jan. 1954; Vol. 59-no. 1

4. *Postscript: Letter to Michigan Alumni,* winter issue: Feb. 1954. MSUA. BOT; Box 1902, folder: 5 sup. mat. 2/19/54

5. *Postscript: Letter to Michigan Alumni,* winter issue: Feb. 1954. MSUA. BOT; Box 1902, folder: 5 sup. mat. 2/19/54

6. Thomas. pp. 261-73

7. *The two schools would also claim federal lands in 1862 with the passage of the Morrill Act.*

8. SBA, 15 Dec. 1954. www.onthebanks.msu.edu

9. SBA, 21 Jan. 1955. www.onthebanks.msu.edu

10. SBA, 18 Feb. 1955. www.onthebanks.msu.edu

11. Hannah to Jenkins. 24 May 1955. MSUA. JAHP; Box 61, folder: 21 name change

12. SBA, 18 Feb. 1955. www.onthebanks.msu.edu

13. Thomas. pp. 265-66

14. Stason to Hatcher, (Memo). 25 Feb. 1955. BHL. HHHP; Box 53, folder: MSU name/letters to Stason. *As the dean points out in a review of the 1908 constitution, Michigan State's current name, approved by the legislature in 1925, may actually be "invalid." He argued that the legal name might still be "The State Agricultural College!"*

15. Stason to Hatcher. 22 Jan. 1954. BHL. HHHP; Box 53, folder: MSU name change, letters Stason

16. Millard to Niehuss. 31 March 1954. BHL. MLNP; Box 4, folder: top. files, 1953-54 (E-P), MSC-name change *(Millard's official opinion 1760 was included in the letter.)*

17. Ibid.

18. Niehuss to Millard. 5 April 1954. BHL. MLNP; Box 4, folder: top. files, 1953-54 (E-P), MSC-name change

19. Stason to Hatcher, (Memo). 25 Feb. 1955. BHL. HHHP; Box 53, folder: MSU name/letters to Stason.

20. Thomas. p. 286

21. "Michigan State: College or University? 10 Answers to that Question." Students and Alumni of Michigan State, circa Feb. 1955. BHL. GMWP; Box 159, folder: boards and commissions: colleges, state, 1955, MSU rename

22. "The Matter of Infringement." Circa Feb. 1955. MSUA. JAHP; Box 61, folder: 19 gen. subject: name change

23. "Confusion." Circa Feb. 1955. MSUA. JAHP; Box 61, folder: 19 gen. subject: name change

24. "On the Matter of Constitutionality." Circa Feb. 1955. MSUA. JAHP; Box 61, folder: 19 gen. subject: name change

25. "The Matter of Precedence." Circa Feb. 1955. MSUA. JAHP; Box 61, folder: 19 gen. subject: name change

26. "On the Matter of Costs Involved in the Change of Name." Circa Feb. 1955. MSUA. JAHP; Box 61, folder: 19 gen. subject: name change

27. Pierson to May. 30 Mar. 1955. MSUA. JAHP; Box 61, folder: 19 gen. subject: name change

28. "Memorandum on the College's Curricular Growth." Circa Feb. 1955. MSUA. JAHP; Box 61, folder: 19 gen. subject: name change

29. "List of Name Changes of Land-Grant Institutions and Other State Institutions of Higher Learning." Circa Feb. 1955. MSUA. JAHP; Box 61, folder: 19 gen. subject: name change

30. Hannah to Christman. 16 Mar. 1955. BHL. HHHP; Box 53, folder: MSU name change

31. (Standard letter from John Hannah). Circa Feb. 1955. MSUA. JAHP; Box 61, folder: 19 gen. subject: name change

32. Ibid.

33. Eisenhower to Hannah. 21 Mar. 1955. MSUA. JAHP; Box 61, folder: 20 name change

34. Hannah to Christman. 16 Mar. 1955. BHL. HHHP; Box 53, folder: MSU name change

35. Ibid.

36. Hatcher to McCune. 28 Feb. 1955. MSUA. JAHP; Box 61, folder: 19 gen. subject: name change

37. Hatcher to Williams. 28 Feb. 1955. BHL. GMWP; Box 159, folder: boards and commissions: colleges, state, 1955, MSU rename.

38. Ibid.

39. "A Statement By The University." *The Michigan Alumnus*, circa Apr. 1955. MSUA. JAHP; Box 61, folder: 20 gen. subject: name change

40. "MSC Students Called 'Kids' in Name Action: U-M Official Says 'They Haven't Grown Out of Short Pants." *Ann Arbor News.* 9 Mar. 1955

41. "University on Solid Ground in Opposing Name Change." *Ann Arbor News*. 9 Apr. 1955.

42. "MSC Students Called 'Kids' in Name Action: U-M Official Says 'They Haven't Grown Out of Short Pants." *Ann Arbor News*. 9 Mar. 1955

43. Brady to Morgan. 16 Mar. 1955. BHL. MLNP; Box 4, folder: top. files, 1953-54 (E-P), MSC-name change

44. "University on Solid Ground in Opposing Name Change." *Ann Arbor News*. 9 Apr. 1955.

45. "A Statement By The University." *The Michigan Alumnus*. Circa Feb. 1955. MSUA, JAHP; Box 61, folder: 20 gen. subject: name change

46. (Standard letter from John Hannah). Circa Feb. 1955. MSUA. JAHP; Box 61, folder: 19 gen. subject: name change

47. SBA. 18 March 1955. www.onthebanks.msu.edu

48. Ibid.

49. Ibid.

50. Ibid.

51. Thomas. p. 254

52. Kuich to Williams. 12 Mar. 1955. BHL. GMWP. Box 159, Boards and commissions, 1955: colleges, state, MSU rename

53. Mossner to Williams. 14 Apr. 1955. BHL. GMWP; Box 159, folder: Boards and commissions, 1955: colleges, state, MSU rename

54. Mossner to Williams. 28 Jan. 1954. BHL. GMWP; Box 159, folder: Boards and Commissions, 1954: colleges, state, MSU

55. Mossner to Williams. 14 Apr. 1955. BHL. GMWP; Box 159, folder: Boards and commissions, 1955: colleges, state, MSU rename

56. VanDusen to Hannah. 22 Mar. 1955. MSUA. JAHP; Box 61, folder: 20 gen. subject: name change

57. Waldron to Hannah. 23 Mar. 1955. MSUA. JAHP; Box 61, folder: 20 gen. subject: name change

58. Brady to Morgan. 16 Mar. 1955. BHL. MLNP; Box 4, folder: top. files, 1953-54 (E-P), MSC-name change

59. "Situation Report, Mar. 30, 1955." MSUA. JAHP; Box 61, folder: 20 gen. subject: name change

60. "University on Solid Ground in Opposing Name Change." *Ann Arbor News*. 9 Apr. 1955.

61. "Attorney General Says Legislature Can Give MSC Title of University." *Ann Arbor News*. 1 Apr. 1955

62. "University on Solid Ground in Opposing Name Change." *Ann Arbor News*. 9 Apr. 1955.

63. Thomas. pp. 255-56

64. Hatcher to Dear Senator. 30 Mar. 1955. BHL. GMWP. Box 159, Boards and commissions, 1955: colleges, state, MSU rename. *All quotes in this section derive from this letter.*

65. "Perry D. Chatterton." *Find a Grave*. 1 Aug. 2009. http://www.findagrave.com/cgi-bin/fg.cgi?page=gr&GRid=40146731

66. Chatterton to Hannah. 12 Dec. 1951. MSUA. JAHP; Box 61, folder 18: gen.

67. Hannah to Chatterton. 18 Dec. 1951. MSUA. JAHP; Box 61, folder 18: gen.

68. "Senate Seem Approving Name Change." AP. 14 Apr. 1955. *Ann Arbor News*

69. Thomas. p. 255

70. Tripp to Fisk. 25 Apr. 1955. BHL. GMWP; Box 159, folder: Boards and commissions, 1955: colleges, state, MSU rename

71. Stason to Hatcher. 10 May 1955. BHL. HHHP; Box 53, folder: MSU name change/letters to Stason

72. Ibid.

73. [Untitled summary]. 14 Apr. 1955. BHL. MLNP; Box 4, folder: topical files, 1953-54 (E-P), MSC-name change

74. Morrill to Hannah. 18 Apr. 1955. MSUA. JAHP; Box 61, folder 21: name change

75. Hannah to Morrill. 21 Apr. 1955. MSUA. JAHP; Box 61, folder 21: name change

76. SBA. 15 Apr. 1955. www.onthebanks.msu.edu

77. SBA. 20 May 1955. www.onthebanks.msu.edu

78. https://www.eff.org/issues/transparency/history-of-foia

79. Howard Remus Smith Papers. http://archives.msu.edu/findaid/046.html

80. http://www.findagrave.com/cgi-bin/fg.cgi?page=gr&GRid=40146731

81. "Facts Concerning the Need to Change the Name of Michigan State College of Agriculture and Applied Science." MSUA, JAHP; Box 61, folder: 19 gen. subject: name change

82. (Standard letter from John Hannah). Circa Feb. 1955. MSUA. JAHP; Box 61, folder: 19 gen. subject: name change

83. Tripp to Fisk. 25 Apr. 1955. BHL. GMWP; Box 159, folder: Boards and commissions, 1955: colleges, state, MSU rename

Chapter 14: Hannah v. Aigler—Case Law for a Rivalry

1. Aigler to Houston ... 26 Nov. 1951. BHL. RWAP; Box 9, folder: corr. 1946-52 Houston

2. MeasuringWorth.com

3. Braunwart, Bob. Carroll, Bob. "The Taylorville Scandal." *The Coffin Corner*. Vol. 2, No. 6 (1980)

4. Ibid.

5. Ibid.

6. MeasuringWorth.com

7. Kryk. p. 97

8. Shuster to Aigler. 16 Dec. 1921. BHL. RWAP; Box 1, folder: 1921 corr. P-Z misc.

9. Griffith to Weaver. 22 Oct. 1935. BHL. RWAP; Box 6, folder: corr. 1934-39 Griffith 4/34-1/36

10. Small Handbook of ICFR. UMA. DICAP; Box 13, folder: small Handbooks 1895-1908, 1930, 41

11. Shuster to Aigler. 16 Dec. 1921. BHL. RWAP; Box 1, folder: 1921 corr. P-Z misc.

12. Aigler to Shuster. 5 Jan. 1922. BHL. RWAP; Box 1, folder: 1921 corr. P-Z misc.

13. Young. pp. 21-22, 24-25. *In November of 1920, Aigler became aware of a subsidizing scheme orchestrated by members of the Detroit Alumni Club that had effectively funneled thousands of dollars to prospective student athletes in order to lure them to Ann Arbor.*

14. Aigler, Ralph W. "Control of Intercollegiate Athletics at Michigan." 10 Aug. 1957, *Michigan Alumnus*, Vol. LXIII, Number 21

15. SBA. 17 Mar. 1926. www.onthebanks.msu.edu

16. SBA. 19 Nov. 1926. www.onthebanks.msu.edu

17. Scott to Hannah. 22 Aug. 1955. MSUA. HP; Box 69, folder: 38

18. Beaumont to Murfin. 27 Oct. 1914. MSUA. ICA; Box 1182-4, folder: 1 corr. 1914-22

19. *Aigler received an LL.B from UM; Hannah received a B.S. from MAC.*

20. *A thorough reading of many Aigler communiqués suggests no prejudice on his part towards people of color or creed. Many of his closest friends were Jewish; at one time, he dated a Jewish woman while practicing law in Chicago.* (Aigler to Salsinger. 19 Mar. 1938. BHL RWAP; Box 7, folder: corr. 1934-39 "S" misc.) *Hannah's record speaks for itself (see below).*

21. Kuhn, Madison. Circa 1976. MSUA. HAP; Box 34, folder: 27 "John Hannah." *Hannah publically supported hiring black professors; rejected minority quotas for the faculty; struck down racial identity on student records; and integrated dormitories as far back as the late 1930s. Lacking conference affiliation, Michigan State was forced to contract with athletic programs embracing Jim Crow practices, a matter that greatly troubled him. This was one of his reasons for seeking membership in the Big Nine. Hannah's racial convictions ultimately earned him chairmanship of President Eisenhower's*

controversial *Civil Rights Commission of 1957—the commission played a major role in helping draft the 1964 Civil Rights Act.*

22. *The Willis Ward incident may have offered a small clue regarding Aigler's conviction on civil rights. As chairman of the Board in Control of Athletics, he was asked by President Ruthven to defend Fielding Yost's 1934 contract with Georgia Tech—an agreement neither Aigler nor Ruthven had a role in drafting. (The BIC and regents typically rubber-stamped scheduling contracts arranged by the athletic director.) The controversial agreement respected the Yellow Jackets' demand that Negroes not participate, let alone dress for the game in Ann Arbor.* (Behee, John. *Hail to the Victors! Black Athletes at the University of Michigan.* Ann Arbor: Ulrich's Books, 1974. pp. 18, 22-30.) *One response by Aigler best sums up his stance, at least as it pertained to the Ward story: "Needless to say, you and some of the others who have been interested in this situation, have been actuated by a sincere desire to be helpful to Mr. Ward and the cause of racial equality. The pathetic thing about the whole matter is that the agitation will almost certainly in the long run have the diametrically opposite effect from that desired."* (Aigler to McGraw. 19 October 1934. BHL. RWAP; Box 7, folder: Willis Ward.) *Aigler apparently felt the legislative/judicial process, rather than civil protest, would better serve the cause of racial justice.*

23. McEwen to Crisler. 16 Dec. 1953. BHL. BICA; Box 6, folder: 1953-1954

24. Crisler to McEwen. 17 Nov. 1954. BHL. BICA; Box 6, folder: 1953-1954

25. *Consistent with conference tradition, Aigler attended meetings with Professor Plant through the end of the 1954 calendar year. His departure coincided with the tedious process of revising Rule 7, the handbook rule spelling out how the conference would provide financial assistance for the non-scholar athlete. The final revision was approved at the May 1957 spring meetings. The new regulation would take effect at the beginning of the 1958 academic year.*

26. Ackley to Hatcher. 2 July 1954. BHL. HOCP; Box 6, folder: UM BICIA Papers 1953-54

27. Aigler to Smith. 23 July 1956. BHL. RWAP; Box 10, folder: corr. 1946-52 personal

28. Aigler, Ralph W. "Amateurism and Intercollegiate Athletics." *The MAQR*, 25 May 1957

29. Aigler, Ralph W. "Control of Intercollegiate Athletics at Michigan." *The MAQR*, 10 August 1957

30. Aigler, Ralph W. "Intercollegiate Athletics and Education." *The MAQR*, 7 Dec. 1957

31. Hannah to Aigler. 25 Oct. 1941. BHL. RWAP; Box 8, folder: corr. 1940-45 "H" misc.

32. Reeves, Floyd. Untitled. 11 June 1970. MSUA. HAP; Box 34, folder: 37

33. Hannah. p. 16

34. SBA. 23 Nov. 1936. www.onthebanks.msu.edu

35. SBA. 18 Mar. 1937. www.onthebanks.msu.edu

36. Huston to Aigler. 4 Dec. 1936. BHL. RWAP; Box 7, folder: corr. 1934-39 NCAA

37. Young. pp. 110-14

38. Hannah to Aigler. 27 Nov. 1941. BHL. RWAP; Box 8, folder: corr. 1940-45 "H" misc.

39. Hannah to Aigler. 13 Apr. 1943. BHL. RWAP; Box 8, folder: corr. 1940-45 "H" misc.

40. Aigler to Hannah. 1 Nov. 1941. BHL. RWAP; Box 8, folder: corr. 1940-45 "H" misc.

41. Hannah to Aigler. 25 Oct. 1941. BHL. RWAP; ox 8, folder: corr. 1940-45 "H" misc.

42. Aigler to Hannah. 30 Mar. 1943. BHL. RWAP; Box 8, folder: corr. 1940-45 "H" misc.

43. Aigler to Richart. 21 Dec. 1948. UIA. Series 4/2/12; Box 3, folder: WIC 1948-49

44. Aigler to Wilson. 12 June 1947. BHL. RWAP; Box 10, folder: corr. 1946-52 Wilson, K.L. 1/2

45. Aigler to Howes. 25 Feb. 1952. BHL. RWAP; Box 9, folder: corr. 1946-52 "H" misc. (HA-HN)

46. Aigler to Howes. 20 Mar. 1952. BHL. RWAP; Box 9, folder: corr. 1946-52 "H" misc. (HA-HN)

47. Adams to Hannah. 17 Oct. 1951. MSUA. JAHP; Box 72, folder: 32 corr. 1951, American Council on Education Policy Committee

48. Aigler to Houston. 19 Feb. 1952. BHL. RWAP; Box 9, folder: corr. 1946-52 Houston

49. Aigler to Houston. 3 Apr. 1952. BHL. RWAP; Box 9, folder: corr. 1946-52 Houston

50. Ibid.

51. Aigler to Howes. 20 Mar. 1952. BHL. RWAP; Box 9, folder: corr. 1946-52 "H" misc. (HA-HN)

52. Howes to Aigler. 24 Mar. 1952. BHL. RWAP; Box 9, folder: corr. 1946-52 "H" misc. (HA-HN)

53. Ackley to Hatcher. 2 July 1954. BHL. HOCP; Box 6, folder: UM BICIA papers

54. Aigler to Houston. 3 Apr. 1952. BHL. RWAP; Box 9, folder: corr. 1946-52 Houston

55. Hannah to Scott. 22 May 1956. MSUA. JAHP; Box 69, folder: 38 Athl. Council, gen. 1954-58

56. *The FRs first entertained revising the handbook rules on financial aid during the spring conference meetings of 1954. It was quite apparent that limiting grants to only those students demonstrating scholarship was not going to keep the Big Ten competitive with other conferences. (See Ackley to Hatcher. 2 July 1954.) The faculty came up with a revised "Rule 7" which allowed various forms of "financial assistance" to "worthy" students, consistent with the Hannah Committee recommendations (ICFR meetings of 6-8 Dec. 1956). That assistance not only was given to scholastically qualified students (academic scholarships) but also to the "needy" athlete desiring a college education (financial grants and campus jobs). The proposal was ultimately approved in Jan. of 1957 with formal enactment scheduled for Jan. of 1958. Hannah's concern with the proposal was that a job requirement was unrealistic for an athlete asked to compete on the practice field and also in the classroom. He favored a full-grant consistent with his old Jenison Awards. There was no mention in conference minutes whether Scott ever followed through on Hannah's request. Regardless, within a few years, the athletic scholarship became a reality for the Big Ten.*

57. Ackley to Hatcher. 2 July 1954. BHL. HOCP; Box 6, folder: UM BICIA papers

58. Thomas. pp. 449-54

59. McQuiston, John T. "John Hannah, 88, Who Headed Michigan State and Rights Panel." *The New York Times* 25 Feb. 1991.

EPILOGUE: EMPLOYMENT CONTRACTS

1. Aigler, Ralph W. "Amateurism and IC Athletics." *The MAQR*, 25 May 1957.

2. "Judge Rules Against NCAA." *ESPN.com News Service*. 9 Aug. 2014. http://espn.go.com/college-sports/story/_/id/11328442/judge-rules-ncaa-ed-obannon-antitrust-case

3. Farrey, Tom. "Ed O'Bannon: Ruling is Tip of Iceberg." *ESPN Outside the Lines*. 10 Aug. 2014. http://espn.go.com/espn/otl/story/_/id/11332816/ed-obannon-says-antitrust-ruling-only-beginning-change

4. "Judge Rules Against NCAA." *ESPN.com News Service*. 9 Aug. 2014. http://espn.go.com/college-sports/story/_/id/11328442/judge-rules-ncaa-ed-obannon-antitrust-case

5. Falla. p. 106

6. "2012-13 Revenue Expense Budget Details." 31 Aug. 2013. http://www.ncaa.org/sites/default/files/2012-13%2BRevenue%2Band%2BExpense%2BBudget.

7. Dahlberg, Tim. "Court Ruling on Paying College Athletes Will Fundamentally Change the NCAA." *Business Insider*, 10 Aug. 2014, http://www.businessinsider.com/court-ruling-on-paying-college-athletes-2014-8

8. Ibid.

9. Ibid.

10. Berkowitz, Steve. "NCAA increases value of scholarships in historic vote." *USA Today Sports*. 1/17/15. www.usatoday.com/sports/college/2015/01/17/ncaa-convention-cost-of-attendance-student-athletes-scholarship.

11. Ibid.

12. Ibid.

13. "Min. of the Conf. Joint Group," Appendix 1: Report of Rules and Revision Committee #2. 10-12 Dec. 1953. BHL. ADUM; Box 84, folder: 1952-1957. *The committee quotes a SUI survey by graduate student Charles Andre Jacot entitled "How Male College Students Use Their Time." He found that athletes have 13.08 fewer hours per week for study compared to non-athletes due to various commitments.*

14. Falla. p. 52

15. Ibid. pp. 51-52

16. Ackley to Hatcher. 2 July 1954. BHL. HOCP; Box 6, folder: UM BICIA papers 1953-54

17. Aigler to Lorenz. 1 July 1936. BHL. RWAP; Box 12, folder: athl. corr: 1933-36 "L" misc.

42987154R00170

Made in the USA
Lexington, KY
16 July 2015